FIGHTING WITH THE FILTHY THIRTEEN

FIGHTING
WITH THE
FILTHY THIRTEEN

*The World War II Story
of Jack Womer,
Ranger and Paratrooper*

JACK WOMER
AND
STEPHEN C. DEVITO

CASEMATE
Philadelphia & Oxford

Published in the United States of America and Great Britain in 2012 by
CASEMATE PUBLISHERS
908 Darby Road, Havertown, PA 19083
and
10 Hythe Bridge Street, Oxford, OX1 2EW

ISBN 978-1-61200-100-5
Digital Edition: ISBN 978-1-61200-112-8

Cataloging-in-publication data is available from the Library of Congress and
the British Library.

10 9 8 7 6 5 4 3 2 1

Printed and bound in the United States of America.

For a complete list of Casemate titles please contact:

CASEMATE PUBLISHERS (US)
Telephone (610) 853-9131, Fax (610) 853-9146
E-mail: casemate@casematepublishing.com

CASEMATE PUBLISHERS (UK)
Telephone (01865) 241249, Fax (01865) 794449
E-mail: casemate-uk@casematepublishing.co.uk

TABLE OF CONTENTS

	PREFACE AND ACKNOWLEDGMENTS	9
	THE 506TH PARACHUTE INFANTRY PRAYER	20
1.	MY EARLY YEARS	21
2.	FIRST JOBS	28
3.	MEETING MISS THERESA COOK: MY FUTURE BRIDE	33
4.	THE OUTBREAK OF WORLD WAR II	39
5.	DRAFTED INTO THE ARMY: PRIVATE JACK WOMER	43
6.	BECOMING A STAGE PERFORMER	48
7.	WAR GAMES IN THE CAROLINAS	53
8.	THE JAPANESE ATTACK PEARL HARBOR	61
9.	OFF TO EUROPE TO FIGHT HITLER	64
10.	ARRIVING IN ENGLAND: FIRST IMPRESSIONS	70
11.	VOLUNTEERING TO BECOME AN ARMY RANGER	75
12.	OFF TO SCOTLAND	79
13.	CAUSING TROUBLE IN DUNDALK!	92
14.	BACK TO ENGLAND, AS RANGERS	94
15.	RANGERS NO MORE	106
16.	THE MAKING OF A PARATROOPER 1, 2, 3!	109
17.	BECOMING ONE OF THE "FILTHY THIRTEEN"	117
18.	LIFE AT THE WILLS' MANOR ESTATE, LITTLECOTE, WILTSHIRE	121
19.	AN ENCOUNTER WITH WINSTON CHURCHILL	127
20.	PRELUDE TO OVERLORD: THE INVASION OF FRANCE	129
21.	D-DAY MISSION DISCLOSED	134

22.	THE INVASION IS ON !	138
23.	OFF TO A BAD START: JAMES GREEN'S PARACHUTE	143
24.	D-DAY	149
25.	D-DAY PLUS ONE	168
26.	NO TIME TO CRY	173
27.	GOO-GOO AND PEEPNUTS ARE KILLED	176
28.	CARENTAN—A RED ROSE FOR A SOLDIER	180
29.	BACK TO ENGLAND	188
30.	OPERATION MARKET-GARDEN: THE BATTLE FOR HOLLAND	195
31.	THE JUMP INTO HOLLAND	201
32.	EINDHOVEN	207
33.	THE KILLING OF CORPORAL JOSEPH J. OLESKIEWICZ.	210
34.	LIFE IN HOLLAND	217
35.	GOODBYE TO HOLLAND	224
36.	ON TO BASTOGNE: THE BATTLE OF THE BULGE	233
37.	A USELESS REPLACEMENT	239
38.	MIKE MARQUEZ AND THE SCREAMING MEE-MEES	242
39.	CHRISTMAS DAY, 1944	245
40.	STAYING WITH CIVILIANS	250
41.	OH THOSE NINETY-DAY WONDERS!	254
42.	TO THE FATHERLAND!	263
43.	LIVING WITH THE ENEMY	268
44.	THE WAR IN EUROPE IS OVER!	274
45.	THE LAST PATROL	279
46.	GOING HOME	283
47.	SETTLING BACK INTO CIVILIAN LIFE	290
48.	BRINGING PEACE TO THE HALE FAMILY	294
49.	THE REMAINS OF THE DAY	301

This book is dedicated to
all American soldiers who served in World War II,
and the people they left behind.

They are not lost who fought and fell,
they only wait ahead.
—Thomas Walbert, 29th Ranger Battalion

PREFACE AND ACKNOWLEDGMENTS

Jack Neitz Womer, a kid from Dundalk, Maryland, was among the first of the millions of young American men who were drafted for World War II. Forced to leave his job with the Bethlehem Steel Company when called to serve his country in April 1941, Jack was drafted into the 29th Infantry Division, trained as an infantryman, and sent overseas in October of 1942. Always wanting to be the best soldier he could become, Jack volunteered for the 29th Ranger Battalion, a new and elite unit trained by British Commandos, and was among the relatively few men who met the extensive and rigorous requirements for becoming a Ranger. After the 29th Ranger Battalion was disbanded in October 1943, he volunteered to become a paratrooper with the 101st Airborne Division. His Commando training was viewed as at least the equivalent to the training the 101st Airborne Division had undertaken in Toccoa, Georgia, and made him eligible to become a "Screaming Eagle." He earned his paratrooper wings by making the five required paratroop jumps within two days, instead of the usual seven.

Jack was assigned to a special demolition section within the 506th Parachute Infantry Regiment of the 101st Airborne, known both famously and infamously as the "Filthy Thirteen." It was with the 'Filthy Thirteen' that he, along with the more than 6,000 other Screaming Eagles, was an active participant in the D-Day invasion of Normandy, the battle for Holland, and the defense of Bastogne during the Battle of the Bulge.

He witnessed firsthand the deaths of many soldiers, both Allied and enemy, as well as civilians, and the destruction and carnage brought about by war. Men who served with Jack will tell you that he was an exceptional soldier, served his country valiantly, and displayed unusually good leadership in combat. After the war Jack returned to his home in Maryland as a local hero. Like most returning veterans, Jack put the war behind him and picked up where he had left off before being drafted. He went back to his job in the steel mills, married his fiancée, bought a house, raised two children, and eventually retired.

But all of the above occurred many years ago. World War II began and ended long before I was born. I had never heard of Jack Womer until one day in the early part of June 2003, when I noticed for sale on the internet an original photograph of some American soldiers training during World War II for "invasion day," in reference to June 6th, 1944, the day Allied forces invaded France. The photo, shown on page 102, is of seven U.S. Army Rangers undergoing Commando instruction with model 1928A1 Thompson submachine guns. I've seen thousands of World War II photos, but few have intrigued me as much as this one. There was something about it that called out to me. I'm not sure what it was, precisely, but I believe it resides in the expressions on the faces of the soldiers and the circumstances in the photo: young men who just a few years prior had endured the hardships of the Great Depression of the 1930s and now, drawn together by destiny, seem proud and willing to defend the United States at great risk to themselves.

I was especially intrigued by the back of the photo, which had a caption listing the soldiers' names and hometowns. The soldiers are identified as: Pfc John Toda of Sharon, Pennsylvania; Pvt. John Dorzi of Barrington, Rhode Island; Pfc Jack Womer of Dundalk, Maryland; Pfc Robert Reese of McKeesport, Pennsylvania; Lt. Eugene Dance of Beckley, West Virginia; Cpl. Dale Ford of Thurmont, Maryland; and Pfc Manuel Viera of Cambridge, Massachusetts. The caption was dated June 16th, 1943.

I purchased the photo and, coincidentally, received it in the mail on June 16th, 2003—exactly sixty years to the day from the date in the caption. That evening my wife and two children went to the local theater to see a movie while I decided to stay at home and read. After a while I took a break and began looking closely at the photo, wondering about the men it depicted. Whatever happened to them? Did they take part in the Allied invasion of Normandy? Did they survive the invasion? Did they survive the war? Were they killed in action? Had they become close friends during the war, and perhaps lost touch with one another afterward? Do they or their families know of the photo? I thought to myself that if any of them are still alive, they would probably like to have a copy. For those that were deceased, I felt that it was important that their families have copies. I resolved to find out what happened to the men in the photo, and to provide them or at least their families with copies.

The only information that I had on each of the men was their name and their hometown. I began my search with two basic, although dubious, assumptions: 1) that each of the seven men survived the war and were still alive; and 2) each man returned to his hometown after the war and still lived there. I arbitrarily decided to start with the soldier whose hometown is closest to Chantilly, Virginia, where I live. I looked on a map and observed that Dundalk, Maryland, the hometown of "Private Jack Womer," was closest, just over an hour's drive away. Using the internet White Pages, I searched for "Womer, J" in Dundalk, Maryland. No luck. I repeated the search for the state of Maryland and, among the "Womers" that appeared was a "Womer, Jack" living in Fort Howard, a small town adjacent to Dundalk.

The next day I set out to dial the number listed for "Womer, Jack." Just before I dialed I became a little nervous since I didn't know what kind of a response to expect. I was concerned that whoever answered my call would immediately hang up after I explained why I was calling, and think that I was odd. I took a deep breath, dialed the number, and after a few rings the person who answered the phone shouted "HELLO." A man had answered the phone, and from his pronunciation of this single word I suspected immediately that he was an older gentleman of the World War II era and an Army Ranger: the Jack Womer in the photo.

"Hello," I said nervously, " I'm looking for a Mr. Jack Womer." "I'm Jack Womer, what do you want?" shouted the voice on the phone. "I have a photo, sir, taken during World War II. It's a picture of seven army Rangers holding Thompson submachine guns training in England for the invasion of Europe, and one of the men in the photo . . ." Before I had completed the sentence the voice on the phone exclaimed "That photo was taken in Scotland!" "It doesn't say Scotland in the caption," I responded. "That photo was taken in Scotland! I was in the 29th Ranger Battalion, and that's where we trained, in Scotland. That's me in the photo," he replied excitedly. "How are you so certain that this photo is of you," I replied. "Look at my left hand, do you see a bandage on it?" "No, I don't," I responded. "Look closer. I remember when that photo was taken, I had a bandage on my left hand," he said. I looked closer at the photo and, to my astonishment, in the photo the left hand of Jack Womer was indeed bandaged. I felt a chill run up my spine.

We continued talking, for well over an hour. Jack told me that he remembered the day the photo was taken, in February of 1943, when he and the other 29th Rangers attended the British Commando Depot School at Achnacarry House at Spean Bridge, Scotland, and how a few days prior to the picture being taken he had injured his left hand during practice with live hand grenades. He went on to tell me many stories about his days in the military during World War II. As with many other draftees from the Baltimore area, Jack was originally drafted into the 29th Infantry Division, and assigned to its 175th Infantry Regiment. He told me how he was sent overseas in October 1942, on the *Queen Elizabeth*, arrived in Scotland, and went to England.

He hated the food he was served in the 29th Infantry Division so much that when he learned that the Army was planning to form the 29th Ranger Battalion he purposely set out to become a Ranger, partly because of the challenge, but also because of the better food Rangers were served. He went on to tell me that after the 29th Rangers were disbanded in October 1943, he and the other Rangers were sent back to their original units within the 29th Infantry, but he later became a paratrooper in a special demolition squad within the famed 506th Parachute Infantry Regiment of the 101st Airborne Division for the extra pay. The special demolition squad to which he was assigned, nicknamed the "Filthy Thirteen," would become famous and the subject of a book of the same name.

His many stories of his combat experiences in Normandy, Holland and the Battle of the Bulge, and his other, more comical war experiences as a soldier, warmed my heart and captured my interest. I could have listened to Jack all day. Since our initial conversation that day in June 2003, Jack and I have become good friends.

Jack has lived alone since 1987, when Theresa, his beloved wife of over forty years, passed away. While he may be alone, he is by no means lonely.

Now an old man, Jack spends most of his time enjoying life by doing the things he loves to do: playing golf, watching televised sports, passing time in his home with a steady stream of visits or phone calls from family, old and new friends, spending time with his lady friend, and catching and eating fish and blue claw crabs with Jules and Gene Franks, two of his childhood friends.

But over sixty-six years later, the war is still with him. On a wall in his family room he has displayed in a framed case the left sleeve of the combat jacket he wore when he jumped into Normandy from his C-47 plane in the early hours of June 6th, 1944. The Screaming Eagle insignia on the sleeve is intact, but the sleeve contains tiny holes from a mortar round that exploded just a few feet away and nearly killed him while he was in a wheat field shooting at Nazi soldiers. Other mementos are displayed throughout his home, and serve as constant reminders of his participation in the war.

He occasionally attends reunions of World War II veterans with whom he served during his time in the 101st Airborne, and enjoys the lifelong bonds he made during the war. He often reminisces about the war, and wonders why he survived and has enjoyed a postwar life missed by those he knew and were killed. I've heard Jack say many times, "When I look back on my war experiences, and all that I went through, I should have been killed a thousand times over. But I wasn't, and I often wonder why I was spared."

Unlike many of the men in the 29th Infantry and 101st Airborne Divisions, Jack was never wounded or seriously injured during the war, despite the innumerable attempts made on his life by enemy soldiers using all sorts of weapons, and all of the dangerous situations he was in. Jack firmly attributes having survived the war unscathed to two factors. First and foremost is the protection that God provided to him throughout the war and, for that matter, his life. Jack said a lot of prayers while in the military, and many of his close friends, family, and his then-fiancée, Theresa Cook, prayed for his safety.

Second was his training as an Army Ranger. In addition to the rigorous physical training Rangers were required to undertake, they also underwent intense training to think and behave intelligently and strategically in combat situations. Ranger training was provided by experienced and combat-hardened Commandos, not inexperienced officers. Jack's Commando training and skills is what most distinguished him and other Rangers from the rest of the World War II servicemen, including his fellow Screaming Eagles.

Conversations between Jack and I have included anything and everything, but always seemed to end up centering on his military service. Jack has many personal stories of World War II, ranging from his experiences in camp, with civilians, during training and in combat. Some of his stories are funny, some are sad, some are quite amazing, and to those who have an interest in World War II, all are worth listening to. Aside from a few anecdotes of Jack that have appeared in a few places, such as the book "The Filthy Thirteen" (by Jake McNiece and Richard Killblane), in some of the writings of World War II historians Mark Bando and Jonathan Gawne, and on some internet pages, most of Jack's war experiences have never been written. I strongly encouraged him to preserve his memories of the war in book form. I even offered to help him find an author to assist him in writing his memoirs.

After considerable coaxing, he agreed, but under the condition that I write his memoirs for him! I tried to wriggle out of it by saying that while I've authored a couple of highly specialized scientific books and a number of articles in scientific journals, I'm only a student of World War II history, and have no credentials as a writer of it, and that he'd probably be better off working with someone who did. He didn't go for my idea, and I knew that the only way his war memories would be penned is if I did it for him, lest they'd inevitably be lost forever.

So I agreed to help write Jack Womer's memoirs of World War II. My biggest concern was really to find the time to conduct the necessary research and write. Being a husband, a father of two adolescent children, working full-time, and maintaining a home does not leave much time in a day to research a topic and write a book about it. Then I realized that this is an issue that many writers are confronted with. Why should I be any different? I viewed the time issue as part of the challenge of writing the book.

After some discussion, Jack and I felt it best that his memoirs be written as if Jack were telling his own story to me. The general approach we used is that every few months I would visit Jack at his home and tape record hours of his verbal recollections. I would then transcribe the recordings, connect his recollections into the form of a developing story told in the first person, edit and polish the text, and mail him the draft for his review and comments.

Prior to my visits with Jack I would familiarize myself as much as possible with details on the topic that we would focus on that particular day. I would use these details to help stir his memories and provide context to the discussion. In addition, prior to my arrival on a given day Jack would pull out from his personal files old newspaper clippings, photos, letters he had written home or were written to him during the war, as well as military books that provided details on his units' activities or whereabouts. These too would serve to bring back memories and provide additional details to his recollections. While Jack's memory of his experiences in World War II is quite remarkable, these additional sources of information helped to fill in some gaps or uncertainties. This overall approach worked very well.

Published reference materials that I found particularly useful in providing background information and context are those written by noted historians of World War II. For information pertaining to the 29th Infantry Division, these include: Joseph H. Ewing's *29 Let's Go: A History of the 29th Infantry Division in World War II*; Joseph Balkoski's *Beyond the Beachhead. The 29th Infantry Division in Normandy*; and Alex Kershaw's *The Bedford Boys*. For information on the 29th Ranger Battalion I found the following sources to be most helpful: Robert W. Black's *Rangers in World War II*; the doctoral thesis of Jerome J. Haggerty, *A History of the Ranger Battalions in World War II* (Department of History, Fordham University); publications by Jonathan Gawne; and the library collection of the Headquarters of the National Guard Association, located in Washington DC.

For general information on the 101st Airborne Division, I relied primarily on Stephen E. Ambrose's well known book *Band of Brothers*, and three of Mark Bando's books: *Vanguard of the Crusade: The 101st Airborne Division During World War II; 101st Airborne: The Screaming Eagles at Normandy;* and *101st Airborne: From Holland to Hitler's Eagle's Nest*. For information on the "Filthy Thirteen," I used the book of that name by Richard Killblane and Jake McNiece as the primary source. Ian Gardner and Roger Day's book *Tonight We Die as Men* was particularly helpful for details on the 3rd Battalion of the 506th Parachute Infantry Regiment, and the mission of the Filthy Thirteen during the Normandy invasion.

I also relied on the personal accounts of men who served side-by-side with Jack during World War II, and knew him well. These men, along with the units in which they served during the war, include: Willard Sparks, Company C, 175th Infantry Regiment, 29th Infantry Division; Sgt. John Polyniak, Company A, 29th Ranger Battalion and Company C, 116th Infantry Regiment, 29th Infantry Division; Lt. Colonel Eugene Dance (retired), Company A, 29th Ranger Battalion and 506th Parachute Infantry Regiment, Jake McNiece, Robert Cone, and Jack Agnew, 506th Parachute Infantry Regiment, and Sgt. John Slaughter, Company B, 29th Ranger Battalion and Company D, 116th Infantry Regiment, 29th Infantry Division. (Sgt. Slaughter underwent Ranger training with Jack Womer, but did not know Jack personally. He provided details on the training he and other Rangers, including Jack, experienced.) I gratefully acknowledge the willingness of these fine men to provide me with relevant details and anecdotes regarding Jack and the war.

I acknowledge the input and photograph I received from Evelyn Moehle and Maggie Moehle Gilbert, the wife and daughter of Ross A. Moehle, who was a paratrooper in the 101st Airborne and was with Jack throughout D-Day. I am grateful to Mr. John Polyniak, Jr. for providing photos of his father, Sgt. John Polyniak, a very close friend of Jack Womer.

Particularly valuable information was provided by a totally unexpected source: Theresa Cook, Jack's long-deceased wife. Jack and Theresa met and fell in love long before Jack was drafted, got engaged during the war, in December of 1941, and married almost immediately after Jack returned home from the war in 1945. Theresa was very much in love with Jack. She faithfully wrote to him almost every day while he was in the service. Jack wrote to Theresa quite frequently as well. In *all* of their letters they express their deepest love for one another, and reflect on the wonderful life they would share together after the war. Theresa kept and compiled in one place their letters (hundreds of them), as well as photos of Jack and clippings from particular issues of local newspapers that contained stories about Jack while in the service.

These letters and newspaper clippings, and even the photos, represent a "gold mine" of information. They not only helped to refresh Jack's memory, but also supplemented it with tidbits and specific details of his war years that he has long since forgotten. Theresa died in 1987 from complications brought on by an infection. I genuinely believe that she somehow knew that someone would one day write a book about Jack, and had the foresight to save and compile the letters, clippings and photos, knowing that they would serve as invaluable reference materials. I am deeply grateful to Theresa, and regret never having had the opportunity to meet her.

In addition to the challenge of finding the time to write this book, the second challenge I encountered was to write the text so that it "sounds" as if Jack Womer were speaking directly to the reader. Jack is extremely intelligent, but when he speaks he tends to become excited, loud, quite vulgar (sorry Jack!), uses a lot of hand gestures, and mixes past, present and future tenses, often within a single sentence.

If I had written this book as a literal transcription of Jack speaking I think most readers would have a difficult time understanding him. I decided that the best way to deal with the matter was to write the book as if Jack had written it. Jack expresses himself quite well when he writes. I realized this after I had read many of the letters he wrote to his family and Theresa during the war. So I adopted Jack's writing style and wrote the book such that it accentuates his intelligence, accurately conveys his recollections of his experiences of World War II, and captures the feelings and emotions he expresses when he tells of his experiences, but without including his vulgarity and blending of tenses. In using this approach I feel that I remained true to the storytelling process.

You may be curious as to why I, a successful white-collar professional of the baby-boomer generation, would bother to befriend an old World War II veteran and retired steel worker, and write a book about him. I very much appreciate the fact that I'm a citizen of the United States, enjoying the freedom that comes with being a U.S. citizen. I don't take my freedom for granted, and I feel indebted to individuals such as Jack, who have fought against foreign enemies to defend and preserve the way of life I now enjoy.

Becoming a friend of a veteran such as Jack Womer, and writing a book with him is my way of showing respect and appreciation, not only to him but to all veterans, for helping to provide the freedom given to me and every U.S. citizen. Also, I wanted to preserve history. I have not only endeavored for this objective, but have discovered new information that I believe will be of particular interest to many World War II enthusiasts and historians.

Throughout the development of this book I tasked a number of people of different perspectives to review and comment on various draft versions. I very much appreciate and gratefully acknowledge the critical input and recommendations provided by: Jo Vleck and her daughter Vanessa; Louis DeVito (my father, and a veteran of World War II); Eileen DeVito (my mother), Colonel Joseph Gesker (retired), noted 101st Airborne Division historians Mark Bando and Richard Killblane; and various members of the Womer family. I am grateful to Ellen Womer (Jack's daughter), for her review of the near final version of the manuscript and providing me with the finishing touches, and for her assistance with the publication of this book. I also acknowledge Teresa Coleman (Ellen's daughter) for her assistance in the work's publication. I especially acknowledge Kenneth Kryvoruka, my dear friend and fellow historian, for his particularly careful review and detailed critique of the near-final draft manuscript.

Developing a book of this type pulls one away from his family. I gratefully acknowledge Kathryn Henry-DeVito, my wife, and our children, Christine and Michael, for their patience and understanding, and recognizing the historical significance of this work.

I cannot overstate my gratitude to the staff at Casemate Publishers, particularly Tara Lichterman, Libby Braden, and Steven Smith for their assistance in developing this book and for their professionalism. In addition I am especially grateful to Colonel Robert Kane (ret.), founder and former head of Presidio Press, who kindly offered to lend his editorial expertise to the preparation of the manuscript.

In case you are wondering, after months of searching I was able to find out about the other men in the above-mentioned photo (shown on page 102). The 29th Ranger Battalion disbanded in October of 1943, and the men in the Battalion returned to their original units within the 29th Infantry Division. Dale Ford returned to the 115th Infantry Regiment and survived the initial assault on Omaha Beach on D-Day, but was killed in action a week later, on June 13th, 1944, as the 29th Infantry was heading inland toward the city of St. Lo, France. Manuel Viera returned to the 121st Engineer Combat Battalion of the 29th Infantry Division, and was killed in action on Omaha Beach on D-Day. He was 24 years old.

The rest of the men in the photo survived the invasion of Normandy as well other battles, and returned home after the war. John Toda returned to Sharon, Pennsylvania, and later moved to Warren, Ohio. John Dorzi (D Company, 116th Infantry Regiment, 29th Infantry Division) returned to Barrington, Rhode Island, and died in the late 1980s. Robert Reese returned to McKeesport, Pennsylvania, and died in 1991. Eugene Dance, like Jack Womer, joined the 506th PIR of the 101st Airborne Division, and participated in the D-Day invasion and other battles as paratroopers. While Jack returned to Maryland after the war, Eugene Dance remained in the military and served in the Korean War, later retiring as a lieutenant colonel. He eventually moved to Lake Worth, Florida. I mailed copies of the photo to the surviving men and to the families of those who were deceased. They were all very grateful for my efforts.

Stephen C. DeVito
Chantilly, Virginia

THE 506th PARACHUTE INFANTRY PRAYER
written by
Lt. James G. Morton
506th PIR, 101st Airborne Division*

Almighty God, we kneel to thee and ask to be the instrument of thy fury in smiting the evil forces that have visited death, misery and debasement on the people of the earth.

We humbly face thee with true penitence for all of our sins for which we do most earnestly seek thy forgiveness. Help us to dedicate ourselves completely to thee.

Be with us, God, when we leap from our planes into the dread night and descend in parachutes into the midst of enemy fire. Give us iron will and stark courage as we spring from the harnesses of our parachutes to seize arms for battle.

The legions of evil are many, Father; grace our arms to meet and defeat them in thy name and in the name of freedom and dignity of Man.

Keep us firm in our faith and resolution, and guide us that we may not dishonor our high mission or fail in our sacred duties. Let our enemies who have lived by the sword turn from their violence lest they perish by the sword.

Help us to serve thee gallantly and to be humble in victory; though Jesus Christ our Lord. Amen.

*An original, typed version of the prayer was included in the same envelope that contained a letter written by Sergeant Jack Womer of the 506th Parachute Infantry Regiment to his fiancée, Theresa Cook, of Baltimore, Maryland. The letter is dated January 24th, 1945.

1.

MY EARLY YEARS

Life for me began on June 18th, 1917 in Lewistown, Pennsylvania, an old Dutch town about 40 miles northwest of Harrisburg. I was the fourth child of Methodist parents, primarily of Dutch descent. My father, William Walker ("Walk") Womer, worked in a steel mill in Lewistown, as did his father and grandfather. The mill was owned and operated by the Standard Axle Works, and my father worked as an open-hearth melter, which in those days was considered a good job.

I never saw much of him when I was young as he was always working in the steel mill. He worked very hard and liked to drink beer—lots of it. Despite the large volumes of beer he regularly consumed, I don't think he ever missed a day of work in his entire career, and he died a very old man. My mother, Roxie, was a housewife.

At the time I was born I had three older brothers, David, Benjamin and Herbert. David was about seven years older than me, Ben about six years older, and Herbert about five. My sister, Dolsie Jane ("Janey"), was born about a year after me. My parents would have another son, my younger brother Douglas, who was born during the 1920s.

AUNT DOLSIE

A few months after I was born my mother took ill, and it became increasingly difficult for her to care for four children. My father couldn't afford to hire a nanny to help manage the household and raise the children, so by the time I was about a year old my parents decided to send me to Sunbury, Pennsylvania to live with my aunt Dolsie, my mother's sister. Sunbury is about 50 miles northeast of Lewistown, right on the Susquehanna River. By this time Janey had been born. Of the five children in my family at the time, I'm still not sure exactly why I was the one who was chosen to be sent off to live with Aunt Dolsie. It may have been because I was still a baby and my parents may have believed that sending me off to live with her would take the most stress off of my mother. While I'm certain that my parents' actions were well intended, I've always held some resentment against them, particularly my mother, for sending me off when I was just a baby to live somewhere else.

My Aunt Dolsie lived alone in a small row house in Sunbury, close to the Susquehanna. Before I was born she had been married to a police officer, "Uncle Billy," who was killed when a car ran over him. When she took me in she lived alone. She didn't have any children of her own, and she liked the idea of caring for me, which she did for about five years.

Aunt Dolsie was a very kind and decent God-fearing woman who gave to this world more than she took from it. She was the salt of the earth, and loved and cared for me not as her nephew, but as if I were her son, and I grew to love her not as my aunt but as if she were my real mother. Let me tell you from firsthand experience that when an infant is given to another woman to be cared for temporarily during the early years of the child's life, that "other woman" *is the child's mother*. In many respects I consider my Aunt Dolsie to be my real mother. Aunt Dolsie never had any children of her own, and from the time she began taking care of me when I was a year old until she died many years later I believe she considered me to be her son. Even years after I had stopped living with her, she often told me and my parents that she was going to leave me her estate after she died. Aunt Dolsie was the world to me. She read incessantly, and had a huge collection of books. She was very intelligent and well-informed, and knowledgeable on just about any subject.

When Aunt Dolsie was in her fifties she married a second time to an older man named Henry Wagner, who was divorced and worked for the railroad. His ex-wife had taken everything from him. Aunt Dolsie never prepared a will, and when she died Henry automatically inherited her entire estate, including everything she had planned on leaving me, which included her house and her extensive collection of books. Henry was well aware of what Aunt Dolsie had intended on leaving me, because she had told him. But after she passed away the old bastard kept everything she owned for himself and told me to get lost. So I wished him bad luck, and not too long afterwards he was hit and killed by a train!

MOVING TO MARYLAND

In 1922, while I was still living in Sunbury with my Aunt Dolsie, my father decided to move the family from Lewistown, Pennsylvania to Sparrows Point, Maryland so he could work in the open hearth furnaces of the Bethlehem Steel Company. Sparrows Point is located about 10 miles southeast of Baltimore, very close to the mouth of the Chesapeake Bay and Patapsco River.

The steel industry in the Baltimore area started in 1893 with the construction of a mill and shipyard by the Pennsylvania Steel Company. During World War I there was a large demand for steel and in 1916 Bethlehem Steel acquired the Pennsylvania Steel Company and increased its production in the Baltimore area. The local economy was soon dominated by the Bethlehem Steel Company. The demand for steel continued to rise after World War I ended in November 1918, and Bethlehem Steel was in need of experienced steel workers to meet this demand. To attract skilled workers such as my father, they offered steady work, more opportunity, higher wages, and a better quality of life for their families.

Along with the mills, Bethlehem Steel established a residential community for its workers adjacent to its steel mills and named it Sparrows Point. Workers could pay low rent (between $4 and $14 a month for a nine-room house) and get free home maintenance, company-subsidized churches and schools, easy access to credit, and a strong sense of community. Many of the company houses had indoor plumbing, gas for cooking and hot water, both gas and electric light connections, coal furnaces, and bathrooms—luxuries in those days that many families had not experienced previously. In return, Bethlehem Steel attracted and secured young, skilled laborers, who were more than willing to work hard and establish their roots in Sparrows Point.

From the time the company first set up its operations in Sparrows Point in 1916 until the 1980s, billions and billions of tons of steel were made by the men who worked there. The steel made at the Sparrows Point mills would be used for all sorts of purposes, such as automobiles, Campbell's soup cans, the hulls of ocean tankers, all sorts of guns and naval ships used during World War I, World War II, the Korean and Vietnam wars, the girders used to construct office buildings, and the wire and girder plates of suspension bridges, to name just a few uses. The steel used in the construction of the Golden Gate Bridge (California), the George Washington Bridge (New York), Chesapeake Bay Bridge (Maryland), and the Mississippi River Bridge at New Orleans was made in Sparrows Point. During the 1950s the Bethlehem Steel mills in Sparrows Point, Maryland was the largest steel manufacturing facility in the world.

So my parents, attracted by Bethlehem Steel's promise of steady work at higher wages, and with the expectations of a better quality of life, moved the family to Sparrows Point. Many other laborers from rural Maryland and Pennsylvania and the South—of Welsh, Irish, German, Polish, Russian, and Hungarian descent, as well as blacks—relocated to Sparrows Point for the same reasons. Bethlehem Steel dominated and controlled the whole area. Even the Sparrows Point High School prepared steelworkers' sons for jobs at the mill. All of my father's sons, as well as the sons (and even grandsons) of many other steel workers, would eventually work for the Bethlehem Steel Company.

My father's superior skill level as a steel worker enabled him to be "assigned" to rent a six-room corner row house located at 1014 H Street, one block away from the section where the negroes lived. Row houses were little more than apartment-sized houses connected side-by-side to one another on a street. Our house was on the corner of the block, which was a little more comfortable than row houses between corner houses.

Of the six rooms in the small house my parents rented from the Bethlehem Steel Company, three were bedrooms, one was the bathroom, one was the kitchen and one was the dining room. At the time my family moved in to the row house there were six Womers living there: my parents, my sister Janey, and my three older brothers, David, Herbert and Ben. I was still living in Sunbury, Pennsylvania with my Aunt Dolsie.

My mother never worked. As did most mothers in those days, she stayed home and cleaned and managed the household, did the shopping, cooked our meals, cleaned our clothes, paid the bills, and tended to the other needs of the family. My father worked as a "first-helper" or "melter" in the open hearth, and his furnace was 69, number one in the plant.

Being an open-hearth melter was not easy, but it was one of the better jobs to have in a steel mill because it involved more responsibility and the salary was higher. It got quite hot in those open hearth furnaces, and a major requirement (and drawback) to being a melter is that you had to be able to tolerate the brutally high temperatures. My father was a cracker-jack open-hearth melter—one of the best that ever worked at Bethlehem Steel's Sparrows Point facility.

In 1922, shortly after the family had settled in Sparrows Point, my mother wrote my Aunt Dolsie to tell her that she wanted to take me back to live with the rest of my family. By this time I was approaching five years of age, and Aunt Dolsie and I had become very attached to one another. Neither she nor I wanted me to leave Sunbury to live with my parents and siblings in Maryland. I wanted to stay in Sunbury in the worst way.

Aunt Dolsie pleaded with my mother that I should stay in Sunbury, and even offered to legally adopt me, but my mother said no. Aunt Dolsie was the world to me, and I've always resented my mother for not letting me stay with her. I cried and cried when I had to leave. From the first day when I arrived at my parents' home in Sparrows Point I felt like an outsider in my own family. My parents, brothers and sister were all close with one another because they had all lived together and had bonded as family members naturally do. But because I had only lived with them for a year and had been separated for four years, I felt that I was viewed and treated more as a close relative rather than as a brother or son. I never did feel right, always as if I were an outsider.

In our house there were only three bedrooms, and there were now seven of us living there. My parents occupied one of the bedrooms, my sister occupied another, and my three older brothers (David, Benjamin and Herbert) and I had the back bedroom. When my younger brother Douglas ("Dogeye") was born he stayed, at first, in my parent's bedroom and then later in my sister's. In those days there was no such thing as air conditioning, and in Maryland the summer months can be quite hot and humid. It got quite uncomfortable in those row houses during the summer months.

Every Sunday we put on our Sunday clothes and walked to the Methodist church to attend the services. My father would come along, but only if he wasn't working that day and food was served after the services. My brothers and I used to collect the donations made during the services.

For awhile I attended Bible school, which was held every Wednesday at the church. My family lived in the row house in Sparrows Point from 1922 to 1930, and then we moved a few miles away to a more spacious, single-family home at 3015 Dundalk Avenue in the town of Dundalk.

LIFE IN SUNBURY, PENNSYLVANIA

Although I had to move to Sparrows Point, to be with my family, I didn't completely stop living in Sunbury with aunt Dolsie. As a compromise for taking me from Aunt Dolsie against her wishes and mine, my parents agreed to allow me to spend the summer months with her. Every June, as soon as the school year ended, my parents drove me up to Sunbury, and I wouldn't return home until the last week or so of August, when the next school year was about to begin. This started from the time I was in first grade until I was in high school. Sunbury was a wonderful place for a kid to live in those days, especially during the summer months. It probably still is.

Sparrows Point and Dundalk were primarily dedicated to the steel industry, and had lots of gigantic ugly brick steel mills with huge smoke stacks that operated 24 hours a day. In Sunbury there was a lot of wide-open space, and plenty to do. There was the Susquehanna River for boating, fishing and swimming, there were forests to hike, mountains to climb, freight trains to ride on, and plenty of other kids to play with. It was up in Sunbury that I learned how to climb mountains, fish, shoot a rifle, sail a boat and hop freight trains! My best childhood friends, Earl, Short, Orville, and Vivian Reichenbach, lived up in Sunbury. We had a lot of fun.

During my teenage years I would often sleep in the Reichenbach's home instead of Aunt Dolsie's house. I used to work as caddy on the golf course that was up there, getting paid 35 cents for nine holes. I gave all the money I earned at caddying to Aunt Dolsie. She never asked for it, but she didn't have very much and I knew that she needed it more than I.

The Susquehanna River runs right along Sunbury, and there were a lot of sail boats and row boats moored right along the shoreline. My friends and I did a lot of boating there, and I eventually became quite skilled at it. We spent a lot of time on the Susquehanna looking for adventure. Our boats had sails that were made out of sugar bags. We'd often sail to the small islands that are all over the place in the river, where we would relax in the summer sun, swim, fish or just sit around and talk.

My favorite childhood memories are hopping onto the freight trains up in Sunbury, which I started doing when I was about 14 years old. We'd hop freight trains going from town and stay on until we felt like getting off. Sometimes we would hop rides all the way to Harrisburg, which is about 50 miles south of Sunbury. It was wild and fun! When the freight trains came in through town they had to slow down, and that's when we would hop on to them. Hopping onto a train is not an easy thing to do, but with a little practice I learned to hop them just as well as any of my friends. It was a matter of running along side of the train after it had slowed down, and knowing just where and when to jump on.

Overall, I'd say I had a good childhood. The only part for which I was, and always remained, bitter was when my parents sent me away as a baby to live with my Aunt Dolsie for a few years. When I returned I never quite felt that I was part of the family. Aside from that, I can't complain about anything and enjoyed my childhood. It's good that I did because little did I know what lay ahead, just around the corner—the Great Depression of the 1930s and World War II.

2.

FIRST JOBS

I got my first real job in the early 1930s while I attended the Baltimore County Public School Number 6. I found work after school in a foundry located on Dundalk Avenue, right across the street from where we lived. They made steel parts for toilets and other things. Once the parts were manufactured they were stacked in a yard behind the foundry. My job was to help stack them, restack any that fell on the ground, and keep the yard clean of debris. I'd work weekdays after school and all day on Saturdays for a few cents an hour. I know it may seem as if I didn't make much money, but in those days earning 30 to 50 cents a week wasn't too bad of an income for a teenager.

After I finished my years at the elementary school I started high school at the Franklin Day School, which was a private Christian high school located at 24 West Franklin Street in Baltimore, Maryland. I was on a partial sports scholarship because I was a good athlete. I was very good at playing football, baseball, basketball, and soccer. I don't remember the exact tuition costs, but I do remember that my scholarship paid for a good chunk of it. My parents were required to pay the rest.

One day, after three years of attendance and with only one more year left until graduation, my parents received a letter in the mail from Mr. J.A. Kershner, Headmaster of Franklin Day School, saying that I could no longer continue on at the school. I had been kicked out. At the time I didn't know why, but I later learned it was because my parents had stopped making payments on the balance of the tuition.

It was 1936, I was about 19 at the time, and I was quite annoyed because I was pretty near to graduating. It was during the Great Depression and my father's income often varied from paycheck to paycheck as he would get laid off from time to time. But I don't think the tuition was unaffordable for my parents because I had the partial scholarship. The hardships of the Depression certainly didn't keep my father from buying beer.

When I left Franklin Day School I needed to find a job. The Depression was in full swing and had taken quite a toll on the economy. The country was in the midst of hard times, and jobs were very hard to find. In addition, the places where I could work were very limited. I had no car so I had to find work in Dundalk or Sparrows Point. Other than the mills owned and operated by Bethlehem Steel there were very few places where a man could work, even if there was any.

Naturally I figured my best chance of finding work was with Bethlehem Steel. At that time when you wanted to get a job as a laborer in the steel mills, you would have to get up early in the morning and walk to the mills and go stand and wait outside of the foreman's office, in rain, snow, the cold of winter, the heat of summer, or whatever it happened to be, and hope that they were looking for help. If they were, a foreman or some representative would eventually come out of his office and announce whatever they were looking for: "crane operator," "observer," or whatever, and when they announced something that you were capable of doing you would raise your hand and hope they would pick you. That's how they hired people at Bethlehem Steel during the Depression. There were no unions to help you, no applications to fill out, no resumes to prepare—none of that.

Of course knowing the right person always helped whenever it came to getting a job, just as it does today. My brother Ben, who was already working for Bethlehem Steel, told me that they needed a "layer-out" helper in the steel plate mill where he worked. I spoke with Ben's boss, and he hired me as a helper in the 110-inch plate mill, working the 11:00 pm to 7:00 am "graveyard" shift. I was paid $ 2.56 per hundred tons of steel. In those days we weren't paid by the hour, we were paid in tonnage, or more simply, in accordance to your productivity. When working, a layer-out helper usually made a little over five dollars a day, which during the Depression was decent money, especially for a 19-year-old such as myself.

What the layer-out helper did was draw lines on hot steel so that it could be cut to the appropriate size. To draw the lines we used square wooden templates that varied in size: six to three feet wide, which we would lay on hot steel that had been rolled out into a long continuous thin sheet. Then while standing on the hot steel wearing wooden shoes, we would take soap stone, and using the templates, we'd draw lines on the steel, remove the template, and other workers would quickly cut the steel into plates in accordance to the soap-stone lines we had drawn. The steel was so hot that if you didn't keep moving the wooden templates would catch on fire. Very often the wooden shoes would also, so you had to work quickly.

I soon learned that steelworkers were seldom referred to by their actual names among one another, but rather by nicknames. An employee's nickname was given by his co-workers, and usually based on some personality trait, characteristic or noticeable attribute. The nickname given me was "Jitterbug," because at the time it was the dance of the day, and I was an outstanding "jitterbugger." Once given a nickname, it stuck with you forever. It is not uncommon for men who for decades worked side-by-side in the steel mill not to know their co-workers real names. Some examples of my co-workers' nicknames during the 1930s and 1940s were Gypsy Booth, Swampy, Dead Man, Homily, and Pappy.

I worked as a layer-out helper in the 110-inch plate mill for a couple of years on the graveyard shift, and in 1938, during the height of the Great Depression, I was laid-off, this time indefinitely. I was about 21 years old. A few months later I got my next job, which was also with Bethlehem Steel, through my older brother David, who at the time was a supervisor in the company store. David had a good friend and golf buddy named Scotty Reid, who helped me get hired to work the graveyard shift five nights a week as an "observer" in the number 54 slab mill. I had worked in the steel mill long enough to know that being an "observer" in the slab mill wasn't the best job to have, but it wasn't as dangerous, dirty, or lowly as some of the other ones, such as being a third-helper in the open hearth furnace. Besides, it paid a bit more, and at the time pay was pretty much all that mattered to me. The year was 1938 and, except for the four and a half years that I would spend in the U.S. Army, I stayed in the number 54 slab mill until I retired in 1982.

It was difficult to work in the steel mill, especially in the 1930s and

1940s. Most people in those days could not afford to own a car and, as with many of Bethlehem Steel's workers, my father and brothers and I would have to walk about two and a half miles to get to work. We'd have to walk in rain, snow, cold weather or hot weather to get to and from the mills. There was a street car in Dundalk, but it wouldn't go to the mills from where we lived. After we got to the mills we'd then work our shifts, and walk the same distance home in the same weather conditions. The temperatures in the mill were stifling. In addition to the constant intense heat, it was usually noisy and dark, and no matter how careful you were, you could count on occasionally being burned by hot molten steel.

There was no job security whatsoever—you were at the mercy of the boss. Neither the Occupational Safety and Health Administration (OSHA) or the National Institute of Occupational Safety and Health (NIOSH) were in existence at that time, so there were few, if any, workplace standards in place. Many workers would get injured in the steel mills. Holidays didn't mean anything if you worked in the mills in those days. There was no negotiating with the boss, and if a holiday fell on a day that you were regularly scheduled to work, you worked as if it were any other day, and received no extra pay or extra day off. Essentially all of the steel mill workers were men, and many had difficulty fathering children. Some attribute this to the constant exposure to the increased temperatures and the destructive effect it has on sperm production. My father was an exception, as he fathered six children.

My mother used my pay from working in the steel mill to help support the household. I never had much money in my wallet. As in most households across the United States during the Depression years, money was usually scarce. We stuck together, took care of one another, and looked for other sources of income during those days. The times were tough.

One of the things we did to make some extra money was look for and sell scrap iron. The iron dealers at the scrap yards would buy it for about $1.20 for a hundred pounds. My brothers and I would look along the railroad tracks for iron, or anywhere else we could find it. We would take any kind we could find (or steal) that wasn't nailed down. We would have torn-up the railroad tracks for the iron if we had had the tools to do it.

We'd borrow a car and load the scrap iron into the car and drive to the dealer. He'd weigh the entire car with the scrap iron in it, and then we'd remove the iron and the scrap dealer would re-weigh the car. The difference between the two weights was, of course, the weight of the scrap iron that we were selling. We learned later that a lot of the scrap metal that dealers in the United States collected was sold to Japan. It is quite possible that the Japanese used some of this scrap metal to construct the fighter planes and aircraft carriers that attacked the United States naval base at Pearl Harbor on December 7th, 1941.

Sometimes when we were about to sell the iron we would take our dog with us. He was a big, heavy mutt and must have weighed close to a hundred pounds. On a couple of occasions we made the dog lie down on the floor when we pulled up to the scrap dealer. We climbed out of the car, leaving the dog in the car to add to its weight. When we unloaded the scrap iron from the car one of my brothers removed the dog in a way such that the scrap dealer didn't see him and we ended up being paid a little extra. We didn't make a habit of doing this with our dog because we figured if the dealer ever realized what we were up to he would no longer buy scrap iron from us. We never got caught.

3.

MEETING MISS THERESA COOK: MY FUTURE BRIDE

It was Friday, August 23rd, 1940, at about 12:00 noon, just two months after my 23rd birthday. My memory of meeting Theresa Cook on that day is as clear in my mind as if it were yesterday. There was a very nice golf course up in Aberdeen, Maryland, and that morning I went up there with a couple of friends to play golf. I was supposed to work the graveyard shift at the steel mill that night. My father taught his children to have a strong work ethic and, like him, I never missed a day of work. Being young and full of energy, I had plenty of time to play a full 18 holes of golf and come home and work all night in the steel mill.

I was out on the course with two of my friends, when about noon I became distracted by the presence of a beautiful young woman wearing shorts and walking along with three little kids. I had never seen her before. My friends and I stopped playing golf and politely introduced ourselves. She told us her name was Theresa Cook and that she was babysitting the children. She told us that she lived in Baltimore with her mother, but that weekend she was staying in Aberdeen in the home of the parents of the children to babysit, as they had gone away for the weekend.

Theresa was Polish. Her real name was Theresa Elizabeth Przewozny. When her parents immigrated to the United States her father worked as cook on the boat that brought them overseas. When the family got off the boat in New Orleans, for some reason their name Przewozny was replaced with Cook. Someone in the registration office must have confused the father's occupation on the boat with the family's last name, so Cook was the name the family usually used from there on.

After we spoke for a while she told us that there was a dance that night at the golf course country club, and indicated that she was available to go. I got all excited about the dance and wanted to go with her, but the problem was that I had to work that night. But there was something about Theresa that, aside from her good looks, I found appealing right from the start, and made me feel that I should get to know her. I wanted to go to the dance with her in the worst way, but I didn't want to miss work either.

I thought about it for awhile, and said to myself to hell with going to work, I'm going to go to the dance with Theresa. I told her I would go, but only if she would be my date. She politely accepted. Then I did something that I had never done before, and seldom ever did in my entire working career: I called the mill and told them I wasn't coming to work that night.

I could tell that Theresa liked me a lot. Aside from thinking that I was handsome and a gentleman, Theresa also liked me because I had a job, didn't smoke or drink, and that I liked kids. We were both Christian, although she was Catholic and I'm Methodist, which didn't matter much to us. I liked her because, aside from being very pretty, she had a nice personality and was a very respectable, fun-loving young lady. She and I were nearly the same age (I was a year older), and we both liked to do the same things.

We went to the dance that evening, and let me just say that she sure knew how to dance and party and have fun! I was light on the feet myself, and we danced the night away and had a great time. One song that was played that evening was Hoagy Carmichael's newly released "The Nearness of You." It's a beautiful song, and as we held each other tight and danced to it we fell in love right there. It became our song. Before we parted that evening I asked her if I could see her again. She said yes, and asked if I would go to her home in Baltimore to meet her mother. I agreed.

Soon afterwards I went to Baltimore to visit Theresa and meet her mother. Theresa had experienced a rough childhood. By the time we met her father was institutionalized in the Spring Grove mental hospital and remained there for most of the rest of his life. One of her two sisters had committed suicide, and the other had already left home. I felt kind of sorry for Theresa, since she had experienced some rough times as a child, and the Depression hadn't made things any easier for her or her mother. She had a dog named Spotty, whom she loved very much.

Theresa lived on the second floor of a building located at 201 N. Washington Street in Baltimore. Theresa's mother owned and operated a saloon, which was on the first floor of the building, directly below their apartment. When I went up to Baltimore and saw where they lived I felt uneasy because it was in a rough neighborhood. The looks of their saloon didn't make me feel any better.

The regular patrons were for the most part functional alcoholics and small-time bookies, served by any one of the six barmaids that worked there. All that the patrons would do in there was sit for hours on end drinking, smoking, talking a lot about nothing, and placing bets. The place was smoked-filled and reeked of stale beer, hard liquor and cigarette smoke. It was a real dive. I didn't like being in the saloon at all because I didn't drink alcohol or smoke, or bet on horses.

Theresa and her mother were alike in many ways. They were both devout Catholics and *never* missed mass on Sunday. They were both friendly, hardworking, outgoing-type people. They got along well with one another and had a lot of friends. I liked that. But the mother, unlike Theresa, cursed like a sailor and was a heavy boozer. She could out-drink any man I knew any day of the week. She especially loved going to the horse races at the local track. When she wasn't able to go the races, she'd bet with the local bookies that hung out in her saloon. I don't think she ever won too much money betting on the horses, and at best probably ended up winning just as much as she lost.

Theresa's mother liked me right from the start. First she was Polish and, while I'm primarily of Dutch descent, she liked the fact that I have some Polish blood in me. She also liked that I was Christian, and didn't seem to mind that I wasn't Catholic. She particularly liked the fact that I didn't drink or smoke, or hang out in saloons, which I found odd because she did all those things. She was always good to me and I was very fond of her.

Theresa and I began to date regularly and had a lot of fun. Those were the days of the big-band era, and jazz composers like Glenn Miller, Benny Goodman, Harry James, Woody Herman, Tommy Dorsey, Lionel Hampton, Gene Krupa, and singing groups such as the Ink Spots filled the airwaves with unbelievably good music. Theresa and I were good dancers,

Jack as a young man in Baltimore, Maryland, circa 1937. *Photo: the Womer family*

Jack, circa mid-1930s, as a student in the Franklin Day School, a private Christian high school in Baltimore. *Photo: the Womer family*

Jack and a girlfriend, Shirley Lewis, circa 1938, all dressed up and ready to go out jitterbugging in the nightclubs of Baltimore. Shirley and Jack were in love and wanted to get married, but her mother was opposed to it since Jack wasn't Catholic, and so put an end to their relationship. *Photo: the Womer family*

Jack's parents, Roxie and William Walker ("Walk") Womer. A few months after Jack was born Roxie took ill, and it became increasingly difficult for her to care for Jack and his three older brothers. In 1918, when Jack was about a year old, his parents decided to send him to live with his aunt Dolsie, who was Roxie's sister. Jack would return to living with his parents in 1922, after they moved to Sparrows Point, Maryland. *Photo: the Womer family*

Theresa Cook, the wind beneath Jack's wings, in a photo taken in September 1942. It was love at first sight when Theresa and Jack met on August 23rd, 1940 on a golf course in Aberdeen, Maryland. From the time Jack was drafted in April 1941 until the time he was discharged in September 1945, Theresa faithfully wrote to him nearly every day, and prayed constantly for his safety. Jack firmly believes that one of the reasons he survived the war is because of Theresa's prayers. They were married in November 1945, and remained together until her death in 1987. *Photo: the Womer family*

and we both loved to dress-up and go out. I was a pretty flashy dresser, and so was she. I always wore a nice stylish suit when we were out on the town, she'd wear a nice dress, and we'd go out by ourselves or with other couples and tear-up the city.

Many of our dates took place in the dance halls and night clubs in Baltimore. I could jitterbug better than anyone I knew, and many of my friends, both male and female, nicknamed me "Jitterbug." Some of the clubs we would frequent were the Ambassador on North Baltimore Street (right across the street from Theresa's saloon), and the Alcazar up on Cathedral Street. I met a very young Frank Sinatra at the Alcazar when Tommy Dorsey's band played there. Sinatra used to sing with Dorsey's band, and when I met him he was just a skinny young kid. He hadn't yet reached superstar status, although he was clearly on his way.

4.

THE OUTBREAK OF WORLD WAR II

By the late 1930s ominous signs began to emerge that the world was heading for another war. In the newspapers and on radio broadcasts, the names Adolf Hitler and Benito Mussolini were mentioned regularly. In 1937 I was 20 years old, and I remember reading that Japan invaded China, and that Hitler was building the Nazi Party and increasing Germany's military strength.

In another year or so, in blatant violation of the Treaty of Versailles, Hitler began to use his military to seize control of territories that had been taken from Germany as part of the terms and conditions of the treaty. In the latter part of 1938 Germany took control of Czechoslovakia. In September of 1939 Germany invaded Poland, and a few days later Britain and France declared war on Germany.

The situation in Europe and in other parts of the world during the late 1930s increasingly became the subject of conversations in my household, in the steel mills, and just about everywhere else. Most of the time the conversations would culminate in one general question: was the United States going to go to war? At the dinner table, or in the evenings while listening to radio broadcasts in our living room, we'd discuss the latest news stories, and each of us would voice their opinion on what the latest stories meant to the United States and to world peace. At work people did the same.

At the time, many of the people in the Dundalk area and who worked in the steel mills were turn-of-the century immigrants (or the grown children thereof) from a country that was now either at war with, or occupied by Nazi Germany. Many of these people felt a strong loyalty to their native country (or to their parents') and were quite angered by the situation in Europe. Some wanted the United States to go to war with Germany and Italy, but I and most people I knew felt differently.

I remember that shortly after Britain and France declared war on Germany, President Franklin D. Roosevelt said that the United States would not get involved in the European war. This announcement made me, my parents and brothers, and many of my buddies at the steel mill, feel at lot better. The next year, 1940, was an election year and the extent of U.S. involvement in the European war a big political issue. I think most Americans at the time did not want the U.S. to get involved, and I remember some people speculated that Roosevelt promised to maintain U.S. neutrality simply to help increase his chances of re-election in 1940, knowing damn well that the U.S. would eventually go to war.

Throughout 1940 the situation in Europe became increasingly worse. Italy declared war on France and Britain. The Nazis invaded and took control of the Netherlands, Belgium, Luxembourg and France, and began bombing England. I think by the middle of 1940 most people, including myself, began to realize that United States involvement in the war was becoming increasing likely. Benito Mussolini signed the Tripartite Pact with Nazi Germany and Japan in September of 1940, forging an alliance called the Axis.

These events undoubtedly caused President Roosevelt to reconsider his position on neutrality and to begin preparing for war. Near the end of 1940, a law was passed that required young men to register as being eligible to serve for 12 months in the U.S. armed forces. Every male within a certain age group had to register for service, but registration alone did not automatically mean you would be drafted. Whether you were called depended upon how you were ranked by your local draft board, which was composed of members of your own community.

I remember registering for the draft, along with a lot of other guys near the end of 1940, and the federal government began drafting men into the service in the early part of 1941. Some guys that I worked with in the steel mill were drafted at that time. What would happen is that you would get called into the main offices of the mill and you would interview with the superintendent and some other managers. They wanted to know if your job, or more specifically your income from your job, was essential to your family. If the superintendent of the mill felt that it wasn't, he would recommend to the local board that you be drafted. If the income from your job was essential to your family the superintendent would recommend that you not be.

Whether you would be drafted was essentially in the hands of the superintendent, and his decision on how you should be ranked or rated for draft purposes was supposed to be based on how important you were to your family's sustenance. I'm convinced, however, that my superintendent was prejudicial when he ranked the guys for draft purposes. It seemed to me and others that if you were Catholic, a Mason, an ass-kisser, or Negro you were given a very low rating and weren't likely to be drafted, regardless of whether you were or weren't essential to your family. I didn't fit into any of those categories.

In my family there were five boys, plus my father, and all of us worked in the steel mill and had incomes. By 1941 my older brother David was married and had a child. Ben was also married and had a few children. Neither my brother Herbert nor I had a wife or children to support so both of us were in line to be rated by the superintendent as A-1 draftees. By now my younger brother Douglas and I were the only two of the Womer brothers still living at home. Douglas was a little too young at the time to be drafted, although he would be later.

One day while I was at work in the steel mill I was called to see the superintendent, whose name was Joe Stokes. He knew me, my brothers, and my father very well because we had been working there for awhile. Joe was smart, but a lot of guys didn't like him because they felt he was underhanded. I didn't have strong feelings toward him one way or the other because I rarely interacted directly with him. I never got the feeling, though, that he liked me.

I knew why I was called into his office that day, and I knew what the outcome was going to be. Joe didn't need to ask any questions, but he did anyway. It was all an act, a formality. I answered his questions nonetheless, and told him I wasn't married, that I had no children, and while I still lived at home and gave most of my income to my mother, she had my father's income to rely on if ever I were drafted. I had no chronic medical conditions, and I was in good physical shape. I had no valid reason for staying out of the service. I knew it, Joe knew it, and he knew that I knew it.

After I had answered all of his questions Joe looked at me and said, while fighting hard to hold back a smile and with a hint of pleasure in his voice: "I've got to recommend to the local draft board that you be drafted. I've got to let you go Womer, I'll see ya." I said back to him, disgustedly, "Yeah, I'll see ya." Enjoying himself, the son-of-a-bitch said to me, "Don't worry, Womer, it's only going to be for one year." I didn't come back until nearly five grueling years of wartime military service had passed, and when I did come back the son-of-a-bitch had written on my papers that I had been terminated. He didn't want me to come back to work in the steel mill. He couldn't and didn't stop me from returning to work, though, for it was illegal for an employer not to hire back a man who was forced to leave his job because he had been drafted into military service.

5.

DRAFTED INTO THE ARMY: PRIVATE JACK WOMER

"Like the draft,
a Birthday's something
That you can't dodge or evade,
So may this one be an army
Of grand pleasures
on parade."
—From a birthday card sent to Jack Womer by Theresa Cook for his
24th birthday, on June 18th, 1941

Not too long after I had met with my superintendent in the steel mill, the local newspaper published a list of the names of men who had been selected for the draft. Sure enough, and as I expected, my name was included on the list. I had been drafted, and there was nothing I could do about it. I was quite annoyed. I was nearly 24 years old, I was working, and, despite the hardships of the Great Depression, overall I was having a good life. Theresa and I were young, going steady and having lots of fun together. We'd date at least once or twice a week, sometimes just visiting friends but usually we'd go out and "jitterbug" our feet off in the nightclubs of Baltimore. Things were starting to go real well for me, and getting drafted meant that everything going on in my life at the time had to be put on hold. I was quite bitter about having been drafted—I was madder than hell!

The paper instructed the draftees to report to a certain location in Dundalk on April 25th, 1941. A streetcar would take us to a check-in enter in Essex, which is a small town located a few miles north of Dundalk. On the morning of April 25th I waited, as instructed, at the streetcar stop. There were a lot of men at the stop waiting for the ride to Essex. Apparently, I had been drafted along with a lot of other guys from Dundalk and Sparrows Point, some of whom I already knew, either from childhood or working in the steel mills. Willard Sparks and Harry Hendricks, two long-time Dundalk buddies of mine, were there. I think it made us all feel a little better to see some familiar faces, to know that we were all in this together. But even the familiar faces couldn't remove the butterflies we felt in our stomachs that morning.

We arrived a little later in the day to the check-in center in Essex. The place was a mad house. It was packed with guys like me who had been told to report for the draft. There were loads of guys standing in lines that circled around all over the place. You couldn't tell where one line began from where another line left off. After checking in we went to the Armory in Baltimore to be examined. I was in superb physical condition, as I had played a lot of sports, and was actively involved with playing soccer and baseball at the time. After examining me they told me they were going to mark me "1-A," meaning that I was a top draft pick. Me and the other men that passed the examinations were then officially sworn in and inducted into the army. The guys who didn't pass the examinations were sent home.

Those of us who were inducted were sent to Fort Meade, Maryland, which is located about about midway between Baltimore and Washington, DC. When we arrived there one couldn't help but immediately notice that the whole place was a big mess. A lot of construction was going on. They were building a lot of barracks and other buildings. At first I didn't know why, but after awhile I realized it was to accommodate the large influx of draftees that they were going to receive. The ground was muddy because of the heavy and frequent April rains and because they hadn't yet planted any grass or trees due to the construction. Practically every square inch of ground at Fort Meade was mud.

After we got settled in and were issued army uniforms we were told that we were soldiers in the 29th Infantry Division. None of us had any idea as to what that meant, as all of the military jargon and way of life was new to us. The 29th Infantry Division was composed mostly of men from different parts of Maryland and Virginia. Some of them were from other states such as West Virginia, Delaware, and Pennsylvania, but for the most part the '29ers were Marylanders and Virginians. Me and a few other guys that I knew were assigned to Company C of the 175th Regiment, which was commanded by Colonel Harry Ruhl.

I learned later that me and the other men with me were among the first draftees of the Selective Service Act to arrive at Fort Meade. Other soldiers were already there when we arrived, but most of them had been in the National Guard units comprising the 29th Infantry Division before the Selective Service Act became law in September of 1940.

I could tell right away that I was going to hate being in the military. Aside from being angry about having been drafted, everything in the military was "yes sir," "no sir," standing at attention, saluting, and all of that formality stuff. I wasn't used to it, and never did get used to it. I had a problem with it. What made the situation a little easier to deal with is that practically everyone in the 175th Infantry Regiment was from the Baltimore area, so we all had a lot in common, plus I even knew some of the guys in the 175th, including Company C. Willard Sparks and Harry Hendricks were in my company. I even knew our sergeant. He had lived in Dundalk, close to where I lived, and was a real nice guy.

Life at Fort Meade wasn't too bad at first. We learned to shoot some of the military firearms, such as the M-1 Garand—a gun which I later would use quite extensively in combat. Afterwards, we'd take them apart and clean them, shoot them again, and take them apart and clean them again. I was an outstanding marksman. I had particularly good vision, which I think is why I was one of the best shots in Company C. We would also go through a lot of physical exercises, all-night hikes, and sometimes we were tasked to help with some of the construction work that was going on.

After a while though, these activities became boring. We were constantly cleaning guns and equipment that didn't need to be cleaned, constantly going through the same exercise routines, and being taught the same things, over and over again. Life at Fort Meade became real dull fast. It seemed the more boring it became the more resentful we became at being in the service. We didn't see any reason or purpose to what we were doing. We wanted to go back to our lives: to our jobs, our homes, our girl friends, our families, or to whatever we had or were doing before we were drafted.

Although things got dull at Fort Meade, we were allowed some privileges that would take the edge off our hatred of being in the army. One of the best privileges was frequent permission to leave the base for one or more days. We'd often get passes to leave the base during the evenings of the weekdays, and even over the weekends. I and many of the other guys in the 175th Infantry would usually go home when we were given weekend leaves, since most of us were from the Baltimore area and Fort Meade was only a few miles away. I could leave Fort Meade on a Friday afternoon at 5:00 pm, hop on a bus and by 6:30 be sitting at the dining room table in my parents' home in Dundalk eating a delicious home-cooked meal. I would then literally spend the whole weekend with my family, friends, and Theresa, leave Dundalk in the evening on Sunday, and be back at Fort Meade that evening well before curfew.

Going home on a weekend pass wasn't as easy for the guys in the other regiments of the 29th Infantry Division, as most of these men were from towns much farther away, such as those in southern Virginia or western Maryland. In those days the roads and transportation services weren't like they are today. Traveling from Fort Meade for a distance as short as 100 miles to a small rural town in the middle of nowhere in Virginia or Maryland was practically a day's trip in itself.

Most of what few roads led to the small towns of Virginia and Maryland at the time weren't paved, and cars or buses couldn't travel as fast on them as today. After heavy rains theses roads would become muddy and flooded, and were difficult to drive on. Nor were rail and bus services efficient back then. I knew of soldiers, though, who lived far away and were so homesick that they often would return home for the weekend—even if only to have dinner with their families, or to just spend a few hours. To them the long and difficult trip was worth it.

In addition to getting frequent passes to leave base we were also allowed to have visitors, and receive and write mail. Theresa was my very first visitor, and the first person to write to me when I entered the service. One of the first letters she sent was during the first week of May, 1941. In that letter she told me that she bought two new records, Glen Miller's "The One I Love" and Woody Herman's "Intermezzo." We planned what we wanted to do that weekend, as I knew I was going to get a weekend pass.

Theresa and I saw each other quite a bit while I was at Fort Meade, as I either got passes to leave base or she'd come to visit me.

When she and I weren't together we would write to each other. Throughout my entire time in the service Theresa wrote me a letter practically every day, telling how much she missed me and loved me, and what was going on back home in Baltimore and Dundalk. Soldiers love to receive letters from home, regardless of how near or far it may be, and I was no exception. My parents, brothers, my sister Jane, and other relatives and friends wrote to me on occasion, but by far Theresa wrote to me the most. Her letters were always quite special, and comforting to me. I lived off of them. I'd write frequently to her as well, but not as much as she wrote to me.

In the latter part of July 1941 we heard word that the 29th Infantry Division was to leave Fort Meade for four months of training elsewhere. We also heard about this time that the draftees' enlistment time, originally only 12 months under the Selective Service Act, was to be extended an additional six months, for a total of 18. This meant, of course, that instead of being released from military service in April 1942, I wouldn't get out until October. (In actuality, I wouldn't get out of the military until September of 1945.)

We became quite angry when we heard this. I hated being in the army. I had already begun counting the days as to when I was going to leave. Even though at Fort Meade I was close to home and was able to regularly see the people that I loved, it still felt like I was in prison. I had about nine months to go, after which I figured my life would return to how it was before I was drafted. Having to stay in the service an additional six months only worsened the already serious problem that most of us were having with morale at the time.

6.

BECOMING A STAGE PERFORMER

Sometime in August 1941, we heard that the senior officers of the 29th Infantry Division wanted to produce a musical revue for the public. The purpose of the musical was to offset anti-war protests that were taking place across the country at the time, and to stir patriotism and arouse public support for the military. The musical revue, called "Snap it Up Again," was a two-act show staged by Gene Ford, and the performers were, for the most part, to be comprised of men chosen from the various regiments of the 29th Infantry Division.

Those wishing to perform in the play had to audition and be selected. At first many of the guys weren't particularly interested in auditioning for the show. However, when we heard that the military planned to take the show on tour across the country many of us became quite interested. We figured those who were selected would spend most of the time traveling and performing across the country instead of undergoing the endless daily drill routines and training exercises—which is what we were currently doing, and anything that would exempt us from the daily grind of army life was a gift from Heaven. By the time the show would have completed its performances, a good chunk of the amount of time we were required to remain in the service would have passed by, even with the six month extension.

The grand finale of Snap it Up Again was to include a Manual of Arms routine in which 36 men known in the show as the "Dandy Fifth" would go through a variety of elaborate movements with their rifles that included such things as twirling them, moving them from shoulder to shoulder, tapping the rifle butts on the floor, parade marching, and other movements—

with all 36 men doing these exercises in perfect unison and formation. We had been taught some of these routines during our basic training at Fort Meade, but the show performance of these and other routines was designed to be much more involved and difficult, but also quite impressive to watch.

It was decided by the organizers of the show that the 36 men required for the Dandy Fifth drill were to be chosen entirely from the 175th Infantry Regiment. A lot of guys in the 175th auditioned for the "Dandy Fifth Drill," and only the guys who were markedly skilled at Manual of Arms exercises were selected to perform. Myself and my buddies Harry Hendricks and Sparky (Willard Sparks) auditioned, and each of us was selected. The audition was quite competitive, and we were proud to be among those selected.

Show rehearsals for Snap It Up Again started in the last half of August 1941 and continued into September. The Dandy Fifth Drill consisted of nine rows of four guys per row and I was chosen to be one of the four in the front row, which was reserved for the best of the best, although there were times during the routine when all of us would be in a single row and take up the whole stage.

Our first performance was held in Baltimore, in the Maryland Theater on Franklin Street. There wasn't an empty seat in the house. The entire performance went very well, and us guys in the Dandy Fifth put on a great show. We looked real sharp in our parade dress uniforms, and we performed our routines flawlessly. The audience was quite impressed. While I was up in the front line performing I winked at every pretty woman sitting within the first few rows that I made eye contact with. A few of them winked back at me! I couldn't get to meet any of them, though, because we had to get up early the next day and travel to our next show. After we finished our performance that night our officers made sure that we immediately dismantled our stage, collected our props, and went back to Fort Meade. No time was allowed for socializing with the audience.

We were scheduled to perform the following evening at the Mosque Theater in Richmond, Virginia. The distance from Fort Meade was about 130 miles, which in those days would easily take about five to six hours to travel. In addition to the long travel time, we also needed a couple of hours or so hours to unload our props, set-up the stage and get ourselves ready for the show. The plan was that we'd get up early, have breakfast, load the

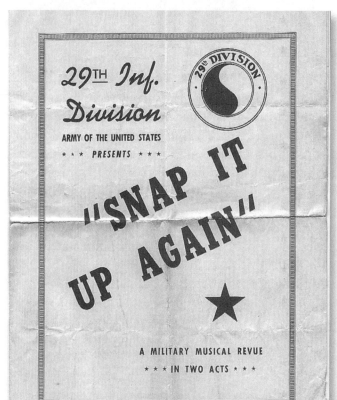

Front cover and page 2 of the original four-page play bill from the musical revue "Snap It Up Again."

29TH Inf. Division

ARMY OF THE UNITED STATES

★ ★ ★ PRESENTS ★ ★ ★

"SNAP IT UP AGAIN"

★

A MILITARY MUSICAL REVUE

★ ★ ★ IN TWO ACTS ★ ★ ★

THE TWENTY-NINTH INFANTRY DIVISION

ARMY OF THE UNITED STATES

Presents

"Snap It Up Again"

A Military Musical Revue in Two Acts

STAGED BY GENE FORD

ACT 1

1. THE TWENTY-NINTH OF 1917
   Commentator—Pfc. Robert C. Warren, 176th Field Artillery
2. SNAP IT UP AGAIN
   (Lyrics by Gene Ford; Music by Leon Dandoy, Jr.)
   115TH INFANTRY GLEE CLUB
3. SALUTE TO GYMNASTICS
   Pvt. Irving Levick, 176th Field Artillery
4. TROMBONIANA
   110TH FIELD ARTILLERY
   Pfc. Robert Delong   Staff Sgt. George Edlund
   Pfc. Everett Snyder   Pfc. Osborne A. Rhodes
   Pfc. Cornelius McQuade   Pfc. John Wilson
5. AT THE RECRUITING STATION
   The Sergeant—Pvt. Arthur C. Boring, 175th Infantry
   The Corporal—Sgt. William Church, 176th Infantry
   The Civilian—Pfc. Robert Dewitt, 115th Infantry
   The Recruit—Pfc. Harvey Barnes, 111th Field Artillery
6. BANG BANG
   (Lyrics and Music by Robert Davidson and Howard Acton of the
   National Press Club)
   MEMBERS OF THE 115TH INFANTRY GLEE CLUB
7. THE NEW RECRUIT
   (By courtesy of Joe Besser and James Little)
8. SALUTE TO OPERA
   Pvt. Martin Willen, 115th Infantry
9. FANFARE OF FANS
   Members of the Ensemble
10. DISCORD IN FANS
    Pvt. Max Zera, Special Troops   Pfc. Larry Smigel, 110th Field
    Pvt. Weldon O'Toole, 175th Infantry   Artillery
    Pvt. Edward Dargan, 176th Infantry Pfc. Walter Model, 111th Field
    Pvt. Ben Suffrin, 115th Infantry   Artillery
11. SALUTE TO JIVE
    110TH FIELD ARTILLERY, DIXIELAND BAND
    The Jitterbug—Pvt. Maurice Sykes, 104th Medical Regiment
12. BALLAD FOR AMERICANS
    (By arrangement with Robbins Music Corporation)
    115TH INFANTRY GLEE CLUB
    Soloist—Pfc. John Wilson, 110th Field Artillery

INTERMISSION
(10 Minutes)

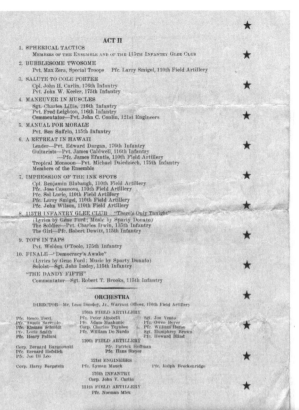

ACT II

1. SPHERICAL TACTICS
Members of the Ensemble and of the 115th Infantry Glee Club

2. BUBBLESOME TWOSOME
Pvt. Max Zera, Special Troops   Pfc. Larry Smigel, 110th Field Artillery

3. SALUTE TO COLE PORTER
Cpl. John H. Carlin, 176th Infantry
Pvt. John W. Keeler, 175th Infantry

4. MANEUVER IN MUSCLES
Sgt. Charles Lillis, 116th Infantry
Pvt. Fred Leighton, 116th Infantry
Commentator—Pvt. John C. Conlin, 121st Engineers

5. MANUAL FOR MORALE
Pvt. Ben Suffrin, 115th Infantry

6. A RETREAT IN HAWAII
Leader—Pvt. Edward Dargan, 176th Infantry
Guitarists—Pvt. James Caldwell, 116th Infantry
        —Pvt. James Efantis, 110th Field Artillery
Tropical Monsoon—Pvt. Michael Dziedziech, 175th Infantry
Members of the Ensemble

7. IMPRESSION OF THE INK SPOTS
Cpl. Benjamin Blubaugh, 110th Field Artillery
Pfc. Jose Casanova, 110th Field Artillery
Pfc. Sol Lurie, 110th Field Artillery
Pfc. Larry Smigel, 110th Field Artillery
Pfc. John Wilson, 110th Field Artillery

8. 115TH INFANTRY GLEE CLUB   "There's Only Tonight"
(Lyrics by Gene Ford; Music by Sparty Donato)
The Soldier—Pvt. Charles Irwin, 115th Infantry
The Girl—Pfc. Robert Dewitt, 115th Infantry

9. TOPS IN TAPS
Pvt. Weldon O'Toole, 175th Infantry

10. FINALE—"Democracy's Awake"
(Lyrics by Gene Ford; Music by Sparty Donato)
Soloist—Sgt. John Insley, 115th Infantry

"THE DANDY FIFTH"
Commentator—Sgt. Robert T. Brooks, 115th Infantry

ORCHESTRA

DIRECTOR—Mr. Leon Dandsy, Jr., Warrant Officer, 176th Field Artillery

176th FIELD ARTILLERY
Pfc. Rosco Tocci   Pfc. Peter Altobelli   Sgt. Joe Vento
Pfc. Angelo Saverolo   Pfc. Adam Mashunic   Pfc. Owen Boyer
Pfc. Khemas Schmidt   Corp. Charles Toynbee   Pfc. William Burns
Pfc. Louis Smith   Pfc. William De Nardo   Sgt. Humphrey Brown
Pfc. Henry Pallani   Pfc. Howard Blind

Corp. Bernard Baranowski   Pfc. Patrick Hoffman
Corp. Bernard Hofelich   Pfc. Hans Steyer
Pfc. Joe Di Leo

110th FIELD ARTILLERY

121st ENGINEERS
Corp. Harry Bergstein   Pfc. Lyman Mauck   Pfc. Ralph Breckenridge

176th INFANTRY
Corp. John V. Carlin

115th FIELD ARTILLERY
Pfc. Norman Mlek

MEMBERS OF THE 115TH INFANTRY GLEE CLUB
DIRECTOR—Pvt. Barr Cannon
MANAGER—Sgt. Robert T. Brooks
MEMBERS OF 115TH INFANTRY

Pvt. George Douglas   Pvt. George Williams   Sgt. Edwin Woods
Pfc. Ferrell Beasley   Pvt. Michael Carpinello   Pvt. Paul Riley
Sgt. John Insley   Pvt. Saul Hineck   Pvt. Louis Hollott
Sgt. Ignatius Keyser   Pvt. H. M. Stevens   Cpl. Alfred Cutsail
Pfc. William Nowell   Sgt. Vernon Ferguson   Pfc. James Donb
Pfc. Frank Young   Pvt. John Fiori   Pvt. Douglas Green
Pvt. Garet Cannon   Pvt. Charles Irwin   Pvt. Ray Miller
Pfc. Phillip Cannon   Pvt. Martin Willen   Pvt. John Edwards
Pvt. Chesney Kramer   Pvt. Edward George   Pvt. Thomas Carney
Cpl. Ivan Moore   Pvt. James Robinette   Cpl. Nolo Shobe
Pvt. Robert Preston   Pvt. George Sparwasser   Pvt. Walter Miller
                     Pvt. Adolph Sanders

MEMBERS OF 104TH MEDICAL REGIMENT
Pvt. Gildo Farrando   Pvt. Edgar Novick

MEMBERS OF 110TH FIELD ARTILLERY REGIMENT
Pvt. Thomas Arena   Pvt. Nicholas Grimaldi   Pvt. David Salina
Pvt. James Efantis   Sgt. Arthur Lambert   Pvt. John Wilson
Pvt. Sidney Fishman   Sgt. Marion Retur
                     Sgt. William Church, 176th Inf.

MEMBERS OF THE ENSEMBLE
Pfc. Harold Bamnan, 176th Field Artillery   Pfc. Eddie Rosick, 110th Field Artillery
Pfc. Frederick Ferraro, 176th Field Artillery   Pfc. Howard Shirk, 110th Field Artillery
Pvt. John Gallo, 176th Field Artillery   Pfc. Paul Stowell, 110th Field Artillery
Pvt. Anthony Lupone, 176th Field Artillery   Pfc. Raymond Algood, 110th Field Artillery
Pfc. Ray Morris, 176th Field Artillery   Pvt. John Edwards, 116th Infantry
Pfc. William Pollock, 176th Field Artillery   Pvt. Francis Saunders, 175th Infantry
Pfc. Walter Strenski, 176th Field Artillery   Pvt. Wilfred Schroeder, 175th Infantry
Pfc. Louis Carlucci, 110th Field Artillery   Pvt. Edward Dargan, 176th Infantry
Sgt. Joseph Giesmondi, 110th Field Artillery   Pvt. Amerigo Battaglia, 104th Medical Regiment
Pfc. Morris Regan, 110th Field Artillery   Pvt. John Fuchella, 104th Medical Regiment

MEMBERS OF THE "DANDY FIFTH" DRILL (175TH INFANTRY)
Pvt. Melvin Augdotir   Pvt. Joseph Kitkowski   Pvt. Charles Perschaks
Pvt. Anthony Barthmaier   Pvt. Nicholas Kissink   Pvt. Melton Price
Pvt. Henry Brachett   Pvt. Jacob Lind   Pvt. Gus Roessler
Pvt. Raymond Resone   Pvt. Grayland Taft   Pvt. John Royall
Pvt. Francis Brown   Pvt. Howard McAlee   Pvt. Jack Silverman
Pfc. Fred Brunngraber   Pvt. McCambridge   Pfc. Walter Soulsman
Pvt. Joseph Deille   Pvt. John McComas   Pvt. Willard Sparks
Pvt. Robert Downan   Pvt. Fred Middleton   Pvt. Howard Stine
Pvt. Joseph Finn   Pvt. Koo Miller   Pvt. Warner Argil
Pvt. Harry Hendricks   Pfc. James O'Mara   Pvt. John Wieland
Pvt. Walter Holland   Pfc. James Peacock   Pvt. Jack Womer
Pvt. William Kassa   Pvt. Clinton L. Zulauf

EXECUTIVE STAFF
29th Infantry Division
Morale Officer—Maj. Samuel R. Turner

General Manager—Lt. Harry Haller, Division Recreation Officer
Company Manager—Lt. Arthur G. Ueberroth, Jr., 175th Infantry
Auditor—Lt. Col. Christian A. Claypoole, 175th Infantry
Chief of Service—Lt. Eccles H. Scott, 116th Infantry

PRODUCTION STAFF

Producer—Mr. Gene Ford
Dance Director—Miss Marion Dufrow Venable, assisted by Pvt. Weldon O'Toole
Musical Director—Mr. Leon Dandsy, Jr., Warrant Officer, 176th Field Artillery
Choral Ensemble Director—Mr. Robert Frederick Freund
Stage Managers—Sgt. Robert T. Brooks, Pvt. Michael S. Gordon, Pvt. Maurice Sykes
Charge of Properties—Pvt. Edwin Bernstein
Assistant Property Man—Pvt. James Laney, 110th Field Artillery
Charge of Makeup—Mr. Bernard J. McConnell
Secretary—Pvt. Richard Kessler
Promotion—Pvt. Jean A. Lowenthal, Pvt. Wilbern Wood
Costumes by Brooks, New York
Scenery from Kaj Velden Studios, New York
Electrical Effects from National Stage Lighting Co., Washington, D. C.
Shoes by Selva, New York
Incidental Wardrobe by Jack Mullane, Washington, D. C.

Page 3 and 4 of the original four-page play bill from the musical revue "Snap It Up Again."

On page 4, note that Harry Hendricks, Willard Sparks, and Jack Womer are listed as members of the "Dandy Fifth."

props, equipment and ourselves onto the trucks and leave Fort Meade by about six o'clock in the morning. We got up at about 5:00 am, had breakfast, and went outside to wait for the trucks that would take us down to Richmond. There must have been some miscommunication between the organizers of the show and the truck drivers, because the damn trucks didn't show up at Fort Meade until about six o'clock in the afternoon!

The show was scheduled to start at 7:00 pm that evening, but we didn't arrive at the Mosque Theater until about midnight! We figured the audience would have gone home by then, but when we walked in through the stage door and peaked into the theater expecting to see a lot of empty seats we were surprised to see that practically the entire audience was there waiting for us. Here it was, midnight, and the place was packed with people who had been waiting patiently for at least five hours to see the show. We couldn't believe it! Inspired by the audience's desire to see us, we quickly unloaded the props and equipment, prepared the stage, got ourselves dressed and finally got the show underway at about 3:00 am. We put on a great performance. The audience loved us!

7.

WAR GAMES IN THE CAROLINAS

In early September of 1941, after about six months of training at Fort Meade, the 29ers were told that they would soon be going somewhere else for additional training. Two weeks later the 29th Infantry Division was sent about 45 miles south to Fort A.P. Hill in Caroline County, Virginia, approximately midway between Washington, DC and Richmond, and just east of Fredericksburg.

Me and the other performers in the show "Snap It Up Again" at first were exempt from the trip because of our show responsibilities. But after the performance at the Mosque Theater in Richmond, which took place about mid-September, 1941, we were told that future performances were put on hold. I never did learn why the show tour stopped after only two performances, but it did. This meant that me and the other performers would have to go with the rest of the division to Fort A.P. Hill for the additional training. In October and November there were some rumors flying around that the show was going to start-up again, but it never did.

We didn't do too much while we were at Fort A.P. Hill. We stayed in tents pitched in a very large corn field. There were seven men to a tent, and being the first time we had ever stayed in tents we weren't used to it. While at Fort Meade we lived in barracks that had hot water and heat, and tents were a big difference. Near the end of September, we left Fort A.P. Hill and headed south by truck for Fort Bragg, which is located in Fayettesville, North Carolina, about 250 miles further south.

After a few days or so at Fort Bragg, we were back on the road and traveled a good 75 miles west to Charlotte. We were now in the deep South and it was 1941. Many of the people that lived in the small rural communities and towns in the vicinity were still bitter over the Northern victory in the American Civil War. Those Southerners still held a grudge against Northern folk, who they seemed to define as anyone who lived north of North Carolina. They looked at us 29ers as Northerners, or Yankees, even though most of us were Southern boys ourselves, from Virginia and Maryland! Many of the local folks didn't like us being in or near their towns, and often treated us unkindly.

The purpose of going to Charlotte was to participate with other divisions in war games or, what I've seen in some books described as "The Carolina Maneuvers." All this was, basically, was make-believe war among the divisions. One or more divisions would be designated as the "Red Army" (the bad guys), and they would have to "fight" against one or more other divisions designated as the "Blue Army" (the good guys). Those G.I.s in the respective armies were given red or blue armbands or cloths to wear or afix to themselves for identification.

We'd typically "fight" throughout the rolling hills, farms, forests, swamps and towns along the border of North Carolina and South Carolina, in the general area south of Charlotte. Referees were assigned to observe the "fighting" and designate the winners and losers. We seldom ever carried real weapons during the war games, for obvious reasons. Instead, we used props, such as use broomsticks for rifles, stove pipes for mortars, and rocks for grenades.

When we did carry real firearms, we almost never carried live or even blank ammunition. We had to simulate the sounds of gunfire vocally. Occasionally we used real firearms loaded with blank ammunition. In doing so we could grow accustomed to the kick of the gun and the sound of gunfire in combat-like settings without the risk of anyone being shot. Live ammunition was used on rare occasions.

"Tanks" were often just a small truck with the word "TANK" written in large letters on each side. Other types of military vehicles were similarly represented. I guess the intent of the war games was to try to simulate combat as close as practical to the real thing, so that in the event we were sent to Europe to fight the Krauts we'd at least have had some experience, even if it was only make believe.

The U. S. military brass must have felt that the war game experience, although artificial, would be better than no experience at all. In reality, the games were a joke. For example, one of the things we used to do is disguise ourselves as being the opposing army, and trick the unit we were fighting against. All you had to do was find out when and where the colored identification material (usually armbands) of the opposing army was being handed out, and go there and act just like the other guys that were supposed to be there. In essence, you were getting false identification, which you would carry in your pocket. During a war game, if you saw "enemy" troops and felt that you were going to be spotted or captured, all you had to do was remove your own identification, hide it, and put on the false colored identification. In doing so you'd trick the enemy into thinking that you were one of them.

All we would do during the war games is run around and either "hide" from the "enemy" or "fight" them by pretending we were shooting real bullets, throwing real hand grenades, killing or capturing them. During "battles" we'd often see civilians or local people going about their daily routines, which would sometimes extend into the battle areas. For example, we'd see children walking to school right between our lines, farmers plowing their fields, and people fishing in ponds—all right where we would be pretend-fighting.

One time during the middle of a "shoot-out" a young boy walked up to me and asked if I wanted to buy some fresh donuts. I bought a couple, ate them, and went back to "shooting" the enemy. On another occasion we were resting in a wooded area after a battle. It had been stifling hot that day, and we were exhausted from the heat. Some local kids came around selling homemade ice cream right there in the woods. They were selling it for 25 cents a half-pint, which at the time was ridiculously over-priced, and those kids knew it too. But we were hot and exhausted, and that frozen ice cream looked so good that, hell, I would have paid a dollar to just get a tablespoonful of it on my tongue. A few of us bought all that they had and we gobbled it right down. It was soothingly delicious! And those kids must have made a fortune that day.

During one war game some of my buddies and I were "captured by the enemy." This is when I found out that getting captured during these war games wasn't so bad. We were shooting the hell out of the "enemy," but we were grossly outnumbered and cornered, so we eventually surrendered. We were put into a "stockade" and given good food and were allowed to sleep as much as we wanted. We were actually treated much better as prisoners than we were back in our camp. We were delighted to have been captured! Again, this just goes to show how ridiculous the war games really were.

Morven, North Carolina is where, as I recall, we had our very first war game. Morven is just within the state, very close to the border of South Carolina. It was a very small town surrounded by miles of rolling corn fields and cotton fields. If you blinked your eyes while traveling through Morven you'd probably never realize you were in it. I don't think the town had changed much since the end of the Civil War.

Morven's inhabitants were almost entirely Negro, who spent most of their lives picking cotton and corn as a means of survival. It almost seemed as if slavery hadn't ended for them. They would hardly ever speak to white people, and when they did their accents were so thick you couldn't understand a word they said.

Morven is where I got my first taste of what army life out in the field is really like. During that war game we camped in the woods or fields, and went for days without shaving or washing. We'd even go for a few days without being given much food, and what little we were given tasted like it was garbage. Camping in the woods was particularly bad because they were loaded with ticks, ants, mosquitoes, and poison oak.

Sometimes we'd sleep at night in the cornfields, which were a little better than the woods, but getting a good night's sleep seldom ever happened no matter where you slept because of the cold and the insects. So this was life in the army. I used to think about the native American Indians, and wondered how the hell they lived their entire lives under similar, even worse, conditions.

It was unusually hot in the south that October, more so than it typically is for that time of year. In the daytime it would be stifling hot, and during the night it would be so cold you'd think it was going to snow. During the day I would walk around in just my tee-shirt and pants, and still feel much too hot. At night I would sleep in my jacket and rain coat, wear my shoes and stockings, cover myself with a blanket, and still feel cold.

Shortly after we left Morven, we went to some other area in North Carolina. I don't know where it was, but I remember that hunting season had just opened and a lot of the locals would go hunting while we were involved with the war games. Once I remember being stationed with my unit between two crossroads waiting for the "enemy." We heard shots in the woods and circled around to get closer to where we thought the "enemy shooters" were. It turned out that the shots had come from some local guys hunting deer. We were damn lucky they hadn't shot us, thinking that we were deer walking through the woods!

One night we were next to an old graveyard. It had been raining for a few days prior, and the ground was quite muddy. I noticed a large tombstone lying flat on the ground. I figured sleeping on the tombstone would be better than sleeping in mud, so I slept on the tombstone that night, and was actually able to get in a few hours of deep sleep.

It was during this war game that my M-1 Garand rifle was replaced with a Browning Automatic Rifle or, as more commonly known, a "BAR." Both rifles fire 30-06 bullet rounds, but with the BAR one has the option of firing the bullets on either full-automatic (continuous) fire or semi-automatic fire (i.e., intermittent fire, as fast as one can pull its trigger). Although heavier than an M-1, I liked the BAR quite a bit. I was designated as an expert BAR shooter.

I truly hated being in the army, and particularly having to participate in the war games, but I will say that life in the fields made us tough. We did a *lot* of hiking. Sometimes these hikes would go for many miles and last well into the night. Then late at night after a long exhausting hike, we'd be told to eat and sleep in the fields or woods, only to be awakened a few hours later and ordered to go on another long hike. We'd often go for days with hardly anything to eat or drink, or change our clothes. I was taught how to take a single quart of water and brush my teeth, shave my face, wash my body, and still have enough left over to boil an egg. I figured if I continued to live like this for a couple of more months I would turn into a caveman, or an animal. I had learned how to survive off the land, and I was determined to withstand anything the army could dish out at me. A lot of us felt the same way.

The war games lasted for periods ranging anywhere from three or four days to about two weeks. Sometimes we'd get weekends off. We did this from the early part of October to about the end of November 1941, when it became too cold to continue. It's good that it was too cold for the war

Private Jack Womer, Company C, 175th Infantry Regiment, 29th Infantry Division, Fort Meade, Maryland, circa May, 1941. Jack was among the first men to be drafted following enactment of the Selective Training and Service Act of 1940. *Photo: the Womer family*

Jack (foreground) in Newport News, Virginia, where the 29th Infantry Division was sent in early April 1942 to guard the naval shipyard. The 29ers stayed there until the mid-June, when they were sent to Fort A.P. Hill, near Fredericksburg, for more training. *Photo: the Womer family*

Jack and his fiancée Theresa Cook on September 27, 1942. About a week later, Jack and half of the 29th Infantry were on the *Queen Elizabeth* heading to Europe. The other half of the Division had left for Europe a few days earlier on the *Queen Mary*. Jack and Theresa would not see each other for again another three years. *Photo: the Womer family*

Jack (left) standing guard over train depots in McKeesport, PA in March, 1942. Between pulling guard duty, the trains coming and going, and boats traveling up and down the river, the men hardly ever got any sleep. The tents were very close to some railroad tracks, and hot, smoldering coal cinders that had billowed out from locomotives that rolled by would occasionally land on the tents and cause them to catch on fire.
Photo: the Womer family

games, because by the end of October we were all getting both bored and tired with them. Sometime near the end of October we were told while in camp that we were going to return to Fort Meade in Maryland around mid-November. For me, this was music to my ears because I'd be close to home again, living in heated barracks with hot running water instead of tents out in fields.

I wrote and told Theresa that we heard that we were returning to Fort Meade and that the play might start back up again. She wrote back and told me she'd read in her local newspaper, *The Baltimore Sun*, that the 29th Infantry Division was soon going to go back to Fort Bragg, North Carolina and remain there until about the 6th or 7th of December, and only then return to Fort Meade. I told her not to believe any of what she read in the local papers. Sure enough, what Theresa read was indeed correct and what we were told was wrong. By about the end of the first week in November I was back at Fort Bragg!

8.

THE JAPANESE ATTACK PEARL HARBOR

We stayed at Fort Bragg for about a month, where we participated in
some more training and war games, until during the first week of
December 1941, when we packed up and headed back to Fort Meade. We
were to make two stops along the way, one of which would be at Fort A.P.
Hill in Virginia, and would reach Fort Meade on the 9th of December.

We arrived at Fort A.P. Hill just before the Japanese Imperial Navy
ruthlessly attacked the United States naval base at Pearl Harbor, Hawaii
on December 7th, 1941, killing several thousand innocent American men.
It was at Fort A.P. Hill that I and the rest of the men in the 29th Infantry
Division learned of the attack. An angry mood fell upon us when we heard
the news on a radio broadcast. I think most Americans felt the same way.

The following day President Franklin D. Roosevelt declared war on
Japan during a radio broadcast to the citizens of the United States. We
arrived back at Fort Meade on or about December 9th, as planned. Then,
just as the situation seemed as if it couldn't get any worse, it did, for on
December 11th, 1941, just four days after the Japanese attack on Pearl
Harbor, German leader Adolf Hitler declared war on the United States.
The *world* was now at war.

It was now clear that the 29th Infantry Division wouldn't remain at
Fort Meade for too long, and that we weren't going to be leaving the army
anytime soon, for the United States was officially at war and we were in
the army, trained and ready for action. We knew then that we were definitely going to be thrown into the fight, and for the full duration, regardless
of how long that would be. What we didn't know was where we were going

to do our fighting, for the United States was going to fight on two fronts: in the Pacific against the Japanese, and in Europe against Germany.

Many people believe the attack on Pearl Harbor was a major victory for the Japanese. In reality I believe it was anything but. The primary objective of the attack was to sink our aircraft carriers stationed at Pearl Harbor. Not one was sunk or even damaged because they were all out at sea at the time of the attack. Many battleships and other warships were sunk or otherwise damaged, but with the exception of the battleship *Arizona* and one or two smaller warships, every ship that was attacked, damaged or even sunk was repaired and put back into service. It is, of course, true that the Japanese brutally murdered or injured several thousand young American naval men, but killing or wounding them was not the primary objective of the attack.

The only thing the Japanese accomplished in their attack on Pearl Harbor on December 7th is that they made the American people madder than hell and woke a sleeping giant; the will of the American people to fight back with everything at their disposal, which included millions of young men, tremendous industrial strength, an extremely large workforce, and the ability to rapidly build a military superior to that of the Japanese. The Japanese would pay a tremendous price for their mistake in attacking Pearl Harbor.

Not too long after Pearl Harbor a new selective service act made men between 18 and 45 liable for military service, and required all men between 18 and 65 to register for the draft. Most American men who were between 18 and 30 years old from 1941 to 1945 served in the United States military during World War II. While most were drafted into the service, there were many who volunteered and couldn't wait to get into the fight.

Women began to fill the jobs that had become vacant by the men who went into the service. Industries within the United States shifted their production toward the manufacture of war materials: planes, ships, uniforms, guns, bullets, bombs, and so forth, and many women went to work in the factories. Not too long after the attack on Pearl Harbor, Theresa took a job in a shipyard in Baltimore, where vessels needed to support the war effort were constructed.

The only good things that happened to me in December of 1941 is that I returned to Fort Meade, where I was much closer to Theresa and my home in Dundalk, and that Theresa and I got engaged during Christmas week. We almost got married during that holiday season, but we decided to postpone our wedding until I returned home from the service for good.

My parents liked Theresa, and Theresa's mother liked me. But Theresa was Catholic and I was Methodist. I know this seems ridiculous nowadays, but back then marrying someone who did not practice the same religion was considered taboo. Our belonging to different Christian denominations didn't matter much to us, as we were very much in love, but it was something that mattered a great deal to my mother and father. My parents, particularly my father, at first didn't approve of my plans to marry a Catholic girl, nor was Theresa's mother happy over the prospect of her daughter marrying a Methodist, although she seemed more willing than my parents to go along with our plans. It was nothing personal against either of us, just strictly religious.

To appease my parents, I asked Theresa to leave the Catholic Church and become Methodist. She politely declined, and said that while she loved me and wanted to marry me, she was not willing to give up being Catholic. I completely understood and respected her position, because I felt the same way about leaving the Methodist Church—it was something that I wasn't going to do. I told her that what was most important to me is that we get married, that we could remain what we were, and as far as I was concerned our children could be raised as Catholics.

My father threatened me by saying that if I ever married Theresa or any other Catholic woman, he would throw me out of the house and would never speak to me again. I asked him: "Dad, how many times in your life have you gone to church? The only time I ever see you go to church is when they're going to serve food after the service, so why are you acting like the Methodist Church is so important to you when it really isn't? Theresa is a good woman, and you know it. Why would any man object to his son wanting to marry such a woman?" My father couldn't answer me, because he knew I was right. After awhile my parents gave in and went along with our plans to marry.

9.

OFF TO EUROPE TO FIGHT HITLER

I remained stationed at Fort Meade into March 1942, not doing a heck of a lot during this time. Occasionally I would mouth-off to a superior and get into trouble, and as a result wouldn't be allowed certain privileges such as passes to leave base, or I would get extra kitchen or other duties. I never did care too much about being punished. Despite it all, I got to see Theresa quite a bit. She would frequently hop on a bus from Baltimore and come and visit me, or I'd visit her or my family. Sometime in February or March of 1942 the commander of the 29th Infantry Division, Major General Milton Reckord, was replaced with a new man, Major General Leonard T. Gerow. Shortly after he arrived the division underwent reorganization.

Near the end of the first week in March, my company and other guys from the 175th Regiment were sent to McKeesport, Pennsylvania, a small town located about ten miles or so southeast of Pittsburgh, at the confluence of the Youghiogheny and Monongahela rivers. The U.S. Steel Company owned and operated a lot of mills in McKeesport. It was a steel town just like Dundalk. In fact it looked and smelled much like Dundalk, and being in McKeesport reminded me of home. The only thing we did there was guard the train depots.

We stayed in McKeesport until the end of the month, and then we took down our tents and headed for Newport News, Virginia. We arrived there on or about April 1st, and set up our tents right along the James River, in a section of town known as Hilton Village Branch. Newport News was essentially a gigantic naval shipyard. The U.S. Navy built battleships and aircraft carriers there. Those ships were huge, and the main reason we were sent there was to guard the shipyard. The only official things I did while in Newport News were guard and kitchen duties, and when I talked back to my superior officers, extra kitchen duty.

We stayed in Newport News for about two and a half months, and about the middle of June 1942 we were sent back to Fort A.P. Hill up near Fredericksburg. Not only did we do more training there, but it was becoming more serious and rigorous. I think this was largely because of our new commander, Major General Gerow, and because by this point we were all pretty certain that we were soon going to be sent somewhere overseas to fight. We'd march a few days a week, anywhere from 15 to 30 miles a day in those hot Virginia temperatures of June.

A lot of guys literally collapsed from heat exhaustion during those marches. I'm proud to be able to say that I never collapsed or fell out of any marches that I went on, although a lot of guys did. At the end of a long march our feet would be covered with blisters. Word got up to General Gerow that we were complaining about the long marches and the blisters on our feet, and his advice to us was, "If you get blisters on your feet just keep walking and you will wear them off." Gerow was quite a character.

We were at A.P. Hill for about a month, and by about the middle of July we were sent back to the Charlotte area for more marching and to participate in more war games. For about the next six weeks we pretty much constantly camped, marched and "fought" in the woods and fields of Dilworth, Peachland, Monroe, and Polkton, small towns in North Carolina that are about 30 to 50 miles southeast of Charlotte.

Again, as at A.P. Hill, we tended to train much harder than we had in the past, and we seemed to do more training at night than previously. We'd march longer distances, were given less food to eat, and we had fewer rest periods. The weather was hot during those weeks, and many guys would fall out or collapse during our long daytime marches. But overall the war games that we participated in during this period were just as much of a joke as the ones the previous fall.

Sometimes men would get seriously injured during the war games. One night John Smolek, a guy that I knew from back home in Dundalk, drowned while we were crossing the Pee Dee River. He was with some other guys and they were swimming across when all of a sudden he said he had become weak and too tired to swim to the other side. The other guys tried to carry him back ashore, but he must have panicked because he started fighting with them so they had to let him go. I hadn't yet tried to cross so I wasn't immediately aware of what was happening to John.

Word soon got back to us on shore. One of my officers, who knew that I knew John, told me to get into a rowboat and look for him. I rowed around calling and looking for John, but I didn't see him or hear him. I figured he might have made it to the other side of the river, so I rowed over to the other bank and just as I stepped out of the boat some "enemy" soldiers came out of the woods and said to me "Ha, ha, you're captured." I said "Go to hell you jerks!! I'm not playing war, I'm looking for a friend of mine who may be drowning!! Now help me look for him or get the hell out of my way!" They got out of my way and left me alone.

I looked everywhere for John along the bank and on the river, but I never found him. He had drowned. An airplane spotted his body the following morning floating along the shore, about five miles from where we had crossed the river. I didn't know John real well, but I did play some ball with him back in Dundalk. He was a good kid. This incident shook me up quite a bit. To learn that someone that you've known since childhood died so unexpectedly while training together was news that I found hard to deal with at the time. We all knew that there was a good chance that many of us would get wounded when we were sent off to fight the real enemy, and that some of us were going to be killed in action. That was expected and accepted. None of us, though, expected that any of us would get killed during a routine training exercise at home in the United States. I think John's death would have been easier for me to deal with if he had been killed in action. He was the first of many men I knew that would die as a result of World War II. A military funeral service was held for John in Baltimore, and I was one of the soldiers that made up the honor guard. The funeral was sad and very emotional.

During the last half of August 1942 we left North Carolina and headed southeast to Florida, where we set up our tents in Camp Blanding. After being there for a couple of weeks or so we heard we were going to be sent overseas. We didn't know exactly when, but we knew it was going to be soon. What we weren't told was where: across the Atlantic Ocean to fight the Nazis in Africa or Europe, or the Pacific Ocean to fight the Japs?

About the middle of September, 1942, after a little more than two weeks in Camp Blanding, we packed our gear and tons of equipment and boarded trains. As soon as we realized we were heading north we knew we were going to be sent to Europe to fight the Krauts. After about two days of travel we arrived at the train station in New Brunswick, New Jersey, about 30 miles south of New York City. We unloaded at the train station and were taken a couple of more miles to Camp Kilmer.

Because our embarkation to Europe was imminent, near the tail end of September up through the beginning of October 1942 the 29th Division command granted everyone at least one 24-hour pass before we left the United States. All of the men in my company were issued passes, but most of them didn't come back on time. Most returned well after 24 hours because they knew it was the last time they'd get to see their loved ones, at least for awhile, if not forever. No one got in trouble for returning to Camp Kilmer beyond their approved 24-hour leave. What the hell was the army going to do to us? Throw us into the stockade so we'd miss the boat overseas?

With my pass I hopped on a train and went back to Maryland to visit Theresa and my family. Within a day or two after I got back to Camp Kilmer I was issued yet another 24-hour pass, for October 1st. I returned immediately to visit Theresa and my family once again. It was a bittersweet visit. Sweet in that Theresa and I loved seeing one another again, but bitter in that we hated leaving one another because neither of us knew whether we would ever see each other again. It was the same with my mother, father and brothers. I didn't know if I would ever see any of them again. I had an uneasy feeling about going overseas.

Theresa came with me to the Baltimore train station to see me off on my return trip to Camp Kilmer. We stood on the station platform, hugged each other as tight as we could, kissed, and said our goodbyes with our eyes filled with tears. Just as the train was about to pull out of the station I jumped aboard. I felt quite sad and lonely as I rode back up to New Brunswick.

The 29th Infantry Division traveled to Europe by boat from the docks on New York's west side, but not as an entire division. We left New York and sailed to Europe in two stages, on the luxury liners *Queen Mary* and *Queen Elizabeth*. This was done for two reasons. First, there probably wasn't a ship large enough to carry the entire division for the trip overseas. Second, even if there was such a ship, it would be foolish to send the entire division on a single ship because if it was sunk by a German U-boat the entire division would be lost. About half the division left Camp Kilmer for New York on September 26th where they boarded the *Queen Mary*, which was docked near the *Queen Elizabeth* in Manhattan.

Me and the remainder of the 29th Infantry Division left Camp Kilmer on October 2nd, within hours after I had returned from Baltimore. We boarded trains at New Brunswick and headed for Hoboken, New Jersey. There we boarded ferries and crossed the Hudson River to Manhattan, and began boarding the *Queen Elizabeth*. On October 5th, 1942 the *Queen Elizabeth* slowly pulled out of New York Harbor and began its long journey to Europe.

As we were leaving New York harbor I wanted to see the Statue of Liberty because we were going to pass right by it. I couldn't though because I was on guard duty seven decks down. By the time my duty had ended we were a few miles out of the harbor and I was only able see it from a distance. I don't remember too much about the trip overseas, only that the ship was quite full with men and supplies. We were packed in like hogs in a slaughter pen. We were unescorted, because we could travel faster than the German U-boats that patrolled the Atlantic. The ship also did a lot of zigzagging to help prevent being torpedoed by a sub.

While there was a sense of excitement and adventure among us as we crossed the Atlantic I spent a lot of time wondering to myself if I would ever set foot in the United States again. I think a lot of the men wondered the same. Many of us would return home, but many others wouldn't. For example, my dear childhood friend and army buddy Harry Hendricks, along with the rest of the 29ers, attacked Omaha Beach, France on June 6th, 1944. He survived the D-Day assault, but was killed eleven days later, the day before my 27th birthday, during the 29th Infantry's inland advance toward St Lo.

A week or two after D-Day Willard Sparks, my other dear childhood friend and army buddy, would get hit in the neck with a piece of shrapnel from a German 88mm cannon. It damn near killed him. The shrapnel fragment is about the size of a cube of sugar. Ever since he returned home from the war in 1945, he's kept it on display in his home and proudly shows it to visitors, family, friends, whoever, despite many pleas from his wife not to.

Many of us who were fortunate to return to the United States alive came back paralyzed, crippled, missing limbs, blind, or, perhaps worse, emotionally disturbed. I, after three long war-ridden years, was among the relatively few G.I.s who crossed the Atlantic in the *Queen Mary* or *Queen Elizabeth* in September/October of 1942 who returned home in one piece.

10.

ARRIVING IN ENGLAND: FIRST IMPRESSIONS

October 15, 1942

Dear Theresa,

Just about everything in England is rationed to support the war effort. There are shortages of sugar, flavorings, flour, spices, fruits, meats, eggs, milk, butter, lard, gasoline, clothing, soap, razor blades and practically everything else because these items are needed to support the English troops. The rationing and the stress of the war has taken its toll on the English people. I can see the stress in their faces, and feel it in the air. Most of the citizens look half-starved because of the lack of food.

> *Private Jack Womer,*
> *C Company,*
> *175th Infantry Regiment,*
> *29th Infantry Division*

The *Queen Elizabeth* arrived safely in Scotland on October 11th, 1942. Our stay in Scotland was very brief, less than a day I believe, and we traveled south by train to Tidworth Barracks, an old military camp in Wiltshire, England, located just a few miles from the famous Stonehenge archaeological site. This was the new home of the 29th Infantry Division. We were the third military unit from the United States to arrive in England during World War II. The 34th Infantry Division and the 1st Armored Division had preceded us.

In Tidworth we continued with the rigorous tactical training and marching exercises that we had done in the United States. The hours spent training and marching were long, and took place seven days a week. Weekends were no different than weekdays for us. What made matters worse is that the weather was usually terrible. For one thing it rained a lot, and when it wasn't raining it was usually overcast, misty, cold and dreary. Having to march for miles and conduct tactical maneuvers through all that mud and cold and damp air was no fun.

In the evenings we watched movies in camp, or were allowed to go to the nearby villages or the many pubs in the area and mingle with the local people. Every now and then we were given a weekend pass, but not as often as when we were in the United States. We were a little closer to the war now that we were overseas, and life had become quite different.

We were allowed to interact with the local people. It was wartime in England. Most of the young English men were away fighting the Nazis, and for the most part the locals consisted of women of all ages and those males too young or too old to fight. Occasionally I would see some English soldiers who were stationed in the area or home on leave, but for the most part there weren't too many other soldiers around where we were.

Just about everything in England was rationed, and this, plus the stress of the war and the bombings and worry about their sons, husbands and brothers fighting overseas showed in the way the local people behaved. I could see the stress in their faces, and feel it in the air. Most of the citizens looked half-starved because of the lack of food. The local people, though, while they didn't have a heck of a lot of food, ate five times a day. They would eat early in the morning, then have a little food at about 11:00 am, and then they would have "dinner" in the mid-afternoon. The next meal of the day was at about 6:00 pm, but it wasn't called supper, they called it "tea time," during which they would drink tea and have very little to eat. Then, at 10:00 pm they would have "supper," which consisted of a little more than what they ate at "tea time." Instead of saying "have you had supper?" the English would say "have you had your tea?"

While I felt sorry for the English citizens because of the hardships they were enduring, I didn't like them at all because they were always trying to take advantage of us Americans. They would try to get all they could from us. When an American soldier went to buy something, or have his pants pressed by a tailor, order a meal in a restaurant, hire a taxi or whatever, the

English merchants would raise their prices every time. We had to be real careful.

What made it worse for us is that we were paid in British pounds, not U.S. dollars. The English knew that we weren't accustomed to thinking in terms of pounds when buying things, so it made it a little easier for them to cheat us. The English knew we made more money than their own soldiers so I guess they figured they would try to take what they could from us. We were over there putting our asses on the line for the sole purpose of protecting them from Hitler's Nazis, and it would piss us off quite a bit when an English merchant would try to take advantage of us. I didn't mind the English soldiers, but I didn't care too much for the English citizens who were always trying to swindle us.

Unlike most of the American G.I.s, I didn't drink or smoke, so I would usually stay out of the many English pubs located throughout the countryside and villages. I used to play soccer with some of the locals, and they were surprised at how skilled I was at the game.

In early December of 1942, I took my first of many trips to London on a pass. I'd usually go sightseeing, go to theatres to see movies, eat in restaurants and visit night clubs where big-band orchestras performed and patrons could dance.

I used to meet a lot of British soldiers in London, and some were Commandos (the elite of the British soldiers), but most were regular infantrymen. Many, by now, were combat experienced, and I used to like to speak with them and hear their stories about the war. They gave me advice on how to stay alive, and on what to do and what not to do during combat. I learned a lot from them.

There were many theaters in London, and they were similar in appearance to the ones back home in Maryland. The only difference is that unlike the movie theaters in Dundalk, which charged 25 cents, the London theaters would charge anywhere from $1.00 to $4.00 to see a movie. Typically, at these prices, you would get to see three films: first a newsreel which usually provided the viewers with an update on the war effort; this was followed by a short comedy film; and lastly you would see the main movie.

The subways in London were just like those in New York City. They didn't have street cars in London, but there were a lot of double-decker buses. Unlike New York, though, everything in London stopped or shut down at 10:00 pm. You couldn't get a ride on a bus or subway, see a movie or get a bite to eat after then. Even the nightclubs would close.

The food in London was terrible. It looked good but tasted awful. It was actually worse than the food we were served in camp. I couldn't eat it. I was constantly asking Theresa and my parents to send me food and goodies, particularly cakes, candies and chewing gum.

Most of the young English women I saw in London wore much too much rouge and lipstick. They looked liked clowns or American Indians. What I found particularly astounding is that the London women thought just as much of the Negro American soldiers as they did of us white guys. The English women didn't seem to view or treat Negro American soldiers any differently than white ones.

For example, occasionally while I was dancing in a nightclub in London, a Negro G.I. would pass by me on the dance floor dancing with a white English woman. It was a shocking sight for us, as such things just wouldn't happen in the United States at that time, especially in Maryland and other southern states. I think the English thought that the Negroes were native American Indians, and that's why they accepted them the same way they accepted us.

I have even seen Negro men cut-in on white fellows dancing with white English women. One time I saw a Negro G.I. try to cut in on a white soldier, and the white guy turned and punched him right in the mouth and knocked him to the floor. The white guy continued dancing as if nothing had happened, and the Negro got up and walked away. That was the last I saw of him.

As far as finding girlfriends in England, the American G.I. had all the advantages. First of all, most of the young and handsome English fellows were away at war, and the only Englishmen left for the young and pretty English ladies were primarily the bums, tramps, or men that were old or no good at all. Secondly, the American soldier had much more money to spend than did the English soldiers stationed in the area or home on leave, and the women knew it too.

A buck private in the United States Army was paid a little over a dollar a day as soon as he entered service. This amount would increase as he was promoted. In terms of U.S. money, a private in the English Army got paid a measly 22 cents a day for the first three months of service. For the next six months he was paid 25 cents a day, and then after nine months of service it was 28 cents per day. He would then have to wait a year before his next raise. I once met a sergeant in the English Army who told me that he was paid the equivalent of 30 dollars per month, and he had been in the service for four years!

In terms of having money to spend on the ladies, there was no way the average English soldier could compete with the average G.I., and it was very frustrating for them. The Americans were also was provided with better clothing than the British soldiers, and, as awful as the U.S. army food could be, it was still better than what was provided to the British soldiers.

11.

VOLUNTEERING TO BECOME AN ARMY RANGER

Jack always impressed me as being a natural born leader. I thought he would be promoted to lieutenant in no time. When it came to military training and thinking strategically he always seemed much more superior then everyone else. That's why I wanted to be his friend . . . I knew he was a good soldier, and when we got into the real fighting, I wanted to be near him because I knew he could defeat any enemy before us.

Sergeant John Polyniak,
C Company, 116th Infantry Regiment,
29th Infantry Division.

Army Rangers are the United States equivalent of British Commandos: soldiers that have undergone extraordinarily rigorous and specialized training to become skilled in weaponry, demolition, hand-to-hand combat, covert operations, stealth attack, and amphibious assault landings, especially those of naturally treacherous, enemy-fortified terrains. As are Commandos, Rangers are especially well trained to think intelligently and strategically under combat situations, and are often given particularly dangerous, high-priority assignments in which failure is not an option. Rangers and Commandos are elite among soldiers, and are held in high esteem within the military.

A Ranger battalion had already been formed in England before the 29th Infantry Division arrived, but it had left in October to join the Allied invasion of North Africa. Some of its members had also participated in the ill-starred raid on Dieppe, France the previous August. Sometime in late

November or early December 1942, word came down that a new unit, the 29th Provisional Ranger Battalion, was to be formed within the 29th Infantry Division, to replace the one that had left, so soldiers in the division interested in being considered for the new battalion were asked to volunteer. We were told that volunteers would first be examined, and only those who met the very strict physical and psychological requirements would be allowed to try out for the Rangers. Those who successfully made it through the rigorous and specialized training would officially become Rangers.

It was obvious that becoming a Ranger was by no means an easy thing to do. I decided to try out, partly because I like challenges, but mainly because I heard that soldiers training to become Rangers were fed much better than the guys in the regular army. The food we were served daily in the regular army tasted awful, to say the least. I couldn't stand eating it. To me, going through the difficult ordeal of becoming a Ranger was worth it if in return I could get better food. I figured even if I didn't successfully get to be a Ranger, I would at least be fed better for as long as I could remain in the training.

So I volunteered for the 29th Provisional Ranger Battalion. I don't know how many soldiers initially volunteered, but I do remember there were quite a few. To qualify to undergo Ranger training you had to be intelligent, in tip-top physical condition, have perfect or near perfect hearing and vision, an aggressive temperament, a killer instinct, and a "there isn't anything-I can't-do" attitude. To evaluate whether the volunteers had these characteristics, each man was examined by about 20 people, who were mostly doctors or other medical personnel.

Each volunteer was individually examined from head to toe, given mental aptitude examinations, personally interviewed, and critically evaluated while performing a variety of physical exercises. In addition, they looked at our military records to review the notes and observations recorded by previous or current officers. They were especially interested to see whether you ever fell out on any of those numerous long, grueling marches we had to do back home in the States and in Tidworth Barracks. This initial qualification procedure took about two weeks. It was quite involved.

Many of the guys that volunteered were disqualified right from the start because they didn't pass the physical exams. Guys that met all of the initial screening criteria and did not have a history of frequently falling out of marches were permitted to continue on and undergo training to become a Ranger. This didn't mean that you were a Ranger, only that you were allowed to begin the training. Of the men from Company C of the 175th Infantry Regiment who volunteered, only me and four other men were chosen to go on with the Ranger training. My old childhood friends Willard Sparks and Harry Hendricks were among those disqualified. Willard's eyesight wasn't quite good enough, and there was something about Hendricks' feet that disqualified him.

The newly formed 29th Provisional Ranger Battalion, composed of volunteers who made it through the initial qualifications, was officially established in the latter part of December 1942. General Gerow had put the battalion under the command of Major Randolph Millholland. The 29th Ranger Battalion was administratively under the 29th Infantry Division, but the battalion's training and tactical control was under the purview of the British Special Service Brigade. This was the outfit responsible for overseeing and training the British Commandos. Since Rangers were the American equivalent of the Commandos, it made a lot of sense for us to be trained as such, as the British Special Service had already had established facilities and procedures, and had available experienced, combat-hardened Commando instructors. They were all set up to train us.

I could tell right away that the 29th Provisional Ranger Battalion was a very good outfit. It was so much better than being in my old company. The Ranger trainees were all excellent soldiers . . . real fighters . . . the best of the best. I got along very well in the Rangers right from the start. I knew I was going to learn a lot of new things, and was quite excited about that prospect.

The 29th Ranger Battalion originally consisted of a headquarters unit and two companies: A and B. A few months later companies C and D were added. I was assigned to Company A, second platoon, and my second lieutenant was Eugene Dance, who was from Beckley, West Virginia. Dance had also been my lieutenant while I had been in the 175th Infantry Regiment. He was a small man, but as tough as nails and very organized and military-like. He was a good lieutenant, and a damn good soldier. I liked him. My first sergeant was William Myers, who was also a good man.

There were no separate barracks for the newly formed 29th Rangers, so at the beginning of our training we continued to house with the rest of the 29th Infantry Division in Tidworth, but trained separately. We continued to train seven days a week just as we had in our regular companies, but it was much harder than before, and we did a LOT of strenuous exercising. The officers trained just as hard as everyone else.

The instructors, who were still American at this point in our training, worked us hard, indeed, but we were served the best meals we'd ever had since being in the military. The meals were surprisingly delicious, nearly as good as home cooked meals. Despite all the training and exercising, I actually gained weight because of the quality and serving sizes of the food they prepared for us. The only drawback about eating while in the Rangers is that we would have to run about a quarter of a mile to get to the mess hall. Every day, three times a day and just before each meal, we were required to line-up and run like hell to the mess hall to eat. At first this was quite annoying but after a while we got used to it. We used our evenings to see movies or write letters to loved ones back home.

During this time I met and became very good friends with John Polyniak, a Ranger volunteer like me. John had been in Company C of the 116th Infantry Regiment of the 29th Infantry Division. John was a real nice guy, as honest as they come. Like me, he didn't smoke or drink, and he was an outstanding baseball player. We hung around each other quite a bit, and in fact, we got along so well that we often roomed together when the Rangers were put up in civilian homes. In civilian life John had worked for a while as a barber, so I had him cut my hair when we were Rangers together.

As a matter of coincidence, John was originally from Shamokin, Pennsylvania, which is only about 18 miles from Sunbury, where I had spent a good portion of my childhood living with my aunt Dolsie. What is even more coincidental is that before John was drafted into the service he had moved to the Brooklyn section of Baltimore, which is only a few miles from where I lived in Dundalk. Like me, John returned to his home in Maryland after the war. We've spent the rest of our lives remaining the best of friends and living just a few miles apart from one another.

12.

OFF TO SCOTLAND

The 29th Ranger Battalion trained in the Tidworth area from December 1942 until about the end of January 1943. During this time more of the initially selected volunteers left the Rangers and went back to their original units, either because they became fed-up with the training and quit, or were forced to leave because they couldn't perform to the required level. In late January 1943, we left England and were sent north to the western highland region of Scotland to undergo about five weeks of intensive training at the British Commando Depot at the Achnacarry House at Spean Bridge in Glen Spean, Scotland. Achnacarry House is actually a good-sized castle whose origins date back to the mid-1600s. It was built by the Cameron clan of Scotland, and generations of Camerons had occupied it for centuries. We never stayed in the actual house; in fact I don't recall ever having been inside it.

The Achnacarry House was surrounded by a wild but lovely landscape of rolling peaks, valleys, pastures, lochs, and streams, and is overlooked by Ben Nevis, the highest mountain in the British Isles, rising over 4,400 feet above sea level. Throughout the general area there were old dirt roads, and the remains of old earthen fortifications at which battles had taken place in previous centuries. It was a very picturesque place, but the natural beauty was undermined by the weather, which was typically cold, wet and windy, at least while we were there.

There were a few small hamlets and villages in the area. Fort Williams was the closest village, but we were isolated from all civilians while we trained at the Commando depot. We weren't even allowed to write home.

With the exception of a period lasting about a week in which we stayed in tents, we billeted in Nissen huts (the British equivalent of Quonset huts) throughout our training in Scotland.

Our British Commando instructors were commissioned and non-commissioned officers of the British Special Services Brigade. We primarily took orders from the Commandos, not from our own U.S. officers. Eugene Dance was still my second lieutenant, but while we were in Scotland he couldn't behave too much like one because he was undergoing Commando training along with us.

It was immediately obvious that the Commando instructors were completely unlike any officers or instructors we had had since entering the military. They were extremely tough, ruthlessly harsh, no-nonsense, combat-hardened veterans. No one, not even me, dared to talk back to them. One reason is that if you did they would immediately beat you to within an inch of your life right there on the spot, or shoot at you with live ammunition. They wouldn't shoot to harm you physically, but they would fire a live round or two near your head or feet to scare the hell out of you if you talked back or caused a problem or even failed an assignment.

They weren't like the officers in the regular U.S. Army, who would put you on report, make you do push-ups, run a couple of miles or give you extra KP, latrine or other duties for infractions. Our Commando instructors dealt with such matters in their own way—with sticks, fists, and firearms loaded with live ammunition. They were unusually strict disciplinarians.

Another reason we didn't talk back to them is that we respected them for what they were, and what they were trying to do for us. They were combat experienced—the first instructors we had who had actually been in combat and fought enemy soldiers. They were men who had been involved with combat missions that either failed or were successful, and had learned firsthand why these outcomes occurred. They knew how to kill, how not to kill, and when and when not to kill. They had witnessed many a man die in combat, either from their own mistakes or those of others. They had already faced the enemy, the same enemy that we were going to fight, and they knew what we were going to be up against.

They knew that we were going to be assigned critical but dangerous missions, and they were going to teach us how to successfully accomplish them and minimize our chances of being killed. Our Commando instructors were tough bastards, but they had to be to train us to succeed against the Krauts. In short, from their own combat experience and mettle, they were going to teach us all that we needed to know to effectively participate in the war, and we knew it. They didn't play favorites with any of the men, and no one was given special treatment. All training was conducted strictly by their policies and procedures.

We had to address the Commando instructors as "Sir" and they addressed us as "bloke" or "blokes." Within the first few days we were at the school they took us to some "graves." They looked like real, fresh graves, but they weren't. There were grave markers erected at the head of freshly turned earth the size of a typical grave, and each marker had something written on it that provided a reason why the "soldier" in the make-believe grave had been killed. The grave markers had statements to the effect of "This soldier didn't hit the dirt when the enemy set off a flare," or "These men were bunched together and were killed by an enemy grenade." The instructors used this cemetery to illustrate what would happen to us if we didn't pay attention to some basic common sense practices during combat.

The physical training at the Commando depot was grueling—by far the most challenging any of us had ever experienced, or ever would. It is very difficult, perhaps impossible, to convey in words precisely how brutal our physical training was. It consisted primarily of a series of obstacle courses, speed-marches that went for miles up and down steep hills, mountain and cliff climbing, simulated combat with and without live ammunition and explosives, boat drills, log throwing and tactical warfare. Near the completion of rough training exercises the instructors often had bagpipe players dressed in Scottish kilts playing old Scottish tunes to help get our adrenalin flowing and give us a boost of energy to complete the task.

In addition to the rigorous physical training, we were given a lot of classroom-type instruction on different topics and scenarios that we could expect to experience during combat, and were taught how to think strategically and rationally during these situations to accomplish our mission. We were taught to read maps written in German, how to use a variety of weapons, including those used by the Krauts, and how to kill someone instantly with our bare hands.

All of our training was mission-oriented. The Commando instructors used to emphasize to us to get the job done no matter what, even if it kills you, and kill *anyone* who caused a mission to fail! They didn't want to hear about problems or hold-ups during training routines, even when we were on the obstacle courses. If something went wrong, or if you got hurt, they didn't want to know about it. In their minds there was no excuse for not getting the job done. They used to say, "You get your mission done even if it kills you!" I admired them for that.

OBSTACLE COURSES

A typical day while we trained in Scotland consisted of getting up early, going outside in the cold, stripping-down to the waist, getting into groups of seven or eight men, and each group would do a series of repetitions of throwing a huge, heavy log over their heads. Then we'd have to run the obstacle courses. There were twenty-eight different courses, and were divided into two sets of fourteen each. We'd have to run the first set in the morning and the second in the afternoon. We ran them every day except Mondays. Some of the courses were conducted under live gunfire by the Commando instructors. Combined, these courses stretched over 5 miles of hilly and swampy terrain. The obstacle courses had walls to climb, log and rope bridges traversing steep ravines, rope swings over water hazards, as well as other challenges.

We had to complete the obstacle courses within a prescribed amount of time. To me, the worst course was the one in which we had to jump into an ice cold creek that had a swift current, swim against the current as fast as we could, climb over rocks and logs, swim again, crawl onto land, and then crawl through mud under barbed wire while under fire with live ammo. Another course that I dreaded was the one where we had to cross a deep rocky ravine by crawling on a single rope that ran horizontal above it. Each end of the rope was tied to a tree on either side of the ravine, and you had to pull yourself across, one leg wrapped around the rope and the other dangling. If you were to fall you'd land on sharp-edged rocks and get seriously injured, if not killed. The worst part of it was when you got to about the middle your body weight would cause the rope to sag, causing you to have to crawl on an upward incline to cross to the other side. It was an extremely difficult obstacle course.

One time a Ranger sergeant tried to avoid having to do the obstacle courses. He was caught hiding and running around the courses instead of running through them like everyone else. The Commando instructors said if this is how you behave in training, this is how you're going to behave in actual combat. They told him he wasn't dependable, a disgrace to the outfit, and kicked him out of the Rangers.

SPEED-MARCHES

We had to make seven speed-marches while at the British Commando Depot in Scotland. We had never heard the term "speed-march" until the Commando instructors mentioned to us that we would have to successfully complete them. I remember asking one of my officers, "Sir, what is a speed-march?" and he said, "You're going to find out what a 'speed-march' is, bloke." I found out alright. Basically, it's extremely fast walking along miles of rough terrain and up and down hills while wearing light gear and carrying a rifle and ammunition. You're practically running when you're on a speed-march.

The rationale for doing speed-marches, as the instructors explained to us, is that when you're on a mission which involves making an amphibious landing on a beachhead, and you realize that for some reason you either can't land at the originally planned location and have to land somewhere else, or you land at what you believe to be the planned location, but afterward realize that you're miles from where you're supposed to be, you'll need to get to your correct designation as quickly as possible so you can complete your mission and meet up with supply lines, reinforcements or whatever, as originally planned. The speed-march training was supposed to condition us to move like hell in the event of either of the above scenarios so we could quickly get to where ever we're supposed to be without compromising the mission.

When on a speed-march we couldn't stop for any reason. Our "rest periods" were when we were speed-marching down a hill. But when we got to the bottom of a hill our "rest period" was over. On a speed-march we had to walk as fast as possible, and then some. The Commando instructors had us throw our arms back and forth real hard and fast to make us move more quickly. At the completion of a speed-march our legs would feel as if they were made of rubber, and our feet ached and were covered with blisters, sometimes bleeding. We hated having to do all those speed-marches.

As I recall, we did the seven-mile speed-march in only 56 minutes! I very clearly remember we completed the 15-mile one in an unbelievable two hours and 29 minutes. On this march I remember we had gone about 7.5 miles and a Commando sergeant said "Reverse!" so we had to immediately turn around and go back. When we were nearing completion of the march we could see and hear men in the distance dressed in Scottish kilts playing bagpipes for us, and we all started to feel real good because we knew the ordeal was almost over.

MOUNTAIN AND CLIFF CLIMBING

We did quite a lot of climbing, again to prepare for amphibious assaults on rocky and hilly coastlines. Using rope tied to grappling hooks we'd scale tall cliffs that were perpendicular to the ground. Other times we'd just hike up a mountain, cross rocky ravines and climb cliffs, and then camp out on the mountain for a few days. One time we went on a three-day exercise on Mount Ben Nevis. It had been quite cold, and there was a lot of snow and ice on the ground when we started.

The Commando instructors told us to take our weapons, but gave the unusual order not to take any ammunition. Most of the guys were carrying M-1 Garands, which weigh about 9 pounds, but I was carrying a Browning Automatic Rifle (BAR), which weighs over 20 pounds. At the time I didn't think too much of the fact that they didn't want us to carry any ammunition, as it meant there would be less weight for us to carry in all that ice and snow.

We later realized that the reason they didn't want us to carry any ammunition was because they were going to put us through such a rough ordeal for three days that if we had been carrying ammunition we would have shot them all! There were British Commando instructors with us, but it was our own officers who were leading the way. The Commando instructors were acting as observers.

After a full and delicious breakfast Company A started out early in the morning at the base of Ben Nevis. It was sleeting, and all we saw around us were snow capped mountains. We were on our way up Ben Nevis, and were supposed to camp in a ravine somewhere up on the mountain that night. On the following day we would continue on. We needed to reach the ravine before dusk because with all the holes, cracks, snow and ice that covered the mountain it would be too difficult and treacherous to get to it safely in the dark.

It took a good part of the day to reach the ravine, and we camped there overnight and into the following day. Afterwards, we were supposed to continue on and move toward the right through another ravine, but for some reason our officers didn't instruct us to go to the right, they instructed us to keep walking straight up the mountain. The sleet hadn't let up for a minute, so the ground conditions kept getting worse and slowed us down. By nightfall we stopped and camped again because it was too dangerous to continue on. For food we had been issued British 14-in-1 rations, which were terrible. There wasn't much for us to eat, and we were getting quite hungry. While we camped overnight it was impossible to get any sleep in the snow, ice, sleet and cold.

On the morning of the third day we broke camp and started to move on, soaking wet from the sleet and without having had a wink of sleep or a decent meal for a couple of days. There were snow caps on the right, on the left, and by now right in front of us, which meant that we had taken a wrong turn somewhere—our own officers had gotten us lost! They had missed a path on the right that we were supposed to have taken the morning of the second day. We had taken a wrong turn, and we were lost. By now there was about two feet of snow on the ground.

The British Commando instructors had known we had taken the wrong path but didn't say anything. They had allowed us to continue on the wrong way. They enjoyed doing things like that. We were quite angry at them. The American officers didn't know what to do, so they asked the British instructors how to get back on the correct path. The instructors pointed to a high, snow covered peak on Ben Nevis and said the only way to get back on track was to cross over that peak.

Me and another Ranger named Stewart Pugh were the lead scouts for the rest of the Company so we had to go first and lead the way. Pugh picked up his M-1 and started moving toward the mountain we had to cross. I picked up my BAR and followed right behind him. Pugh and I walked slowly up the mountain slope through two feet of snow. Behind us was the rest of Company A walking in single file in our footsteps. We needed to reach and cross the mountain peak before it got dark, so we walked as fast as we could. About two hours before dusk Pugh slipped on the icy snow and slid like a bowling ball down the mountain on his back right past me with his eyes as wide open as silver dollars. He slid down quite a ways, and knocked over a few guys before stopping. I think he may have been injured by the fall.

So now it's just me leading the way with my BAR, and I was determined not to slip and slide as did Pugh. I used the bipod (the two legs) on the front-end of the BAR as a climbing tool. I'd plant the bipod into the snow, and then used the BAR itself as a pole to pull myself up a couple of feet, and kept repeating this process to climb up the peak. Everyone behind me placed their feet in my footsteps, so they didn't need to worry as much as I did about falling and sliding down the mountain. The only reason why I was able to move along is because of the BAR.

I finally reached the top of the peak, and boy the wind was sure howling up there. I looked down at the other side of the mountain and, strangely, I noticed there wasn't any snow on that side, meaning of course that it would be easy for us to move down the slope and get back on the correct course. So we moved down the mountain slope, and our own officers came around and said, "Okay men, you guys need to rest now, so build all the fires you want, get warm, and try to get some sleep. We'll stay here for the night."

After having not slept for three days the orders to rest and get warm from our officers was music to our ears, for we were completely exhausted, cold, and mentally drained. We started building fires and setting up camp, when all at once the British Commando instructors attacked us with smoke bombs! They were simulating an enemy attack. We had to quickly put the fires out and run for cover and hide for several more hours.

We were mad at the Commando instructors, but the lesson we learned from them is that we had let the exhaustion and being on edge cause us to let our guard down. If this had been an attack from the real enemy we would all have been killed. It turned out that we had moved in a circle on the mountain, and were only a short distance from the huts where we lived. After the "attack" we went down to the huts and finally got a decent meal and some sleep. The British Commando instructors had known all along what was going to happen, and that's why we weren't allowed to bring live ammunition with us, because they knew we were going to reach our breaking point and figured that we would have shot them if we had real ammo.

The following morning the British Colonel in charge of the Commando depot called Company A into a meeting hall they had up there to discuss our training exercise on the mountain. The first thing he did was chew out our own American officers for getting us lost on the mountain. We all loved watching our officers get yelled at for a change.

Then he addressed the rest of us, asking, "Don't you have a sport in your country called boxing?" "Yes Sir," we all replied at the same time. Then he said, "Well in your case, the Commando instructors who threw those smoke bombs at you had gone through everything that you had gone through on that mountain. They too were tired, had not eaten, were cold, and yet they had attacked you. If they had been German soldiers they would have wiped out all of you!" He went on to say that "In war nothing ever works the way it is supposed to. Things go wrong, mistakes are made. Things never go the way as planned. Just as in boxing, what wins a war is the determination that one must have to defeat his enemy, no matter how exhausted or tired you are." He was absolutely right. To defeat your enemy you must be more *determined* than he in order to win. If you're not, you're doomed to fail.

INJURED BY A HAND GRENADE, LUCKY ME

Once during training I was injured by a hand grenade. Captain Hoar, a British Commando instructor, handed me a non-fragmenting grenade and said, "Here's the situation, bloke. There's a Kraut machine gun nest manned by two Krauts on top of a hill that is covered by rough terrain. Your mission is to capture the machine gun nest and take the two Krauts as prisoners. Now, as a Ranger, you're going to think intelligently and act strategically to accomplish this mission. You know that the Krauts aren't expecting anyone to climb the hill to sneak up on them because in their minds it is impossible to do because of the terrain. You also know that you can climb that hill because as a Ranger you can do what other soldiers in the regular army can't do. So now you have just climbed the hill and have snuck up on the Krauts and are hiding in the brush, and are ready to accomplish your mission. Here's how. You're going to throw the non-fragmenting grenade into the machine gun nest. The Krauts in the nest are going to think it is a fragmenting grenade that is going to kill them, and they are instinctively going to dive flat on the ground immediately. So once you've thrown the grenade you run in and capture the Krauts."

Now throwing a live hand grenade is one thing, but throwing it and then running towards it when it's about to explode is another, even if it is a non-fragmenting grenade. So I'm standing there with Captain Hoar and I am still confused as to why he wants me to throw the grenade and charge in after it. The scenario didn't make sense to me. I thought to myself, "What if the Krauts don't hit the ground after I have thrown the grenade? What the hell am I going to do then?" I can't tell a Commando instructor that because he doesn't want to hear it.

So I took the grenade and threw it. It goes into some trees, and I froze. After a couple of seconds the grenade explodes, and I still haven't moved a muscle. "What's the problem, bloke?" Captain Hoar asked. "I haven't figured it out yet, sir, about the Krauts supposed to be going down like you say. I'm not so sure that they will, and if they don't they are going to kill me." Captain Hoar didn't want to hear this! So he said, "I'm going to give you another grenade, and I want you to throw it and then charge in and get those Krauts!" "Yes sir," I replied. I took the grenade, threw it, and then charged in towards where I had just thrown it. It hits the ground and explodes. The fuse of a non-fragmenting grenade contains a lead ball. When the grenade exploded it sent the lead ball and some stones on the ground flying into my left hand. I'm dying in agony from it. My hand swelled up like a balloon and was bleeding profusely.

I thought to myself, "Well, Jack, when you were a little boy and got hurt you would always run to your mother. But where is mother now, when you are in Scotland undergoing Commando training?" I went over to Captain Hoar and said to him "Sir, when the grenade exploded some stuff hit me in my left hand. I'm hurt really bad." I showed him my hand. He looked at it and said "You know bloke, you're lucky." "Why am I lucky, sir?" I replied. Hoar's answer was "Because there was a class training here this morning, doing the same exercise, and two blokes in that class had to be taken away in ambulances, and here you are standing here talking to me." So, I was lucky!

BOAT DRILLS

We underwent a lot of amphibious (boat) training while we were in Scotland. After all, the only thing separating France from Britain was the English Channel, and everyone, including the Krauts, knew that the eventual Allied assault would come in the form of a massive amphibious attack on the coast of France. I remember one night we practiced a mission to capture and destroy some enemy gun emplacements located about 100 yards inland from the beach. It was a covert mission that would require a stealth beach landing, stealth inland movement and location of the enemy guns, and endure a surprise enemy attack. Initial "intelligence reports" gave us the approximate location of the gun batteries, and indicated that there were rows of barbed wire up and down the beach, so we'd have to quietly cut our way through the wire to move inland. It was pitch black outside, and after we landed on the beach we began our approach to the barbed wire in complete silence.

For a minute or so everything appeared to be going as planned, but all at once the British Commando instructors began firing a bunch of flares that lit up the whole area. The entire beach was so brightly lit, it was as if a night ball game was going on. We immediately dove onto the ground, but we were completely exposed. The next thing I knew there was a solid line of live .50 caliber machine gun fire with tracers coming at us from the beach. Even though the bullets were flying about 10 feet over our heads, it was still quite a frightening experience.

We couldn't remain on the beach because if this were actual combat we would be shot to pieces. We couldn't stand up and cut through the barbed wire and charge inland for the same reason. The only option was to crawl inland on our bellies, underneath the barbed wire and machine gun fire. Some of the barbed wire was attached to land mines, and if you raised the barbed wire just a little bit as you crawled underneath it you would set off a mine. What you had to do was quickly remove your back pack, push it under the wire and then crawl under the wire without touching it. There were Commando instructors positioned near where the mines were located to evaluate our movement under the wire and to stop any of us from accidentally setting off a mine.

After we crawled under all of the barbed wire the Commando instructors inspected our guns to make sure that we had kept them free of sand and that they would still fire. We were evaluated on how quiet we were when we landed on the beach, how quickly we dove onto the ground when the flares were set off, how carefully we moved under the barbed wire, and how clean we kept our guns. The ultimate purpose of this sort of training, as difficult and as frightening as it was, was to prepare us for the real thing—and it did.

Another type of boat drill that we had to do was a race on one of the nearby lakes. We would be placed in these large, Viking-like rowboats that would hold thirty-two men each, sixteen on each side, two men to an oar, eight oars on each side of the boat. The boats would compete in 15-mile boat races: 7.5 miles out, and 7.5 miles back. They'd had us row as hard as we could, and the freezing cold water would spray and drip all over us as the oars were lifted out of the water. We absolutely hated having to do this boat drill, but the Commando instructors didn't want to hear complaints.

On other occasions we'd have to go down to a jetty on one of the lakes or lochs, jump into the freezing water, swim to shore and then run about two miles back to our hut. We were like icicles when we got back to our huts. They wanted to prepare us for having to jump, without hesitation, into ice-cold water, and to show us how cold water can affect you. What I learned is that as soon as you jump into cold water, your mouth flies open and stays open. You can't close it for a while. Under these conditions you can swallow a lot of water if you're not careful.

THE VALUE OF OUR RANGER TRAINING

I strongly believe the training we undertook throughout our length of service in the Rangers, particularly during our stay in Scotland, was more difficult than the training the paratroopers received. I eventually joined the 101st Airborne and became a paratrooper during the war. I've seen the movie "Band of Brothers" and have been to Mount Currahee in Toccoa, Georgia, where the 101st Airborne Division originally trained in World War II, so I'm familiar with the types and level of training paratroopers undertook during the war. There is no question that the paratroopers had to endure a lot of hard training, but I'm convinced that what the Rangers had to endure was by far more difficult. I'm also thoroughly convinced from firsthand experience that my Ranger training saved my life during combat. While fighting later on there were many occasions when I depended upon my training as a Ranger to complete missions and get myself or other G.I.s out of certain-death situations.

IT'S OFFICIAL, WE'RE RANGERS!

During the early part of March 1943, we had completed our training at the British Commando Depot in Scotland. A number of the Rangers, I'd say at least half, who had started the training at the Depot five weeks earlier, either dropped out or were kicked out of the battalion and sent back to their original units. The men who had successfully completed the training, including myself, graduated from the British Commando Depot, and were issued 29th Ranger Battalion insignia, which meant that we were now officially Rangers! The insignia was a red arch-shaped piece of felt about a half-inch wide and three to four inches in length with "29th Rangers" sewn across it in blue thread.

The insignia was nothing particularly fancy to look at, but it was something we were all very proud of, knowing what it took to earn the privilege to wear it. To us our 29th Ranger insignia tabs were more like medals than insignia. When we left Spean Bridge we were given a few days of leave. Many of us, including myself, went to London to rest, relax, and celebrate our becoming Rangers! And as Rangers, we were shown a lot of respect from the regular G.I.s and British soldiers.

13.

CAUSING TROUBLE IN DUNDALK!

The Baltimore Sun, *March 5, 1943*
Say, you know what? The other day when I was out on a speed march somebody
swiped all my pictures of my girl. I've been writing to my girl asking her for
more pictures. She says I've got enough. Sure ought to send me another now.
Wonder if you know my girl, Theresa Cook.
 She lives at 201 North Washington Street [Baltimore].
 I'd sure like to have another picture.·

 Private First Class Jack Womer
 Company A, 29th Ranger Battalion

One day in late February, 1943 near the end of our stay in Scotland,
some reporters visited our camp and interviewed us. Lee McCardell,
a reporter from *The Baltimore Sun* interviewed me, and one of the questions I was asked was to mention something I would like to have from
back home. I told Lee that what I wanted most was a photo of my fiancée,
Theresa Cook, of Baltimore, wearing the dress and necklace that I had
paid my mother to buy her as a Christmas present. I explained that I had
lost my wallet, in which I had all of my photos, so I no longer had any
pictures of Theresa.

 I went on to say that I had been asking Theresa since Christmas to
send me pictures of herself in the dress and necklace, but she would not
do it because she had put on a little weight since I last saw her (in early
October 1942) and she was too embarrassed to send me a recent photo of
herself. I had told her in several letters written before I went to Scotland

that I didn't care about her weight, and that I really would like to have a photo of her.

I had forgotten about the interview, but some of the statements I made were published in the March 5, 1943 issue of *The Baltimore Sun.* The story disclosed the fact that I was training in Scotland, which it shouldn't have, and was interpreted by many as here I was, a hard-training soldier a long way from home, and all I wanted was a picture of my girlfriend but she wouldn't send me one. The article made Theresa seem like a real bitch, and me like a poor lonely soldier who missed her. It was the talk of the town for awhile.

Everyone in the Baltimore area reads the *Sun,* and a lot of people who read the article confronted Theresa about it. People that knew us would stop her in the street or at work and say, "Why won't you send Jack a picture of yourself? He really loves you and misses you." Theresa had read the article as well, and was fuming mad over what I had said. She told everyone in town that I had lied about having lost my wallet, and that what I had told the reporter was just a ploy to put pressure on her to send me a photo of herself being overweight. But none of what she said was actually true.

Then *The Baltimore Sun* interviewed Theresa about my request. In this article Theresa said that I would have to wait a long, long time, and that I must have been joking because according to her I had several photos of her. In fact, she told everyone we knew not to believe anything that I said, and that the only reason why I wanted a picture of her in the dress and necklace that I had my mother buy for her was so that I would know the photo was genuinely recent, so that I could see how much weight she gained. Theresa was quite embarrassed about the whole thing, and extremely mad at me. She didn't write to me for weeks after the original story was published.

But I got what I wanted. Theresa's interview was published by *The Baltimore Sun* in their Sunday, March 14th, 1943 edition, and they accompanied it with a photo of her. Lee McCardell sent me a copy!

14.

BACK TO ENGLAND, AS RANGERS

During the first or second week of March 1943, the 29th Ranger Battalion was sent to Eastleigh, located in the Hampshire section of England. The military had no barracks for us in Eastleigh, so arrangements were made again to put us up in civilian homes. John Polyniak and I were assigned to stay in a home owned by a 60-plus-year-old English woman named Frances Rowe, who at the time lived alone. She had five sons, two of whom were away at war, and the other three no longer lived at home and served in the English Home Guard. Her house, like most in the area, was a small but cozy two-story row house. It had three small rooms downstairs and three more upstairs. There was no electricity in the house, but there were gas lights. Each room had its own little fireplace for heat. John and I slept in the front upstairs bedroom where her two sons had slept before going into the military.

I could tell that John and I reminded Mrs. Rowe of her two sons who were away at war. She was good to us—very motherly—and we did all could to help her. She washed our clothes, did our sewing, prepared many of our meals, things that went far beyond what the military was paying her to do for us. John and I tried to pay her extra but she refused to accept any money from us, even though she needed it. Some of her neighbors told me that ever since John and I started staying with her all she did all day while we were out training was play her piano and sing songs. We had made her very happy just by staying with her.

John and I eventually got to meet her two sons who were in the military. One particular morning, I think it was a Sunday, John and I dug a garden bed for Mrs. Rowe. When we finished we came back in the house and were having tea with her, when all of sudden her two sons walked into the house. They had come home on leave and wanted to surprise her so they had not notified her in advance. She hadn't seen her sons for months. Once she saw them she began to cry tears of joy, and hugged and kissed both of them. She introduced John and I and then, without saying a word, one of her sons picked up my teacup, which I had just emptied, and without washing or even wiping it, poured some tea into it and drank. I thought what he did was quite odd, something I would never have done.

Near the end of March 1943, while the rest of the 29th Infantry Division was still training in Tidworth, the 29th Provisional Ranger Battalion was sent to Dartmouth to undergo additional training with the British Commandos. Dartmouth is located right on the English Channel in the southwest portion of England. The military had no barracks for us to stay in while we were there, so arrangements were made to put us up in civilian homes. We trained in and around the Dartmouth moors. The training was difficult, but only about half as much as what we had gone through a month earlier in Scotland. We continued to undergo a lot of night amphibious landing exercises.

During our stay in Dartmouth we were issued ration cards, the same type the English civilians were issued, which meant that we'd be on the same diet as them. The cards were issued once a week, just as with civilians, and they weren't good for getting a whole lot. They put us on English rations for training reasons. When we were on our own rations we ate pretty well, but on the civilian diet we nearly starved. While we were in Dartmouth some of us Rangers were chosen to go on some small military raids. I was never picked to go on any, but I would have loved to have participated. My second Lieutenant, Eugene Dance, went on at least two that I'm aware of. The raids were all hush-hush, we never heard too much about them.

We also stayed for a while in Torquay, an elaborate, well-to-do kind of town located on the English Channel, about 10 miles north of Dartmouth. Anyone who lived there had money. John Polyniak and I lived together with an elderly woman while in Torquay. In early April we rejoined the 29th Infantry Division back in Tidworth, and I was able to spend some time with my old buddies in Company C of the 175th Infantry and show-off my Ranger insignia. During this period we learned a lot more about assault tactics and guns.

Near the end of May, most of the 29th Infantry Division left Tidworth while the 29th Ranger Battalion remained in the area, along with some men from the 175th Infantry, to participate in a tactical training maneuver with some British units. The British were to represent themselves, the Allied forces, and the 29th Rangers and others played the part of the Krauts. The scenario of this maneuver was that British units occupied a beachhead in an area controlled by the Krauts, and their objective was to infiltrate inland and take further control of the area.

As "Krauts," the guys from the 175th Infantry were supposed to stay put and use traditional tactics to prevent any attempt made by the British to move off the beach and head inland. Meantime the 29th Rangers, using stealth and other Commando tactics, were given the mission of infiltrating the British position and disrupt their attempt to move inland. Within the three days given to the exercise, the 29th Rangers made a 40-mile sweep around the British flank, infiltrated their position from the rear, raided and destroyed their command post, and captured their attack plans! The entire maneuver made the 29th Rangers look like super soldiers. We were given high scores on that exercise.

BUDE, CORNWALL

In the early part of June the 29th Rangers were sent to Bude, located on the southwest coast in the Cornwall section of England, for more amphibious warfare training. Bude is a vacation resort town located right on the Atlantic Ocean. It's a beautiful place. There were top notch hotels, golf courses, first-class restaurants and the seacoast, with miles of magnificent beaches.

The Rangers were boarded in one or two of the more exquisite ocean-front resort hotels. John Polyniak and I shared a room. It was quite a nice place. We trained hard, as usual, seven days a week, mainly speed-marching, amphibious landings and cliff climbing along the ocean fronts in and around the Bude area.

While in Bude we were also assigned to test the affects of different ration formulations used by G.I.s on body weight and overall soldier performance under field and simulated combat conditions. Each of the four

29th Ranger companies were given a different ration formulation. Company A was prescribed C rations. We weren't allowed to eat any extra foods or snacks, and each Ranger in each company had to give his word that he would only eat his assigned ration and nothing else for the duration of the test, which I think lasted about three weeks.

The overall goal of the experiment was for the military to determine which ration formulation was the best at providing a soldier's nutritional needs while under combat conditions, as measured by weight lost, or lack thereof. That diet which resulted in the least loss of body weight would be viewed as the preferred diet for soldiers under field conditions.

The experiment took place while we were on maneuvers in the open, foggy and marshy wasteland area in Cornwall known as the British moors, away from our luxury hotel rooms in Bude. The experiment was for us to live off our assigned rations while we undertook tactical manuevers and long speed-marches through the moors. The ground was quite soft, and there was a lot of quicksand. We carried tents with us to sleep in, but trying to set up a tent in a marsh is like trying to nail a board to air. Half the time we'd simply unravel our tents flat out on the marsh and just lie on them to rest for a while, as it was pointless to try and set them up.

Every morning some guys would come around in trailers and would individually weigh us, question us as to our likes and dislikes of the ration diet, and observe us for any changes in our performance as soldiers. We all lost a lot of weight quite quickly. I seem to recall that the men on the 5-in-1 rations lost the least weight. I was on the C-rations, I distinctly remember that the men who were on the C-rations and K-rations lost the most weight. We nearly died being on those rations while on maneuvers in those swamps for three weeks. We were practically emaciated at the completion of the test. After our ration test stint in the British moors we returned, on foot, to our luxury hotel rooms in Bude and were served some of the most hearty and delicious meals I had ever eaten!

FINDING A LADY FRIEND

One day shortly after we arrived in Bude, me and a few Ranger buddies were having a catch with a baseball when a young lady called out to us from the balcony of her hotel apartment, which was close by. She said "Would any of you like to play tennis or golf with me?" Since I was longing for female companionship, and figuring this was a good opportunity to become friendly with a nice young lady, I immediately answered, "Yes, I'd love to play golf or tennis," before any of my buddies could open their mouth. She came down and met me, and we played golf.

Her name was Kwatie, and she was a very beautiful and lovely woman. She told me she was married to a British officer who was stationed off the coast of Africa on a cruiser. She had a son named Peter, who was about six years old. We became quite friendly, and we'd frequently get together to play golf or tennis, or just talk or go out for walks or take in a movie, sometimes just the two of us and other times her son would come along. She was my girlfriend while I was in Bude.

I felt a little sorry for Kwatie because of the rationing and that she had a little child to feed. The people were restricted in the types of foods they could buy, and how much. Chocolate was rationed at 16 ounces per month. Even getting a hearty meal in one of the many first class restaurants in Bude was difficult because of the rationing. We used to have to bribe some of the restaurants to get a decent meal. We use to say things like "I promise to come back tomorrow and have dinner here again if you'll serve me an egg today."

Whenever I had kitchen duty I would go into the pantry and steal whatever wasn't nailed down and bring it to Kwatie. I'd steal flour, apples, peaches, sugar, eggs, bread, butter, whatever was there, and give it to her. She was very appreciative, as she couldn't buy too much of this sort of stuff because of the rationing. She had a damn good set-up with me stealing for her, and she knew it. She ruined it for herself, though, when she started to include her mother, father and then her siblings in on this. She expected me to steal goodies not only for her, but for them as well.

I told her I couldn't steal for her and her entire family, because if I did there would be nothing left for us Rangers to eat! I also pointed out to her that I hadn't gotten a God-damned thing from her or her family for all of the stealing that I had done for them. I got angry at her because I felt I had been used. So I told her that there would be no more goodies for her, no more paying her way to see movies, no more nothing! I ended the situation I had with her.

Several weeks had passed, and I hadn't seen or spoken to Kwatie. One day I was outside playing ball with some of the guys when all of a sudden

I see Kwatie walking towards me with her son Peter and crying her eyes out. At first I ignored her, but she stood right in front of me crying hysterically. I finally asked her what was wrong. She didn't say a word. Instead, she handed me a telegram, and it said something to the effect:

> Ship was sunk off the coast of Africa. We are sending you notice that we are trying to locate/find your husband. More information will follow on your lost husband.

She was all upset. She thought that me being a man of "distinction," that is being that I could get away with stealing all those goodies for her and that I knew how to operate within the system, that maybe I could help expedite the military's effort in trying to locate her husband. As angry as she had made me, I couldn't help but feel sorry for her. So me being the "Sir Walter Raleigh" that I am, I told her I would try to help.

I thought for a moment, and then remembered that whenever I watched a movie in the local theaters different types of local announcements would appear on the screen. One of the announcements was that of a local person who could provide advice or assistance on just about any topic. So I said "Kwatie, let's go see that person in town who can help people who are having a problem or are troubled about something. I've seen his name appear on the movie screen in the local theaters. Maybe he can help you." She agreed so we went to this person's house: Kwatie, myself, and her son, Peter.

We got to the house and Kwatie and Peter knocked on the door and went inside. I remained outside. After a while they came out and she's crying her eyes out again. I said to her, "Well, what happened?" She said, "He said that everything and anything that can be done is already being done, as stated in the telegram, and that he couldn't do anything."

As I'm trying to console her, I noticed two British two-star army generals that were Commandos and were walking down the street right towards us. Now of course I didn't send for the two generals, but Kwatie seemed to think that I had. The two generals saw me and they noticed the Ranger patch on my shoulder, so they knew I was trained as a Commando as well, and I knew that they would respect that and speak with me. I figured if I could stir their British pride a little, maybe they would be moved

The Achnacarry House at Spean Bridge, in Glen Spean, Scotland, as it appeared in February 1943. In late January 1943, Jack and the other men who qualified for the newly formed 29th Provisional Ranger Battalion were sent to the British Commando Depot at Achnacarry House to undergo five weeks of intensive training. *Photo: U.S. National Archives*

The "cemetery" at the British Commando Depot at Achnacarry House. Make-believe graves of soldiers were constructed, and each marker had an explanation for why the "soldier" in the grave had been killed. *Photo: U.S. National Archives*

Log throwing during a typical day of training at the British Commando Depot at the Achnacarry House. There were twenty-eight different obstacle courses on the grounds, divided into two sets of fourteen each. The men would have to run the first set of fourteen in the morning and the remaining set in the afternoon, six days a week. *Photo: U.S. National Archives*

Crossing a fast-moving river: an example of one of the obstacle courses set up at the British Commando Depot at the Achnacarry House. *Photo: U.S. National Archives*

Seven men of the 29th Ranger Battalion undergoing instruction with model 1928A1
Thompson submachine guns at the British Commando Depot at the Achnacarry House. The
men in the photo, taken in February 1943, are (from left to right): Pfc. John Toda of Sharon,
PA; Pvt. John Dorzi of Barrington, RI; Pfc. Jack Womer of Dundalk, MD.; Pfc. Robert
Reese of McKeesport, PA.; Lt. Eugene Dance of Beckley, WV.; Pfc. Dale Ford of Thurmont,
MD.; and Pfc Manuel Viera of Cambridge, MA. The 29th Ranger Battalion disbanded in
October of 1943, and the men in the Battalion returned to their original units within the
29th Infantry Division. Each of the men in the photo participated in the Allied invasion of
Normandy on D-Day. Dale Ford returned to the 115th Infantry Regiment and survived the
initial assault on Omaha Beach on D-Day, but was killed in action a week later, on June
13th, 1944, as the 29th Infantry was heading inland toward the city of St. Lo, France.
Manuel Viera returned to the 121st Engineer Combat Battalion of the 29th Infantry
Division, and was killed in action on Omaha Beach on D-Day. He was 24 years old. The
rest of the men in the photo survived the invasion of Normandy as well other battles,
and returned home after the war. See pages 18–19 for more details.
Photo: U.S. Office of War Information

Jack Womer proudly posing as a member of the 29th Ranger Battalion after successfully completing his training. (Note the 29th Ranger shoulder insignia partially visible in the photo.). This picture was probably taken in August 1943, as this date appears on the rear of the photo.
Photo: the Womer family

John Polyniak also volunteered for the 29th Ranger Battalion, where he met and became very good friends with Jack Womer. John had been in the 116th Regiment of the 29th Infantry Division and was from Baltimore, not far from Jack's hometown of Dundalk. After the Rangers were disbanded John went back to his regiment and was in the first assault wave of the D-Day invasion on Omaha Beach. He survived that day but was later seriously wounded near St. Lo. After the war Jack and John remained the best of friends, living just a few miles from one another in Maryland. John died on June 7, 2011 at the age of 92.
Photo: the Polyniak family

to help her, seeing her crying her eyes out and that she had a young son, and that her husband was a British officer.

I walked up to the two generals, saluted, and said to one of them, "Sir, we're running into a little problem. This young lady is married to a British officer who is stationed off the coast of Africa on a cruiser. She received this telegram that says that her husband's boat was sunk and that he's missing, and that they're trying to locate him. She's having a hard time getting more details from the British Navy as to the status of her husband. I'm trying to help her the best that I can. I believe the British Army should be able to do much better that the British Navy in getting some more information on her husband and the ship he was on."

After I said this I could tell that they were thinking on what they could do for Kwatie. One of the generals said, "Soldier, since you've gone out of your way to try to help this English lady, we will see what we can do. Come with us." We followed the two generals back to their headquarters, as instructed. They get on the radio with the rescue and recovery personnel off the coast of Africa to get some details on her husband. They learned that her husband had been rescued, that he was alive and well, and that he would be home in two to three weeks. She was more than relieved, as you can imagine.

Now for all my efforts in helping her, along with the fact that my 26th birthday was coming up, you'd think that Kwatie would do something special for me, or give me something special. As a token of her appreciation for my efforts, her little boy, Peter, bought me a handkerchief for my birthday. That's all I got out of it! I never saw her again.

THE GOOD LIFE IN BUDE

While the training we undertook in Bude was rough, and usually took place seven days a week, the living conditions and food were, for the most part, outstanding. Actually, things were quite good there. I became friendly with a young married couple that had two children. The wife did all my sewing, washed all my clothes, and did my ironing. In return I'd get the husband American made cigarettes, and I'd give the two children my weekly issue of cakes and candies. They would loan me their tennis rackets and golf clubs, fed me supper, or "late tea" as the British call it. They were a nice family.

I also played quite a bit of baseball while in Bude, as did John Polyniak. Some of the guys in the 29th Rangers formed a couple of baseball teams. A Company had its own team, for which I played second base and pitched. John was also on the team, and played in the infield as well. He was a quite a good ball player. The other team was composed mostly of guys from Companies B and C, and a few guys from Company D. We used to play each other all of the time. We'd also play other teams from other parts of the military, such as Air Corps teams. Some of the teams we played had guys who played on semi-pro and, I think, professional baseball teams before entering the service, but we usually won nevertheless. Our games became quite popular among the other Rangers. They'd come and bet on who would win.

15.

RANGERS NO MORE

> *October 4, 1943*
> *Theresa, the General came down this morning and told us that the 29th*
> *Rangers have been disbanded . . . After 9 months of hard and very good train-*
> *ing, they are sending us back. The General said there was nothing he could do*
> *to stop it, although he tried.*
>
> Pfc. Jack Womer
> Company A, 29th Ranger Battalion

In early September of 1943, some new Ranger recruits who had not yet undergone any training at the British Commando facilities were going to be sent to Scotland. Promotions were promised to guys like me if we agreed to accompany these new recruits, to mentor them and undergo Commando training with them. I agreed to do it, under the understanding that in return I would receive a permanent promotion to sergeant.

We didn't go back to the British Commando Depot at the Achnacarry House at Spean Bridge. Instead we went to the Depot at Dorlin House, a large castle in Acharacle, Argyll, located about 35 miles west of Spean Bridge and just a few miles from the Atlantic Ocean. For nearly three weeks we trained with other British Commando and Royal Marine units in amphibious assault landings at the six very tough assault courses in the area. The courses concentrated on dealing with natural and artificial beach defensive obstructions. Our landing exercises were carried out on mined beaches with incoming live 3-inch mortar shells and live ammunition.

The training was quite dangerous, but it had to be as the intention was to create as close as possible the conditions we would face when we inevitably would have to approach and land on the heavily defended beaches in enemy occupied territory. While at the Dorlin House I achieved "sharpshooter" status with the M-1 Garand rifle, and "expert" status on the Browning automatic rifle (BAR). I performed so well with the BAR that the British Commandos made me a BAR instructor.

As difficult as the training was at the Depot at Dorlin House, it still was not as difficult or demanding as what we undertook at the Achnacarry House at Spean Bridge—no training I ever experienced was as grueling and difficult as that. The sad part was that none of us who agreed to go back to Scotland to help train the new recruits were permanently promoted as promised.

THE END OF THE 29TH RANGER BATTALION

The rest of September was unremarkable for the 29th Ranger Battalion. I went to London and Exeter on passes. We were all delighted when we heard that Italy broke away from the Axis and surrendered to the Allies, because it weakened the Nazis' military strength. Near the end of September we were living in civilian homes somewhere near Southampton, England. At about this time we had begun to hear through the grapevine that the U.S. military might disband the 29th Provisional Ranger Battalion. At first we thought this sort of talk was nothing more than rumor, but it soon became clear that the military was seriously considering mustering the 29th Rangers out of service.

Official word that the battalion was no more came to us on the morning of October 4th, 1943, directly from General Leonard T. Gerow, commander of the 29th Infantry Division. He told us that starting immediately there would no longer be a 29th Provisional Ranger Battalion and we would return to our original units within the 29th Infantry Division. He said he was very pleased with the work we had done, and that he was proud of us, and that he had tried hard to persuade his superiors to keep the battalion. But his superiors felt that our kind of outfit was not needed within the 29th Infantry Division, and there was nothing he could do or say that could help keep it in existence.

General Gerow genuinely felt badly about it, as did Major Randolph Millholland, the battalion's commander. Millholland was a good man, I liked him. When I heard the news about the 29th Rangers being disbanded I told him that I would soldier under him any day of the week. He looked straight into my eyes and shook my hand, and then we parted.

After nine months of tough and excellent training, they told us there was no longer a 29th Ranger Battalion and that we'd all have to go back to our original units. The news nearly killed us. Most of the 29th Rangers, including myself, became quite blue when General Gerow told us the news, and we felt badly about going back to an outfit we once left. I removed my hard-earned 29th Ranger patches from my clothing, mailed them to Theresa, and instructed her to keep them in a safe place. I was sure proud to have worn those patches. They were like medals I had won.

I heard later that disbanding the outfit was intended all along. The theory was to provide a certain number of men with specialized, realistic training and then send them back to the division so that they could provide a hard nut of skill and savvy to the rest of the soldiers in the 29th Infantry. But in my opinion this theory didn't take into consideration the personal feelings of the men who had worked hard to become elite, only to be sent back to their regular units.

It was a shame that we disbanded, because we were a well trained outfit, and it took a tremendous effort for us to become Rangers. Whenever we did anything hard we always put everything we had in it. But after all that good training we received, we had to go back to where we had been before. Even during all of those grueling training exercises when I thought I couldn't go on anymore, I just tried a little harder and prayed a little, and before I knew it, whatever we were doing could always be finished.

I can truly say that despite how hard our Ranger training was, I never missed or fell out on anything we ever did. Even all of those grueling speed-marches and the mountains we had to climb, when a lot of guys would fall out from exhaustion, I was never one of them. I'll admit that there were many times I thought I couldn't take another step, but still I went on, figuring that a good Ranger has to finish the job and complete his mission. Afterward I would always feel proud of myself, especially when other guys had to drop out. I loved being in the Rangers because they did things that most other soldiers couldn't do.

16.

THE MAKING OF A PARATROOPER 1, 2, 3!

December 31, 1943
Theresa, I like this new outfit that I'm in, I swear that I do! I like the men
especially. They all look like good fighting men—I mean men that will be there
when things get a little tough in action.

> Pfc. Jack Womer
> Demolition Platoon, Regimental
> Headquarters Company
> 506th Parachute Infantry Regiment,
> 101st Airborne Division

In October 1943, after the 29th Ranger Battalion disbanded, I was sent back to my old outfit, the 175th Infantry Regiment of the 29th Infantry Division, which at the time was located in Saint Ives, Cornwall, an old fishing village on the southwest coast of England close to Lands End. It had been about 10 months since I had left the 175th Infantry Regiment. While it was nice to be back with my old buddies, returning after all of the training that I had been through, I couldn't help but feel out of place in my old unit. I felt as if I no longer belonged there, like I had outgrown it. I wanted to be back in an elite military unit, not a regular outfit.

Me and other guys that were in the 29th Rangers were hoping to get back into an existing Ranger battalion or one that was going to be formed, but we had no luck. What added to my misery was that it rained practically every day in St. Ives that October, and those cold, fall ocean winds would chill us right to the bone. Every day was cold, gray, rainy, and dreary. There was nothing to look forward to. I had to get out of the regular army and into something with more prestige.

In mid-November 1943, there appeared some hope in getting myself into an elite outfit. While on a two-day pass I went to Reading, a small town about 30 miles west of London. There was a Red Cross station there that served excellent food to G.I.s, and I had gone there just to get a good meal. I went into the station and I saw a first sergeant with the airborne Screaming Eagle insignia on his left shoulder, sitting alone at a table having dinner. He was a paratrooper. He was wearing paratrooper boots, the same kind of boots the Rangers wore. I didn't know too much about the paratroopers, but after looking at him I figured the paratroopers are probably an elite group.

I sat down at the table and started talking to him. He mentioned that he was in the 101st Airborne Division and told me a few things about what it was like to be a Screaming Eagle. Becoming a paratrooper sounded exciting, but what really caught my attention is when he told me that a paratrooper who was a private in an airborne division got paid 50 dollars more a month than a private in the regular army. The extra 50 dollars was hazardous duty pay.

I liked hearing that. A private in the regular army was paid about 30 dollars a month, while a paratrooper was paid about 80, which was the same pay a sergeant in the regular army received. So I decided to become a paratrooper. I would be in an elite military group, plus I'd make more money. What could be better than that? I asked the sergeant if the 101st Airborne Division was looking for additional paratroopers. He said "Heck yeah!" He told me the headquarters of the 101st Airborne Division was located nearby, in Newbury.

When I got back to St. Ives I told my captain that I wanted to leave the 29th Infantry Division and become a paratrooper in the 101st Airborne. "Absolutely not!" he said. The official reason that he gave for denying my request is that the 29th Infantry Division couldn't afford to lose a BAR man, especially one who is designated as an expert, such as me. There's no doubt that was one of the reasons why he didn't want to let me go, but the other reason was that he knew I was a Ranger—a well trained soldier, but he couldn't use that as an excuse to keep me. I spoke with my sergeant and lieutenant about wanting to leave the 29ers and become a paratrooper, and asked them to speak with the captain about letting me go. Neither of them had the balls to go against the captain, so I went back to my captain and pleaded with him to grant my request. He again flat out denied it.

I decided to speak to my regiment's chaplain, because I had no one else to turn to for help and by this time I had become quite depressed about the whole thing. My chaplain was a real nice man. The local English people got to know him, and liked him so much that they asked him to preach on Sundays at the English Methodist Church in St Ives. When I met with him I explained how proud I was to have become a Ranger, how disappointed I felt when the 29th Rangers were disbanded, and how I needed to get back into an elite military unit. I told him that I wanted to join the 101st Airborne, but my captain wasn't going to release me from the 29th Infantry.

The chaplain told me he understood how I felt, and said he would talk to my captain about allowing me to go to the 101st Airborne Division to become a paratrooper. The following day they spoke, and the captain told the chaplain, "No! He ain't going. He's the only BAR man I have." But after a while the chaplain somehow talked the captain into letting me go. I couldn't believe it!

Early in December of 1943, shortly after I was given permission to leave the 29th Infantry Division, I was given another two-day pass. I hopped on a train and traveled about 200 miles east to Newbury, in Berkshire England, where the headquarters of the 101st Airborne Division was located at the time, with the intent of getting the ball rolling with becoming a Screaming Eagle. Not knowing exactly where to go or who to speak with, I walked up to the entrance gates to the 101st Airborne Division headquarters to inquire how I could join the Division.

The military police (MPs) at the gate asked me if I had an entrance pass, and I said "No." They asked me what I wanted, and I replied "I want to join the 101st Airborne Division." They looked me over, asked me a few more questions, and checked my identification. Then one of the MPs said to me, "Do you see those officers up there in the distance?" I said "Yes." He said, "You go up and talk to them about how you can join the 101st because the headquarters is up there, just past where they're standing right now."

When I approached the officers I noticed that there were three of them: two colonels and a two star general. It was General Lee himself, the commander of the 101st Airborne Division! I saluted and told General Lee that I would like to become a paratrooper with the 101st Airborne Division, and showed him the memo written by my captain saying that he agreed to release me. He stared directly into my eyes for a few moments, and then he looked me over from head to toe. Keep in mind I was in tip-top physical condition, having just left the 29th Rangers. He turned my left arm so he could see my insignia, and said, "Are you with the 29th Infantry Division?" I said "Yes sir, and I was also in the 29th Ranger Battalion, before it disbanded." He said "You go over to that building over there and tell them that General Lee said he'll permit you to sign up in the 101st Airborne Division. We'll have to check you out before you can come on board with us, but in the meantime they'll get things started."

I saluted the general and thanked him. Here I was, just a lowly private, talking to General Lee! I didn't say one word to the colonels. I went over to the headquarters building and signed up to become a paratrooper with the 101st Airborne Division. The headquarters personnel said to me, "All right, Womer, you go back to your outfit, and we'll get in touch with you."

About a week before Christmas, 1943, I was officially transferred into the 101st Airborne Division. I wrote my mother and father to tell them I had joined the paratroopers. They had no idea what a paratrooper was or did. One of my older brothers, either Ben or David, explained to them without using any tact whatsoever that being a paratrooper meant that I would be jumping out of airplanes behind enemy lines and right into the fighting. My mother broke down and cried when she heard what I had done. I wrote them again, only this time I tried my best to soften the dangers of being a paratrooper and told them there was no need for them to worry. They, of course, worried anyway. My entire family thought that I had gone mad. Theresa was a little more understanding about me becoming a paratrooper, but she too was quite worried. I know it may sound crazy of me to join the paratroopers, but that's the kind of thing I wanted to do.

EARNING MY WINGS

Although I was now in the 101st Airborne Division, I still had one thing left to do in order to be officially called, and accepted as, a *paratrooper*. I had to earn my silver paratrooper insignia wings by undergoing paratrooper training and successfully completing the five required qualification jumps from an airplane. Most of the men in the 101st Airborne stationed in England at the time had fulfilled the paratrooper requirements in the United States, in which following their basic training they spent about three weeks in paratrooper school and were given an additional week to make the five required jumps.

However, in my case and that of the other 200 or so new recruits in the 101st Airborne Division, it was going to be more of a challenge to earn my wings because the paratrooper training had been put on the fast track. Apparently, training new prospective paratroopers had become backlogged in England, and the 101st had to streamline the training. Instead of taking the usual three weeks or so of paratrooper training and being allowed an additional week to make the five required jumps, someone such as myself would only be allowed about a week or so for training, and then only two days to make the jumps. I was given about ten days to earn my wings instead of the usual thirty.

I had heard that a lot of the new recruits weren't able to earn their wings under the streamlined training, but I wasn't concerned about it. I had just completed extremely rigorous Commando training, and I knew that anything the 101st Airborne Division was requiring me to do I could do standing on my head. I could run backwards faster than any paratrooper could run forward.

My paratrooper training began around Christmas, 1943, about a week after I entered the 101st Airborne Division. It wasn't much, really. We learned how to fold and pack our main parachute and our reserve chute, and practiced jumping from a make-believe airplane. They had a makeshift training area that had half of a C-47 airplane on the ground, with the doors open and a pile of sand about four feet below. The way that we practiced jumping was to get into the doorway of the plane wearing full gear, place our right hand outside of the plane along the outer edge of the doorway, look straight ahead, yell Geronomo!, jump out, land onto the sand pile on both feet and then roll. We did this for about a week, and that was about the extent of the practice that I had jumping out of an "airplane" before attempting to make the required five qualification jumps.

During the first week of January 1944, is when we were to make our qualification jumps. We would have to make them over the course of just two days. Just as in practice, we would jump in paratrooper sticks of six men per stick. We were originally supposed to make three jumps on the first day and the remaining two on the second day, but for some reason it was changed such that we had to make four jumps on the first day and the fifth on the next.

We were told that we could back out at anytime, but anyone who did would automatically be disqualified from becoming a paratrooper. I told them I wanted to do the jumps and that I had no intention of backing out. The night before, we packed our main and reserve parachutes, and went over some last-minute details with the instructors.

I didn't like the idea of having to jump using a parachute that I had folded and packed. I would have preferred to use one that had been packed and folded by someone who had more experience than I, such as a rigger. The instructors told us that before we jumped we would attach a cloth hook-up line from our main parachutes to a metal anchor line that ran down the length of the ceiling of the fuselage of the plane, and once we jumped this line would immediately tighten and automatically pull open our main parachutes.

The instructors pointed out that there was a small chance that the main chute would fail to open, and if this happened we had to open our reserve parachute to avoid being killed. The instructors told us the moment we jumped from the plane to start counting in our heads "one one-thousand, two one-thousand, three one-thousand, four one-thousand, five one-thousand. . . ." If by the count of "five one thousand" the main chute had not opened, it wasn't going to open, and at that point we should immediately pull the cord on our reserve parachute.

While we were packing our parachutes in preparation for our jump the next day, for the hell of it I said with a straight face to the guy next to me, "Hey you, you're packing your death chute." As soon as I said this he became all upset and fell apart. I had frightened him with my comment, and now he was too scared to jump. A sergeant came over and wanted to know what was going on. The soldier told the sergeant that I had frightened him with my comment, and the sergeant chewed me out for upsetting the soldier, but the soldier still flat-out refused to jump. He was petrified. I never saw him again, and I don't think he ever went through with making his qualification jumps. Who knows, I may have saved his life by saying what I said to him!

I made the four jumps on the first day, and the last of the five qualification jumps on the second day. On the first jump I wasn't as nervous as I thought I'd be, but by the time I landed I was quite nervous. I jumped out of the plane, my parachute opened immediately, and I thought everything was going well until I looked up at my parachute and noticed five of the twenty-eight cloth panels of the chute had somehow ripped away. Then I heard one of the trainers on the ground shouting "Pull your reserve! Pull your reserve!" I didn't know who he was talking to—me or one of the other five guys that had jumped with me. I assumed he wasn't talking to me because everything seemed to be going smoothly and none of our instructors ever said anything about what to do if some of our parachute panels ripped out during a jump.

It turned out the trainer was yelling to me. The loss of the panels in my parachute was causing me to descend too fast, but I didn't realize it because it was my first jump. I then drifted over the parachute of another paratrooper who had jumped before me and was by now right below me. I could see that my feet were going to hit the top of his parachute, and when it did it would cause my parachute to collapse and I would crashland onto the ground. As I was about to slam into his parachute I pulled my feet up as far as I could and I just made it past him. I finally hit the ground, but it was a hard landing. I thought to myself, "I don't think I'm going to survive doing this stuff."

On the second jump I was nervous as hell because of what happened during the first one, but I made it without problems. My third jump went well too, but I didn't think I had it in me to complete the fourth one because a jump takes a lot out of you. It really does. There were a number of guys that dropped out after their second and third jumps, but I hung in there and made my four jumps on the first day as required. Boy was I tired that evening. Those four jumps weren't easy, but I did it, and felt good about it.

I made my fifth jump the next day without any problem. They issued me my silver wings, and I was now officially a Screaming Eagle! I was quite proud when I pinned those wings on my chest and sewed the 101st Airborne Division's Screaming Eagle insignia on my clothing. I felt like a million bucks. I was rewarded with a four-day pass. What a way to start the New Year!

MARY EDWARDS—A LADY FRIEND

Every paratrooper that I knew in the 101st Airborne Division had a girl-friend in London. I was no exception. Right after I got my wings I went straight to London on my four-day pass to celebrate and show off my silver paratrooper wings. During that trip to London I met a beautiful young Welsh woman named Mary Edwards. Mary was in the English Army's Auxiliary Territorial Service, or ATS, as it was called. The ATS was for women only, and had been formed specifically to allow English women to participate in the war effort as military personnel.

Mary lived in London, and worked under Supreme Allied Commander Dwight D. Eisenhower in the Allied forces intelligence headquarters. The intelligence headquarters office was located in a bunker forty feet under-ground right in the heart of London, across from Buckingham Palace and close to Westminster Abbey, Scotland Yard and Big Ben. I couldn't get near to where she worked because there were steel gates and guards that kept out anyone who didn't work there.

Mary's family was dirt poor but they were very nice people and, despite the war, a very happy lot. After that trip I found myself developing strong feelings for Mary, and I would go to London every chance I had just to be with her. She had strong feelings for me as well. She would be there to greet me when I arrived at the London train station, and there to see me off when it was time for me to go back to camp. We fell in love, and she wanted to marry me. Part of me wanted to go along with the idea, but another part of me didn't, as I was already engaged to Theresa, who was faithfully and patiently waiting for me to return home to her.

I told Mary about Theresa and that we were engaged, and I even showed her Theresa's photo. But Mary didn't seem to be discouraged by it. I guess she felt that so long as I wasn't married I was fair game. Mary and I would date for more than a year, just about up to when the war ended. I wasn't the only G.I. that had an English girlfriend who wanted to marry him. Girls in London were always trying to meet and marry an American soldier. I knew of a lot of G.I.s that went over to Europe to fight the Nazis and returned to the States with a wife. It was fairly common.

17.

BECOMING ONE OF THE "FILTHY THIRTEEN"

I depended on Jack Womer quite a bit because he knew what he was doing. He had undertaken a lot of specialized training with the 29th Ranger Battalion, and it showed. He was a leader . . . he knew how to handle men, and they had a lot of confidence in him. Our junior officers didn't like Jack because he was smarter than they were and a better soldier, and they knew it. As for me, I never fought with a better soldier.

> Sgt. Jake McNiece,
> Demolition Platoon, Regimental
> Headquarters Company
> 506th Parachute Infantry Regiment,
> 101st Airborne Division

The 101st Airborne Division was composed of three parachute infantry regiments (PIR): the 501st, 502nd and the 506th PIR, plus the 327th Glider Infantry. When I joined the 101st Airborne they wanted to know what my expertise was so that they could place me in the appropriate group. They wanted to know whether I was machine-gunner, a mortar man, a sharpshooter, demolitions expert, whatever.

I had learned beforehand that William Myers, my former first sergeant in the 29th Rangers, had joined the 101st Airborne. I liked Myers, and was hoping I could be placed in his unit within the 101st. I asked them what group Myers was in, and they told me he was in the demolition platoon of the 506th PIR. So I told them I was a demolitions expert, which of course I wasn't, and they assigned me there.

The demolitions platoon was part of the Regimental Headquarters Company of the 506th PIR, which meant that I'd be in close contact with Colonel Robert Sink, commanding officer of the 506th, and other top brass. The platoon consisted of three demolition sections: the First, Second and Third. Each section was commanded by a second lieutenant and contained thirteen men: a buck sergeant, two corporals, and two squads of five men per squad. The platoon had over forty men.

The captain of the demolitions platoon was William H. ("Dapper") Daniels, and the first lieutenant was John H. Reeder. It turned out that Myers' section of the platoon was full, but Jake McNiece, the buck sergeant of the platoon's First Demolition Section, noticed me and asked about me. He'd heard that I was an army Ranger, and requested that I be assigned to his section, which at the time was short of men. So at Jake McNiece's request, I was placed in the section of the platoon known officially as the First Demolition Section, but more infamously as the "Filthy Thirteen." It wasn't the same section that William Myers was in, but at least I was in the same platoon as him, and I felt good about that.

Since the demolitions platoon was part of the 506th PIR Headquarters Company, it was not under the purview of any of the battalions. Each demolition section, however, would support a battalion during training exercises or missions. The Filthy Thirteen section was generally assigned to support the 1st Battalion of the 506th PIR.

The Filthy Thirteen got its name from the type of men that comprised the section. They were primarily men that other officers didn't want in their own outfits—either because they didn't obey orders or follow military procedures, frequently got into trouble, or were just otherwise difficult to handle. And to be plain about it, hygiene wasn't their specialty. The origins of the Filthy Thirteen date back to the latter part of 1942, about a year before I transferred to the division, when the men of the 506th PIR undertook basic training in Toccoa, Georgia. Men in the Filthy Thirteen would come and go throughout the war, as many would get killed or wounded, and were subsequently replaced. From the time the Filthy Thirteen formed in 1942 until the war in Europe ended in May 1945, about thirty men would pass through the section.

When I joined the Filthy Thirteen the second lieutenant was Charles Mellen. He had come on board with the 506th PIR at about the same time as me. The buck sergeant was Jake McNiece, and the two corporals were John Hale and Brincely Stroup. The other men of the Filthy Thirteen, aside from myself were: Joe Oleskiewicz, Louis ("Loulip") Lipp, Charles ("Mauh") Darnell, Jack Agnew, Robert ("Ragsman") Cone, George ("Goo-Goo") Radecka, Roland ("Frenchy") Baribeau, and James ("Picadilly Willy") Green. Another member, Chuck Plauda, joined the group after me. The guys nicknamed me "Hawkeye" because I had unusually good eyesight. I gave John Hale the nickname of Peepnuts, because he had kind of a high voice with a pitch similar to that of a chicken.

The guys were a rowdy bunch alright, and the name "Filthy Thirteen" was quite appropriate for the section. The behavior of most of the guys in the "Thirteen" was influenced quite a bit by Jake McNiece. Jake wasn't big on taking orders or following military rules and regulations. He'd talk back to officers, and wouldn't always salute or address them properly. He would bend and break rules, and didn't seem to care if he got into trouble for it. McNiece liked to get drunk, fistfight, raise hell, and preferred to shave or bathe only when he planned to chase women while on pass in London or elsewhere.

Sergeant McNiece's habits and behavior naturally rubbed off on the corporals and privates in the section. I was never quite as influenced by McNiece as were the other guys in the Filthy Thirteen. I was probably one of the "cleanest" in the section, as I didn't drink or smoke, was always clean shaven, kept my body and clothes washed on a regular basis, and was better at obeying orders. I was also a bit more mature, as I was a little older and had been in the service longer than most (if not all) of them.

Yet despite our few differences, McNiece and I had a lot in common. We were both good soldiers. Neither of us were big on military formality, nor did we respect the authority of officers who were idiots. I was very impressed with Jake's ability to raise hell and get away with it. I admired how he didn't take any crap from officers, no matter what their rank may have been.

Jake was also impressed with me because of my Ranger training. Most of our officers hated him, but the men in the Filthy Thirteen, including myself, were quite fond of him. We quickly became good friends, and remained so the rest of our lives. I also became very good friends with John Hale ("Peepnuts"), and George Radecka ("Goo-Goo"). Unfortunately, the time I was able to spend with Peepnuts and Goo-Goo was short, as both would be killed in action within months after I had joined the Filthy Thirteen.

The Filthy Thirteen, and the men in the whole 101st Airborne Division, for that matter, were well-trained fighters. They were the kind of men I knew I could depend on to support one another and fight to the death, if necessary, when we got into combat with the Krauts. Frankly, that's all that mattered to me. I fit in very well with the Filthy Thirteen, and with the rest of the 101st Airborne Division right from the start.

Not only did I like the men in the 101st Airborne, I also enjoyed the nature of the work of my demolitions platoon. I've always liked fireworks, as well as learning new things, so it's only natural that I would like becoming a demolitions expert. I became quite good at setting explosive charges on bridges, damns, buildings, vehicles and other things, plus searching for and defusing explosive devises. It was dangerous and difficult work, but it was important and I liked it. We'd periodically go on outings where we would practice our demolition skills, bivouac, hike, or participate in tactical maneuvers. The training was hard, but none of what I undertook while in the 101st Airborne Division was ever as difficult as the training I had experienced while in the 29th Ranger Battalion.

18.

LIFE AT THE WILLS' MANOR ESTATE, LITTLECOTE, WILTSHIRE

At the time I entered the 101st Airborne Division, the 1st and 2nd Battalions of the 506th PIR were billeted in Alderbourne, England, and the 3rd Battalion in Ramsbury. The 506th Regimental Headquarters Company, including its demolition platoon, stayed at the estate of Sir Ernest and Lady Wills in Littlecote, Wiltshire. Sir Ernest Wills was the heir to the Wills' cigarette empire in England. He was filthy rich. His Littlecote estate was just a couple of miles or so from the towns of Hungerford and Ramsbury, about 60 miles west of London. The officers and other regimental staff of the 506th Headquarters Company lived in one portion of Sir Wills' huge Tudor-style manor house, while Sir Ernest and Lady Wills and their family lived in another other part of the house.

The Wills' large staff of butlers, maids, and other personnel lived in the mansion or in one of the smaller houses on the estate grounds. The three sections of the 506th demolitions platoon stayed in Quonset huts set up side-by-side along the main drive between the house and the east lodge. Each section of the platoon had its own hut. We were allowed to roam the estate grounds, but the house was off-limits unless we were standing guard duty or serving as orderlies to our officers.

The Wills' manor house was more like a castle. (Today it's a hotel known as the Littlecote House.) It was centuries old, and about every hundred years or so the owners at the time would add another wing onto it. By the time Sir Ernest Wills' assumed ownership it consisted of dozens of rooms, many of which were quite large and contained detailed mural paintings on the walls and ceilings, hand-carved decorative moldings, marble and tile floors, and other features that only the extremely wealthy could afford. It had a dining room that contained a table that could seat thirty-two people comfortably. The ceiling of the dining room was affixed with the body armor of knights. The house was unbelievably magnificent in appearance, and, despite being centuries old, had many amenities that were way ahead of the era. It even had a heated swimming pool.

The bathrooms had beautiful marble sinks and bathtubs that were decorated with magnificent fixtures. On the first floor, near the dining room, was a room that contained many marble bathtubs. It was specifically set up for washing oneself and one's boots and equipment after horseback riding. Practically every room in the house had 24-hour maid service, and signaling a maid to come to one's room was rather simple. In the cellar there was an entire wall covered with light bulbs, with each one representing a particular room. In the rooms there was an electric button that when pressed would light the corresponding bulb in the cellar and summon the servant. There was always a person on duty in the basement monitoring the light bulbs who could dispatch a maid or butler immediately.

In addition to the main house, the grounds held many other buildings that served as guest houses, lodges or stables. The gatekeeper, as did many of the servants and other employed personnel of the manor, had separate living quarters right on the estate. There was even a chapel in the northwestern portion of the house. It was located directly behind the heated swimming pool. The Wills' Littlecote manor estate was quite a place.

NUDE POOL PARTIES AND STEALING BEER

While we were billeted at Sir Wills' Littlecote manor estate the officers of the 506th Regimental Headquarters Company frequently arranged to have women brought onto the grounds of the manor house to participate in nude pool parties. The officers and women would be in or around the pool, stark-ass naked, laughing and drinking and having a grand old time as if they were at a Roman orgy. Privates and buck sergeants were barred from attending the parties, but were ordered to stand guard in the general vicinity when these parties took place. A lot of the privates would often volunteer to stand guard during a pool party just so they could stare at the naked women walking around.

The pool was located in the southwest portion of the house, on the same side as the main entrance. One afternoon I was standing guard while a nude pool party was going on, and an army truck pulled up and delivered twenty barrels of beer. A lieutenant came over to me and said very sternly: "Private! Don't let ANYONE touch any of these barrels. Keep close watch on them!" "Yes sir," I replied. I had about an hour left of my guard shift, and then I'd be off for a while, and then I would return for another shift. I immediately began thinking of a plan to steal one of the barrels and sell it to earn some extra cash. I figured with all of the beer-guzzlers in the demolitions platoon, particularly the Filthy Thirteen, I should have no problem making some easy money.

I thought for a while, and noticed that the beer barrels had been placed on a portion of ground that was at the top of a slight incline. At the base of the incline, about twenty feet away, was a rather large pile of kindling wood, to be used to start fires for cooking and heat. I carefully nudged one of the barrels to get it to roll down the incline and into the pile of kindling wood. Once it came to rest I meandered down and nonchalantly covered the barrel with the kindling wood to hide it. My plan was to come back for it later when it was dark, when I was to do another shift of guard duty.

After I covered it up I continued standing guard near the rest of the barrels until I was relieved. I said to the soldier who was to take my place "You better keep close watch on these beer barrels. The officers don't want anything to happen to them. There are nineteen of them in all. Make sure no one but the officers in the house takes any of them." He said "Alright, I'll make sure nothing happens to them."

I walked over to the Quonset huts used by our demolitions platoon, and went into the one that housed the Filthy Thirteen. Jake McNiece was there, and I said to him "Jake! You like to drink beer. How would you like to have an entire barrel of the same beer that the officers drink?" He said "Hell, yeah." I said, "Well, being that you're my buddy, I'm going to give you the first opportunity to buy it." Jake asked: "How much do you want for it?" I said "As much as I can get! What's your best offer?" He knew that I'd have no trouble selling the beer to someone else, so he had no choice but to offer me an attractive price. He said "Would twenty bucks be enough?" "It's a deal." I replied. "Get a couple of guys to come over when I return to guard duty, and you'll get your barrel of beer."

When I returned to my guard post it was night time. By this time the nineteen barrels of beer that had been outside when I was relieved had been brought into the manor house. But the barrel I had stolen and hid under the kindling wood was still there. The soldier who had relieved me didn't make any comment about a barrel being missing, so I knew that none of the officers suspected anything was wrong. After the soldier left, the two guys that Jake had sent came by for the beer. I told them where they could find it, and they carried the barrel back to their Quonset hut and the Filthy Thirteen had their own beer blast!

AN UNGRATEFUL EMPLOYEE

Near the chapel in Sir Wills' manor house there was a little shop or area where hot drinks and small pastries could be obtained by guests at the estate. During one brutally cold winter night I was standing guard at the northwestern portion of the house, in the general vicinity of the chapel. I had my M-1 Garand, as I was on guard duty, but I didn't have any money on me. I was cold, and I went into the shop and asked the shopkeeper behind the counter for a cookie and a cup of hot chocolate.

"Get out of here!" the shopkeeper shouted. The shopkeeper refused to serve me. He claimed he wouldn't serve me because I didn't have any money, but I know that the real reason was because I was just a lowly private. He was used to serving English aristocrats and the officers in the 506 Regimental Headquarters Company, who, by the way, I knew never had to pay for hot chocolate or cookies at the shop. They got it all for free because they were guests of Sir Wills.

The man tending the shop that night was one of those Englishman who just didn't particularly care for American G.I.s. In his mind we were beneath him. I said to him "Why you God-damn son-of-a-bitch! I was sent over here to fight for you and your country, and right now I'm standing guard outside of your shop freezing my ass off while I'm protecting your cozy English ass from the Krauts, and you won't so much as give me a God damn cup of hot chocolate and a cookie?" He again refused to serve me, and told me to leave. I again called him a God-damned son-of-a-bitch, and he again told me to leave.

At about the same moment Jake McNiece happened to be walking by, and saw me and came inside the shop. He too was carrying a rifle. Jake sensed that there was some friction between me and the shopkeeper. I said,

"Jake, I've been standing outside for hours freezing my ass off on guard duty, and I asked this guy to give me a cup of hot chocolate and a cookie. I explained to him that I have no money, and that I'm cold and hungry. This son-of-a-bitch won't serve me!" Jake said to the shopkeeper "What do you mean you won't give one of my men a cup of hot chocolate and a cookie on a cold night like this? Why you've got enough cookies in here to feed an army, and there's enough hot chocolate in that pot to bath in. Now be a nice guy and give Private Womer what he wants." The shopkeeper ordered both of us to leave his shop.

Jake's face suddenly took on a mean-looking expression. He shouted to the shopkeeper "If you don't serve Private Womer a cup of hot chocolate and cookie immediately, I will personally pour that entire pot of hot chocolate onto the floor, smash all of the cookies and other pastries, and destroy this entire shop with my bare hands. If you try to interfere, I'm ordering Private Womer to blow your God-damned head off!" To add to Jake's theatrics I pointed my rifle at the shopkeeper's head.

Off course Jake wasn't serious with his threats, nor was I about to shoot, but the shopkeeper must have felt otherwise because he began to shake like a leaf on a tree during a hurricane. He quickly poured me a rather large cup of hot chocolate and gave me a cookie. With my rifle still pointed at his head, I said to the shopkeeper, "Thank you. But since you've caused so much trouble for us, I feel that you owe me two more cookies, and Sergeant McNiece a free cup of hot chocolate and cookies too." Without saying a word, the shopkeeper gave me two extra cookies, and gave Jake a cup of hot chocolate and cookies, at no cost. I thanked him again, being the gentleman that I am, and Jake and I left the shop.

The next day the shopkeeper filed a written complaint to Sir Wills about what had happened. In his complaint he gave a detailed description of the incident, and insisted that both Jake and I be arrested for our actions. Word about the incident got back to "Dapper" Daniels, our captain, and Jake and I were called into Daniels' office. Jake explained to Captain Daniels that the shopkeeper was completely out of line for refusing to serve me a hot cup of chocolate and a cookie on a brutally cold winter night while I was guarding and protecting the estate grounds. Jake made the shopkeeper seem like a bastard (which he was), me like a dedicated soldier doing his job, and himself like a responsible sergeant looking out for the welfare of one of his men.

After Jake finished speaking Captain Daniels said to us, "I'm going to look further into this, and decide whether any disciplinary actions against you two are warranted!" I don't know what, if anything, was said or done between Captain Daniels and Sir Wills, but Jake and I never heard a word about the matter again.

19.

AN ENCOUNTER WITH WINSTON CHURCHILL

I made my sixth jump on March 2nd, 1944. It was just a practice jump. There was nothing special about it, but I carried about 20 pounds or more of TNT and that extra weight made a noticeable increase in the jump velocity and the force of the landing impact. I would make my seventh jump that same month, on March 23, only this was going to be a demonstration jump for the United Kingdom's Prime Minister Winston Churchill, Supreme Allied Commander Dwight D. Eisenhower, and General Maxwell Taylor, the new general of the 101st Airborne Division.

Apparently, General Taylor wanted to impress General Eisenhower and Prime Minister Churchill by showing them how well we had been trained as paratroopers. So a bunch of men from the 101st Airborne were ordered to jump for the sole purpose of putting on a show for Churchill and Eisenhower. Our officers told us that once we landed on the ground, in a large open field, we were to report back to the assembly area right away. I hated having to do this jump. I didn't see any point to it. I don't think any of us wanted to do it, but we had to.

On the day of the jump a light rain began to fall as we went onto the airfield and boarded our C-47s. The planes took off, and when we reached our respective drop points we jumped. Another paratrooper and I landed close to each other in the field. There was nothing but open field all around, but I noticed a haystack not too far from us. So I said to the guy with me, "To hell with reporting back to the assembly area in this rain. Let's hide in that haystack over there and we'll report back later. No one will notice we're gone."

We quickly removed our parachutes, rolled them up and ran over to the haystack, which was less than 10 feet from a dirt road. We buried our parachutes in the haystack, and then crawled inside it to hide and get out of the rain. I was sitting in a crouched position in the haystack, with my knees resting against my chest. My feet were flat on the ground at the very perimeter of the stack, but were covered with hay, as was the rest of me. I was able to peek out between the strands of hay that covered my face.

We were in the haystack, just relaxing and waiting for the rain to stop. After about an hour or so a command car came down the dirt road heading towards us. Judging from the direction the car was traveling it appeared to have come from the assembly area. I didn't know who was in the car and, frankly, I didn't care because I just assumed it would drive right by us. Just as the car got close to us, however, it slowed down and pulled off the road, right at the haystack in which we were hiding. To my utter disbelief, sitting in the car were General Eisenhower, General Taylor, and Prime Minister Winston Churchill!

At first I didn't know why they had stopped right at the haystack. Then I thought they somehow must have known that we were hiding in there, and General Taylor had ordered the driver to stop so he could chew us out for not obeying orders. I said to myself, "Boy, Womer, you sure picked the wrong time to screw-up! General Taylor, Eisenhower, and Churchill are going to chew your ass out but good for not getting back to the assembly area as ordered. You're in deep shit now."

Churchill stepped out of the car and walked up to the haystack right in front of where I was hiding. Expecting him to tell me to come out, instead, to my surprise, he unzipped his trousers, pulled his penis out of his pants and peed on the haystack, directly over the spot where I was hiding! His urine trickled down through the hay and onto my boots. I just sat there, not moving a muscle or making a sound, and watched the Prime Minister of the United Kingdom pee on me. I could see that he hadn't been circumcised. He took this rather long pee, shook his penis, put it back into his pants, zipped up and got back into the car. The car pulled away and continued on with its journey down the road. I could not believe what had happened!

20.

PRELUDE TO OVERLORD: THE INVASION OF FRANCE

Mother, please stop worrying about me, I'll be alright. I'd much rather be a live soldier than one who died being a hero. So don't worry, I won't take any chances. But I will do my job, the best I can possibly do it, regardless of the cost.
Pfc. Jack Womer, 506th PIR

We all knew that in order to defeat Hitler's Third Reich and the Nazi war machine the Allied forces would sooner or later have to invade Europe. What we didn't know was how, when or where such a large-scale Allied invasion would take place.

From the time Hitler declared war on the United States in December 1941 until the spring of 1944, hundreds of thousands of Allied troops, tanks, warships, bombers, fighter planes and other weaponry had made their way across the Atlantic Ocean to Great Britain. This massive build-up of soldiers and equipment was no secret to Hitler or his generals, nor was the fact that the Allies intended on using this military strength for a large-scale invasion. Much of the training that the Allied forces were undertaking in Great Britain was invasion-oriented. What was not as obvious to Hitler was where the invasion would take place, but certain locations could be assumed to be unlikely from common sense alone.

That the Allied forces were concentrated in England, that the Allied attack force would be extremely large, and that the success of the invasion was, to a large extent, dependent on keeping the date, time and exact location of the assault a secret right up until the opening moments naturally limited the invasion location to an area that was in close proximity to

Great Britain, namely the northwestern coast of France.

The question that both Hitler and the Allied commanders needed answered was *where* along the hundreds of miles of coast was the preferred spot for the invasion. The closest point of France to England was the Pas-de-Calais, so the Germans naturally needed to prioritize their defenses there. But ultimately the French region known as Normandy was chosen as the invasion site. The plan, codenamed Operation Overlord, was that the Allied forces would launch a massive amphibious attack of unprecedented magnitude on about a fifty-mile stretch of beachfront along the Normandy coast.

The invasion would also utilize Allied paratroopers, specifically the British 6th Airborne Division and the United States 82nd and 101st Airborne Divisions, to land behind the German lines before the seaborne troops came ashore. The overarching objective of the two U.S. airborne divisions would be to protect the western flank of the invasion front from a Kraut counterattack. The invasion of Normandy would be the first combat mission of the 101st Airborne Division.

For security reasons the specific details of the invasion, such as when and where it would take place, and the missions of the different divisions were kept secret from practically everyone involved. None of us knew any of the specific details about the invasion or what any of us were supposed to do, or what our specific assignments were until just a few days, even hours, before D-Day.

DON'T WORRY MOTHER, I'LL BE ALRIGHT

By about the end of February, 1944, we began to sense that the invasion was going to take place soon. By this time we began to notice firsthand or hear from other soldiers that tons and tons of equipment and gear were being allocated and stored in such a way that it could be put into use at a moment's notice. We were told that there was a good chance that soon we would not be allowed to write home for a while. The training in my demolition platoon had transformed from general activities to more mission-oriented or tactical type activities. We practiced at night, during the day, and under stealth conditions, setting explosive charges on bridges and inside of buildings. We also practiced locating and deactivating charges such as those the enemy might set.

In mid-April 1944, we jumped into a simulated combat zone. We put down a lot of smoke from smoke grenades, and it was quite elaborate in a military sense. It was my eighth paratroop jump and I carried, among other things, an 80-pound flame thrower. It's quite tough jumping from a plane with a flame thrower. But once I hit the ground and got it going, I had a lot of fun using it. I practiced shooting flames at make-believe enemy fox-holes and positions. I wondered whether I would have to carry one when we actually jumped for the invasion.

Near the end of April, 1944, the 82nd Airborne, the 101st Airborne, and the 4th Infantry Division undertook invasion practice for our concerted attack of the Normandy beachfront, code-named Utah. The practice exercise was held in southwest England, in Slapton Sands, Devonshire. This location was chosen because its terrain was similar in many respects to that of Utah Beach and the surrounding area.

In about the middle of May, the 101st Airborne Division held an actual dress rehearsal for D-Day. For this the Filthy Thirteen, as did the other groups in the division, assembled and packed all our invasion gear into a C-47 aircraft, became airborne sometime that evening, remained aloft for about the same duration as would our actual invasion flight across the English Channel, and jumped from our planes in the early morning darkness somewhere in England. Then we reassembled and simulated fulfilling our primary D-Day mission, which was to assist in securing two bridges.

It was a rough rehearsal, and a lot of guys got hurt from the jump alone. Brincely Stroup, one of the two corporals in the Filthy Thirteen, broke his ankle during this rehearsal jump, and it was obvious that he would not be able to jump with us on D-Day. Jake McNiece promoted Joe Oleskiewicz to corporal to backfill the vacancy created by Stroup's injury.

After the rehearsal we returned to our Quonset huts on the manor estate of Sir Ernest Wills. By this point we were no longer allowed to listen to the radio, but we still had access to newspapers, which in subtle ways hinted that the invasion was just around the corner. But despite all the invasion hype that we were hearing and seeing, we were still issued passes for rest and relaxation purposes. When on leave I would usually go to London to spend time with my girlfriend, Mary Edwards. Mary, too, was of the impression that the invasion was going to happen pretty soon.

By about mid-May, 1944, air raids by the German Luftwaffe, which had started earlier in the month, were occurring almost daily. Kraut fighter planes would fly overhead and shoot the hell out of our camp for about a minute or two, even drop a bomb, and then leave. These attacks would usually occur at night, and were dangerous. A couple of times I damned near got hit from the Kraut machine-gun fire. We knew that we couldn't withstand such attacks for very long, and that we'd have to invade soon.

Near the end of May I was issued a leave pass and went to London to see Mary. When I returned to camp we were told that the invasion was now imminent. I knew this was true because I had noticed tons and tons of blood plasma arriving and being stockpiled. The plasma was coming from the American Red Cross, who obtained it from volunteer donors. Precisely when or where the invasion was to occur, or what we would do as part of the invasion force were still unknown to us, but we knew for certain it was going to happen real soon.

We were encouraged to write home while we still could, as we would soon be relocated to a highly restricted airbase at which outside communications would be strictly forbidden. We were ordered, of course, not to disclose the fact the invasion was about to take place, but it seemed as if the word was already out, for I began to receive many letters from family members, friends and neighbors from back home wishing me well.

Dear old Mrs. Parker, a sweet and kind elderly woman who was a neighbor of mine in Dundalk, Maryland, wrote me a very nice letter. But I was stunned by her request in which she asked me to kill two German soldiers for her when we attacked. I never expected such a request to come from a sweet old lady like her. I wrote back to Mrs. Parker, saying that I would do my best to honor her request, and that I would try to add some "interest."

Once we heard that the invasion was just around the corner I began to seriously wonder about my destiny. We were told that we would soon no longer be able to write home for awhile, but I wondered how many of us, including myself, would ever have the opportunity to write home again. I didn't know what was going to happen to me once we invaded Europe— whether I was going to get killed, be wounded or survive it all. While there was still time to do so, I wrote a letter to my mother. It was kind of a goodbye letter in case I was killed, but I tried my best not to be obvious about it. In this letter I told my mother not to worry about me, that I would return home after the war, and all of the usual stuff a son about to go into battle tells his mother.

I also confessed to having a serious relationship with a woman (Mary Edwards) in London, and that she wanted to marry me, despite that fact that I told her I was already engaged to Theresa Cook. As ashamed as I felt about admitting this relationship, I wanted my mother to hear about it from me, because I knew it would hurt her feelings if I were to get killed and she heard about it afterward from Mary.

In the same letter I included my original silver paratrooper wings and asked my mother to keep them for me until I returned home, so that they wouldn't get lost while I was overseas. The real reason why I sent her my original wings is that I wanted her to have them as a keepsake in the event I wouldn't return. My original wings meant a lot to me, and I was concerned that if I were killed they'd get lost. I obtained replacement wings for myself. I also wrote a letter to Theresa. It, too, was kind of a goodbye letter. In it I admitted to having dated another woman, but I didn't go into the details. I told Theresa that I loved her very much, and not to worry about me.

21.

D-DAY MISSION DISCLOSED

Either at the end of May or the very beginning of June, 1944, we left Sir Wills' estate and traveled about 100 miles southwest to a highly restricted airbase in Exeter. The entire base was fenced-in and heavily guarded. No one was allowed on or off unless specifically ordered to do so. Communication of any kind with the outside world was strictly forbidden.

There was an area within the airbase where a bunch of large tents were set up, within which were dozens upon dozens of large sand-filled wooden tray-like structures. Each of these "sand tables," as they were called, displayed a scaled-down replica of the locations within the invasion area where the paratroopers would be dropped to fulfill their missions. For each location there was a sand table that portrayed every road, trail, house, building, hill, stream, forest and field in the form of an extremely accurate, miniaturized model. The pre-invasion reconnaissance must have been performed very carefully to get the level of detail portrayed on the tables. They were quite remarkable.

As we studied the tables, the details of where the invasion was to occur and our specific invasion mission were disclosed to us. Beginning at daybreak on D-Day, thousands of Allied troops would come ashore at five designated beaches along the Normandy coast to defeat the German forces and move inland. To help ensure a successful assault, the 82nd and 101st Airborne Divisions were to protect the western flank of the Allied invasion front from a German counteroffensive. The overall plan for the two airborne divisions was that in the early morning hours of D-Day, prior to any

Allied shore landings, the 82nd and the 101st, with a combined force of over 13,000 paratroopers, would be dropped from the sky behind enemy lines over the part of Normandy known as the Cotentin Peninsula, around the areas of St. Mere Eglise and Carentan and about five miles or so inland from Utah Beach, where the U.S. 4th Infantry Division would come ashore later in the morning. Once on the ground, the individual units in the two airborne divisions would proceed to fulfill their specific missions. The paratroopers and glider infantry units would be the first combat soldiers to take part in the invasion.

The 82nd Airborne Division was to parachute onto both sides of the Merderet River, capture Sainte-Mere-Eglise and two roadways at La Fiere and Chef-du-Pont, destroy bridges over the Douve River at Etienville and Beuzeville-la-Bastille, and establish a defensive front west of the Merderet River. A primary objective of the 101st Airborne Division on D-Day was to seize and hold the four inland roadways that headed inland from Utah Beach.

The Cotentin Peninsula is composed largely of low-lying ground in which there is a network of rivers and man-made canals. The peninsula naturally contains a considerable portion of marshes and swamps, which would restrict the ability of the 4th Infantry Division to move inland. It was absolutely essential to the infantry that the four roadways coming from Utah Beach, between St. Martin-de-Varreville and Pouppeville, would no longer be under the control of the Germans when they assaulted the beach. Taking control of the roadways from the Krauts was assigned to the 101st Airborne Division's 502nd Parachute Infantry Regiment (PIR) and the 1st and 2nd Battalions of the 506th PIR.

Once ashore, the 4th Infantry Division would move inland a few miles and join forces with the men of the 1st and 29th Infantry Divisions, who would come ashore at Omaha Beach, about ten miles to the east of Utah. Once joined, these Allied forces, along with the 82nd and 101st Airborne Divisions, were to take control of the entire Cotentin Peninsula and begin moving into the interior of France.

The only problem was that between Utah and Omaha Beaches was the relatively small, yet strategically important, Kraut-occupied town of Carentan. The significance of Carentan with regard to the Normandy invasion is that it would be difficult for the 4th Infantry Division to join with the 29th and 1st Infantry Divisions and take control of the Cotentin if Carentan remained occupied by the German forces. Carentan Highway, the main road in the area, ran along the coast of Normandy and passed through Carentan as it entered the Cotentin Peninsula. Allied forces landing at Omaha Beach would need to use this highway to head into the peninsula.

Another primary objective of the 101st Airborne Division during the invasion of Normandy was to keep the Nazi forces positioned in or near Carentan from interfering with the infantry landings. This objective was to be accomplished by: 1) destroying the German heavy artillery battery at Saint-Martin-de-Varreville and a building complex at Mezieres; 2) capture the La Barquette lock to prevent the Nazis from using it to cause further flooding of the area; 3) destroy or take control of the bridges over the Douve and Taute Rivers in and around Carentan; and 4) organize a defensive line to protect the southern flank from a Kraut counteroffensive. Once the 101st Airborne met up with some of the Allied infantry units that had come ashore, they were then to seize Carentan.

The 501st PIR of the 101st Airborne was assigned to destroy two bridges on the Carentan Highway and the railroad bridge that traversed the Douve River to the west, and seize and hold the LaBarquette Lock located just north of the town. The 3rd Battalion of the 506th PIR was assigned to seize and control the two wooden bridges that traversed the Taute River about two miles northeast of Carentan, just west of the villages of LePort and Brevands. The wooden bridges were located about 1,000 yards apart, and their importance was that they offered a detour route off of the Carentan Highway to enter or leave the Cotenin Peninsula without having to go through Carentan. It was essential for these bridges to be in the hands of the Allied forces, not only to keep the Krauts from using them in a counteroffensive, but also in case Allied forces needed to use them.

To accomplish its mission of seizing the Taute River bridges, the 3rd Battalion of the 506th, under the direction of Captain Charles Shettle, would be supported by one platoon from the 326th Airborne Engineer Battalion and two sections of the 506th Regimental Headquarters Company's demolitions platoon. The specific role of the demolitions sections was to help seize the bridges from the Krauts, set explosive charges, help hold the bridges from the enemy, and blow them to smithereens if the attempt to hold them from the enemy failed. One demolition section was assigned to each bridge, and one of them was my section, the Filthy Thirteen.

In a nutshell, here is what the Filthy Thirteen was supposed to do on D-Day. We were to board our C-47 plane and, along with hundreds of other paratrooper-filled planes, debark from the airbase in Exeter late in the prior evening. Once airborne, we were to head in a southwesterly direction over the English Channel for about 100 miles, make a 90–degree turn to the left and fly past the Channel Islands just off the western coast of the Cotenin Peninsula, then head inland in an easterly direction. Since this was to be a night jump, Pathfinders would parachute in the area about an hour ahead of us to set up visual and radar signals in the specific drop zones.

The Filthy Thirteen paratrooper stick was supposed to jump over "drop zone D" in the vicinity of Angoville au Plain, along with the 1st and 2nd Battalions of the 501st PIR, the 3rd Battalion of the 506th, and the 326th Airborne Engineer Battalion. Drop zone D was located about two miles north of Carentan and about a mile west of where the two wooden bridges traversed the Taute River near Le Port. Once we hit the ground, we were to immediately head east toward the bridges and assist the 3rd Battalion in seizing and holding them and, if necessary, destroy them. On the sand table displays, our assignment seemed pretty straightforward. It turned out to be entirely different.

22.

THE INVASION IS ON!

After a day of standing ready during lousy weather, on June 5th, 1944, official word came down that the invasion was on, which for us meant that we'd fly out of Exeter airfield that evening, and jump into France and begin fighting the Krauts early in the morning of June 6th. That afternoon we gathered our equipment and prepared for our date with destiny. At this point, because of Brincely Stroup's injury, the Filthy Thirteen consisted of only twelve men: myself, Sergeant Jake McNiece, Corporal John ("Peep-nuts") Hale, Corporal Joe Oleskiewicz, Louis ("Loulip") Lipp, Mauh Darnell, Jack Agnew, Robert ("Ragsman") Cone, George ("Goo-Goo") Radecka, Roland ("Frenchy") Baribeau, James ("Piccadilly Willy") Green, and Chuck Plauda.

In anticipation of heavy casualties, other paratroopers were added to our stick and would assist us in fulfilling our mission. One of these was a Navy lieutenant. His mission was to coordinate with the fleet offshore in the event that heavy naval artillery support was needed. The Navy lieutenant had with him special equipment that would enable him to contact our warships and provide them the specific coordinates of Kraut targets.

Including our second lieutenant, Charles Mellen, there were a total of seventeen men in our stick when we jumped. Also on board were the pilot, co-pilot, and the jump-stick man (the man that stands by the doorway and kicks out any paratrooper who hesitates or freezes).

The C-47s that would carry the paratroopers across the English Channel to France had wide black and white strips hastily painted on the tail and wing portions, and a number hand-written in chalk near the loading doorway. The stripes were painted on so that the planes could easily be identified by Allied forces as friendly aircraft, thereby minimizing the chances of being mistakenly fired at. The number near the loading doorway designated the paratrooper stick that was to use the plane. The chalk number written outside near the jump door on our plane was "21," which I felt was a lucky number.

The mood among us paratroopers was upbeat. Most of the guys in my stick gave themselves, or each other, Mohawk-style haircuts and used some of the white and black paint to draw images on their faces so they would look like American Indians going into battle. I guess they figured there was a certain shock value in looking like a wild Indian on the warpath, that it would frighten the Krauts and cause them to hesitate or run away rather than fight.

My Ranger training told me that such a thought was absurd. The British Commando instructors I had would have ridiculed any soldier who did such a thing. The Krauts wouldn't be afraid to shoot and kill a G.I. sporting a Mohawk haircut and a painted face. In fact, if painted faces were to have any effect at all, it probably would be to compel the Krauts to shoot such G.I.s first, since they'd stand out and also the white paint would be more noticeable during the night. I was the only one of the Filthy Thirteen who jumped into France that night without sporting a Mohawk haircut or wearing "war paint."

I distinctly remember one of the guys in our stick had large boils all over his butt. I forgot who he was, but his boils were painfully infected and caused him to develop a fever. He was in a lot of agony. Lieutenant Mellen told him he could be excused from having to jump but, much to his credit, the guy insisted on going despite his condition. He did jump, but his infected boils and fever got the better of him because I later heard from some of the other guys that he was found crawling around aimlessly on a dirt road in Normandy burning up with fever and rambling on incoherently about baseball. The fever brought on by his infected boils made him go out of his mind. I never saw him again.

I packed myself with two 18-pound packages of C-2 explosives, detonator fuses, and other explosives-related items. I would need these in order to help complete our mission. Figuring it would be awhile before I could get extra supplies, I purposely packed my musette bag with extra clothing,

K-rations and extra quantities of other necessities. I carried a gas mask and an M-1 carbine that had a collapsible stock, along with two bandoleers of ammunition. The M-1 carbine is a small, lightweight 30-caliber rifle. It's easier to carry than the larger and heavier M-1 Garand, but it doesn't have the same killing or stopping power because of the smaller bullet size. In addition, its effective range is considerably less than that of the Garand. But I carried one anyway because I figured I'd be doing a lot of close-range fighting and I was already loaded down with a lot of other stuff. The last thing I needed was extra weight.

Between my main and spare parachutes, explosives, M-1 carbine, ammunition and other supplies, I must have been carrying well over 100 pounds of equipment, as did most of us. We could hardly move with all of our gear and equipment strapped on. In addition to what we paratroopers carried on ourselves, our C-47 aircraft carried a package containing an additional 600 pounds of explosives that was supposed to be dropped down with us.

CROSSING THE ENGLISH CHANNEL

It was just before nightfall when we boarded our C-47. I was the sixteenth man in the stick, and the Navy lieutenant, who sat next to me, was the last man. Our plane remained motionless for awhile on the tarmac, while the aircraft's twin engines roared like lions until it was our turn to take-off. At about 11:00 pm on June 5th our plane accelerated down one of the runways at Exeter airbase and became airborne. The C-47s needed to fly across the English Channel in formation, and since there were so many planes that needed to take off, those that had already become airborne couldn't start their way across the Channel until all of the planes were in the air. To deal with this matter once the planes took off and became airborne the pilots would continually circle around the base until every plane on the field was airborne. That's what we did for a while, just circled around the base. Then the pilots took their spots in formation and started across the English Channel.

It was a clear night. As soon as we were over the water I peeked out of one of the small windows along the side of the plane and looked down. I didn't see a single Allied boat or warship. After awhile I looked out again and there, below us and as far as I could see in the distance, were hundreds upon hundreds of Allied ships of all different sizes heading for France. I knew the invasion was going to be big, but never imagined how big until I saw all of those ships. The sight of literally thousands of Allied ships heading towards France was both breathtaking and reassuring.

The flight across the English Channel to our drop zone in Normandy took about an hour. As we flew to our destination the moods among us ranged from excited and upbeat to somber. Some guys chatted with the guys sitting next to them. Others nervously laughed and joked. Others didn't say a word, and some even nodded off. I think most of us did a little of each. My mind was filled with thoughts of home, God, and our mission. I suspect that many of the other guys in my stick had similar thoughts.

Everything seemed to be going smoothly until we flew over the Channel Islands, which are just off of the western coast of the Cotenin Peninsula. As we approached the islands the pilot turned on the red light by the jump door. That was the signal for each of us to stand, get into formation and connect the cloth hook-up of our main parachute to the metal anchor line that ran along the ceiling of the plane, and be prepared to jump.

At about the same time the Krauts positioned on the Channel Islands began firing anti-aircraft weapons at our planes. At first it wasn't too bad, but as we continued to head inland the 20mm anti-aircraft fire became more intense. With the tracer rounds the 20mm fire looked like a steady stream of colored water coming at us. We could hear rounds hitting our plane, and we could see from our windows the sparks from rounds as they penetrated the planes near us.

The whole situation of being cramped inside that plane while under heavy 20mm fire was quite unnerving, to say the least. Although we were all terrified, we just stood in formation trying our best to pretend we weren't frightened. But each of us couldn't wait to get the hell out of that plane.

To reduce the chance of being shot down our pilot reduced our altitude to below 400 feet to get out of the range of the Kraut radar, and increased our air speed so as to reach our drop zone sooner. Despite these measures, the anti-aircraft fire kept coming at us. As bullets from enemy machine guns ripped through our plane like a hot knife through butter, each of us continued to stand in formation, trying our best to pretend that there was no need for concern.

The green jump light finally went on, much to our relief, and we began to jump one-by-one, under the steady stream of 20mm fire. This is when our game plan for the invasion of Normandy began to unravel.

23.

OFF TO A BAD START: JAMES GREEN'S PARACHUTE

February 2, 1945

To the family of Pfc. Jack Womer

Dear Friends

I saw this name as one of a group of 13 or 17 there were of Paratroopers who went on a suicide mission on D-Day.

I do so hope that your dear one is safe. My Son James E. Leech was also one of this same group, and was reported missing at that time, but has since been located as a prisoner of war in Germany.

I do not know if I am writing to a mother or wife of this boy, I'm only taking this chance that it reaches you and I would love to hear from you and the welfare of your dear one. I have had a card and letter from James and he says he is alright.

This [enclosed] Article was written in the "Stars and Stripes," a newspaper printed for the armed forces in the European Theatre of Operations, and gave an account of each of the boys in that group.

I have heard from two of the mothers. Mother of James Green of Norwood, Ohio, who was reported as not having left the plane as he had trouble with his reserve chute. But in a letter that I received today from her she said that he did get out and is also a prisoner of war in Germany at the same camp as my son.

Hoping to hear from you soon I remain Sincerely

Mrs Blanche Leech,
528 Grand Ave
So. San Francisco, Calif.

We didn't know it at the time, but when our stick began to jump we weren't over our designated drop zone. Many of the Pathfinder sticks that were supposed to parachute ahead of us to set up visual and radar signals to aid the pilots were either shot down or became scattered from the anti-aircraft fire and were unable to complete their mission.

The lack of radar and visual signals coupled with the foggy conditions along the coast of the Cotenin Peninsula, and the fear of being shot down, caused many of the pilots of the paratrooper sticks to become disoriented. The pilots were forced to estimate using eyesight alone in the dark of night where they were to drop their loads of paratroopers. This caused many of the paratrooper sticks, including the Filthy Thirteen's, to be dropped in the wrong place on D-Day!

We later heard horrific stories of pilots who became so frightened by the anti-aircraft fire as they flew near the Channel Islands, that instead of continuing inland or even turning around and heading back to England, they turned on the red and green jump lights while still over the English Channel. Not able to see that they were over water, the paratroopers jumped, landed in the Channel, and drowned! The pilots then returned to England without the paratroopers, giving personnel back at the airfields the false impression that they had fulfilled their mission. Fortunately for us, the pilots of our stick didn't do that, but we still didn't jump where we were supposed to.

To add to our D-Day chaos, many of the guys in our stick would become separated from one another as they jumped. What happened was James Green's reserve parachute was struck by the anti-aircraft fire. While Green wasn't injured, it caused his reserve chute to open inside our packed plane. The plane traveling at a high speed and the side jump door being open created a partial vacuum inside the plane, which kept pulling Green's open parachute and its cords toward the doorway. This caused some of the guys in our plane, including me, to be delayed a bit in jumping and to become separated after we jumped.

We originally thought that Green couldn't jump because of this incident and that he remained in the plane and went back to England. About a week or so after D-Day I met up with some of the guys in the Filthy Thirteen and one of them said that after he jumped he saw a plane in our group right above him go down in flames. Since none of us had seen Green on the ground, we just assumed that the plane that had gone down was our plane, and that Green, the pilots and jump stick man were killed when it went down.

In addition, Chuck Plauda claimed that he saw our plane explode within a few seconds after he jumped, implying that he was the last man to jump from the plane. I always suspected that Plauda's claims weren't true. First of all, the Navy lieutenant who sat next to me was the last man in the stick, not Plauda. Second, even if Plauda had been the last man to jump from the plane, his claim that he had been out of the plane no more than a few seconds before he saw it explode seems questionable since he would have had to have been very close to the plane when it exploded and would almost certainly have sustained injuries. Yet he wasn't hurt.

Also, when a paratrooper jumps from a plane during a combat mission, he is concentrating on the ground below, not the plane from which he jumped. There would be no reason for Plauda to turn his head and look up to watch our plane after he jumped from it. It's something a paratrooper wouldn't do during combat. I believe he may have seen or heard another plane explode and just assumed it was ours.

Nevertheless, about a month after D-Day we received official word that Green never returned to England and that he was missing in action. When we heard this, we were convinced that our plane had been shot down. However I found out a few months later, around March or April of 1945, that Green somehow was able to jump from the plane after all. In February of 1945 his mother sent Mrs. Blanche Leech, the mother of James E. Leech, who also jumped from our plane, a letter. Mrs. Green said that her son had in fact jumped from the plane after he had the problem with his parachute. He had been taken prisoner by the Krauts and was being held in Germany, in the same camp as Mauh Darnell (another Filthy Thirteener) and James Leech who were also captured in Normandy.

Hearing this news from Mrs. Green, Mrs. Leech wrote a letter to my parents on February 2nd, 1945, and wrote a separate one to my sister Jane (dated March 19th, 1945), in which she relayed what she had heard from Mrs. Green and from her own son about him being a POW. My sister and my mother then wrote to tell me what they had heard from Mrs. Leech. In her letter to my mother Mrs. Leech indicated that she had written similar letters to the families of the other Filthy Thirteeners, informing them

A view of some of the Filthy Thirteen on June 5, 1944, preparing for their jump into Normandy on D-Day. *Photo obtained from U.S. National Archives footage*

A nervous looking James (Picadilly Willy) Green doing an equipment check. During the Filthy Thirteen's jump into Normandy, Green's reserve parachute would open in the plane causing part of the stick to be scattered. Green was taken prisoner. *Photo obtained from U.S. National Archives footage*

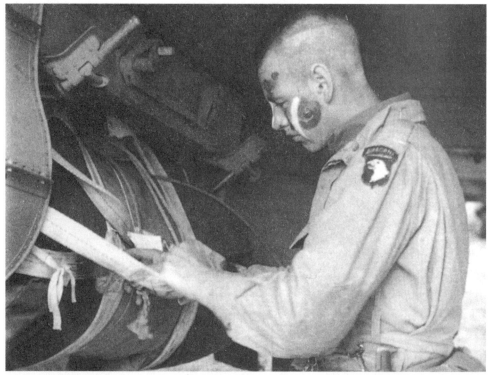

Jake McNiece (right) applies warpaint to Sergeant Mariano Ferra of the 326th Engineers. In the background is Joe Oleskiewicz. Joe survived Normandy, but was killed in action in September 1944, during Operation Market-Garden. *Photo obtained from U.S. National Archives footage*

Robert Cone making a last-minute check of equipment. Cone was taken prisoner. Jack would not see Cone again until November 7, 2008. *Photo obtained from U.S. National Archives footage*

of what she had heard. She had obtained the addresses of the families from the November 30th, 1944 *Stars and Stripes* article.

Green must have jumped from the plane after me and the Navy lieutenant. He must have been captured by the Germans soon after hitting the ground, because no one remembered seeing him in Normandy. He was released from the POW camp after the war ended in May 1945, and weighed only 82 pounds when he was released. From what I understand he never spoke much about the war after he returned home, nor did he contact me or any of the other Filthy Thirteeners. He died in 2002, at the age of 79. I never saw him or spoke with him since June 6th, 1944, while we were still in the plane that carried us to Normandy.

I don't know what happened to James Leech, whether he survived the prisoner camp, and whether he returned home after the war. As for Mauh Darnell, from what I've heard he survived the POW camp and returned home, but he developed a serious alcohol problem, presumably from the emotional and psychological impact of being a prisoner. I found out many years after the war that our plane was not shot down, and made it back to England.

24.

D-DAY

As I approached the doorway, Green's parachute was still blowing around uncontrollably, getting in the way. After a couple of seconds it was clear of the doorway, and I stepped up and positioned myself to jump. The bullets and tracer rounds coming up from the Kraut defenses on the ground were so thick they looked like streams of colored water spraying at us under high pressure. We were flying quite low. Our plane couldn't have been anymore than 400 feet in the air, so I knew it wouldn't take very long before my feet were on the ground, which was fine with me given all the bullets flying out there in the night sky. I glanced at my watch, noticed that the time was 1:17 am, and then I jumped into the night air.

I was one of the last men out of the plane. The Navy lieutenant jumped after me, and I assume that James Green must have jumped after him.

My parachute opened immediately and as I descended to earth all I kept saying to myself while looking head-on at the tracers and bullets coming up was "Keep your feet together . . . keep your feet together." It never entered my mind about those bullets just missing me. Between the anti-aircraft fire coming up at us and planes getting hit and exploding it was just like a 4th of July celebration out there in that night sky.

JUMPING INTO A SWAMP

Within seconds of jumping I was up to my nostrils in water. I was no longer in any immediate danger of being shot by anti-aircraft fire, but I had landed in a swamp and I was now drowning. Prior to D-Day, German Field Marshal Erwin Rommel had wisely anticipated the possibility of an

Allied strike on the Cotentin Peninsula. He ordered many of the fields and low-lying areas of the peninsula, such as those around Carentan, to be flooded to impede Allied paratrooper landings and the movement of other forces into the peninsula in the event of an invasion. It turned out that I was one of the many paratroopers Rommel had in mind.

It was a real struggle to keep from drowning in that swamp. I couldn't stand up straight because I was way off balance with all the gear I was carrying. I instinctively tried to walk to a shallower spot while keeping my head pointed upward, but my feet kept slipping on the muddy bottom, and my head kept going underwater. I then quickly but reluctantly discarded the two 18-pound bags of explosives I was carrying to help regain my balance, but even after doing so I was still drowning.

What saved me was that my parachute had not yet fully collapsed and, by the grace of God, a wind kicked up and filled it and pulled me across the swamp like a surf board. After a few seconds the wind died down and left me in a shallower area of the swamp where I was able to stand about neck high in water.

Then suddenly the wind started to pick-up again, and began to pull my parachute and me further. At this point I was fighting like hell to get my chute down because I was concerned the wind would drag me to a deeper part of the swamp where I would drown. I had a small knife tied around my neck on a shoe string, and I used it to cut myself loose from the chute. I would have drowned right there in the swamp if it were not for that first wind. All around me in the darkness of the night I could hear the frantic splashing of other paratroopers as they landed in the swamp and struggled to rid themselves of their parachutes. A lot of paratroopers did drown in the swamp that night.

As I was standing up to my neck in water assessing my situation, I couldn't help but notice the dozens upon dozens of C-47 planes flying overhead with paratroopers jumping out under heavy anti-aircraft (AA) fire from the Krauts. The night darkness was periodically overshadowed from the illumination created by exploding C-47 aircraft. This occurred when the AA fire hit a plane's gas tank or explosives on board. A big flash would appear when a plane got hit and exploded. I saw three planes blow up, and when each exploded I prayed to God that the paratroopers had already jumped out.

For a brief moment my family back home in Dundalk, Maryland crossed my mind. I thought here I am, stuck in a swamp at 1:30 in the morning behind enemy lines in France in Kraut-infested territory, while the rest of my family is safe back home in Dundalk where it's only about 7:30 in the evening. Right now they have no idea what I'm up against, but tomorrow morning they'll hear on the radio and read in the paper that the invasion has started, and they'll be worried sick about me, especially my mother. I prayed to God that I wouldn't be killed, not so much for my sake but more for hers.

I quickly abandoned my brief thoughts of home when I heard the screams of enemy soldiers off in the distance. They were screaming like wild pigs. I estimated from their noise that they were about two hundred yards away. I thought to myself "Why the hell are they screaming if they're supposed to be super soldiers?" They must have been scared. What I didn't know at the time, was that those particular enemy soldiers were primarily Russian Mongolians. They weren't Krauts but they were fighting for the Krauts. At this point, standing neck-high in water, I was in no position to do any fighting. I wasn't even sure if my rifle would work. In addition, given the distance and the darkness, there was no way I could shoot them from where I was. My first priority was to get the hell out of the swamp, and then focus on the enemy and keeping myself alive.

In the darkness of night I had no idea which direction to head to get out of that swamp. I'd take a few steps in one direction and I'd be in over my head. Then I'd take a few steps the other way and again I'd be in over my head. The only thing I knew was that there was some higher ground nearby that was occupied by the enemy. I figured I'd better find and join up with other paratroopers who had landed in the swamp, as there is strength in numbers, and maybe I'd find a guy that knew of a way to get out of there.

I took out my clicker or "cricket," and began to move around in the swamp, stepping very carefully. The cricket was to help identify someone near you, especially in darkness. One click on the cricket was to be answered by two clicks. That was the signal telling you that a person near you was on your side and not the enemy. Every few steps I'd click once on my cricket and wait for the response.

After moving about twenty feet or so I heard out of the darkness two

clicks in front of me. I met up with the soldier. He was a paratrooper with
the 501st PIR of the 101st Airborne. He and I continued to circle around
together in the swamp, and after a while we must have found and picked
up about thirty men, all of whom were from the 501st PIR. One of them
was a lieutenant. Most of the guys that I found seemed to know one
another, which meant they were in the same outfit, but I didn't know any
of them. But I also found the Navy lieutenant who had sat next to me on
the flight over and jumped after me. He had lost all of his equipment in
the swamp.

In just a few hours it would be daybreak. We had to get out of that
morass, otherwise come daylight we'd no doubt be shot and killed by the
enemy. It would be like shooting ducks on a pond, only we'd be the
"ducks." None of the thirty men that I picked up in that swamp knew how
to get us out. I asked if there were any Rangers present. No one responded.
I was the only Ranger there, and here is where my Ranger training began
to pay off. My training told me to look around and analyze the surrounding
terrain in the context of the situation, and the secret to getting out of the
swamp would come to me.

The natural light from the moon was augmented intermittently by the
light created from exploding Allied aircraft, which enabled me to peer
through the night darkness and catch glimpses of some of the nearby terrain. I noticed the silhouette of a tree near me. Instinctively, I thought, in
a swamp the number of trees should naturally thin out as one proceeds
from land into the water. Conversely, as one proceeds out of the swamp
towards land, the trees should become more numerous. I figured I'd look
for trees, to try and see where they were growing more numerous or less. I
told the guys to wait there in the swamp while I found a way out. I headed
toward one tree, and when I reached it, I'd look for the next one, then the
next, and the next, etc., walking in the direction in which the trees were
becoming more frequent.

It wasn't too long before I reached the edge of the swamp and was
standing on dry land. I looked around and noticed there was a road close
by. I was worried that the Krauts might have planted land mines in the
road, and I was quite concerned about going out on it, because I didn't
know who or what might be out there. I crawled carefully onto the road
on my hands and knees, and found a roll of telephone wire. That told me

that a paratrooper must have been there, because I knew that many of the paratroopers who jumped that night carried telephone wire to establish communications and command posts. I surmised other paratroopers must have already been on that road, and since I hadn't heard any explosions coming from the road, it wasn't mined.

THE KILLING FIELDS

I went back into the swamp the same way that I had come out, and brought the other paratroopers out safely in a single file onto dry land. Soon I ran into a paratrooper there that I knew. His name was Ross Moehle, who'd served with me in the 101st Airborne Division's 506th PIR's Headquarters Company, I think as a runner or messenger of some sort. I don't remember whether Moehle had been in the swamp or had been out on the road, and was alone and saw us and decided to join us. All I remember is that he was with us when we got out of the swamp. Moehle was a good man. He was kind of short, but he was fast as lightening and as tough as nails. He was a damn good baseball player too. That's how I knew him. I had played a lot of ball with him in the 506th PIR. Just seeing him there among us was reassuring to me, and made me feel good.

When we got onto dry land I told the lieutenant about the road that I found, and why I didn't think that it was mined. At that point I wanted to leave him and the rest of the guys and get to my outfit, the Filthy Thirteen, to carry out our assigned mission. The lieutenant said to me " Nothing doing! You're staying with us. I think the road you found leads near a lock over the Douve River. Our mission is to see to it that the Krauts don't blow up the lock and flood the area. We need to get to that lock." He wasn't sure which way on the road led to the lock so he told me: "I want you to take some men and head up the road a little ways to see what's up there, and I'll take some men and go in the opposite direction, and we'll both see what the hell is out there and what we're up against. We'll meet back here and decide what to do next."

Why is he telling this to me? I said to myself. I'm not an officer, I'm just a private, and I'm not even in the 501st PIR! Since I had figured out a way to get him and his men out of the swamp, he looked upon me as a leader and was willing to put me in charge of some of his own men, even though I was just a private in the 506th PIR. I really wanted to find the rest of the Filthy Thirteen and help fulfill its mission, but the lieutenant ordered me to stay with him. Besides, I didn't know where the Filthy Thirteen were, even whether they were alive, and if so, where to begin looking for them. Here I was in the opening act of the Normandy invasion and so far nothing for me had gone as planned.

My British Commando instructors had forewarned me of this during Ranger training. Now I knew exactly what they meant. In subsequent battles I learned this is typical of war. In battle things seldom ever go as planned. Soldiers going into combat need to expect this to happen, rather than be surprised and panic or become indecisive when it does. They need to adjust to the situation by doing things that will contribute to fulfilling the overall mission at hand. This is precisely what I did.

While I knew I wouldn't be able to contribute to the specific mission given to the Filthy Thirteen, I was certainly in a good position to contribute to the overall mission of the 101st Airborne on D-Day, and to the Allied invasion of France itself. I decided that at least for now I'd stay, as ordered, with the thirty or so men of the 501st PIR and follow the instruction of the lieutenant.

I led about eight men down the road as the lieutenant asked me to, and he took another eight and went in the opposite direction. The rest of the men stayed where they were. What I didn't know was that in the direction I was heading the enemy had set up with mortars and a heavy machine gun. But as I led the eight paratroopers in single file down the road, I heard a "voice" that I believe came from Heaven that said to me, "What are you doing out here on this road? Get off of the road!" Knowing that I was in enemy territory, I wasn't about to "argue" with the voice.

I jumped down into the ditch that ran along the side of the road and stayed there without moving any further ahead. The eight men caught-up to where I was in the ditch and stopped on the road. One of them said to me, "What are you waiting on down in that ditch?" I said to them, "I'm not waiting on anything, but I'm not going to walk any further on the road because I don't know what the hell is up there waiting for us. I'm going to walk in the ditch instead. What are you waiting on?" They said they weren't waiting on anything, and continued walking down the road. I watched the men walk by me and moments later, just as they were out of my sight, a heavy machine gun opened up. It killed them all in just a few seconds. If I had not listened to that Heavenly voice I heard, I would have been killed as well.

I ran through the ditch back to the spot where I had parted with the lieutenant. He ran back to the same spot with his eight men. I told him what had happened. Neither the lieutenant nor anyone with him had been shot, but we were all quite rattled by our encounter with the heavy machine gun, particularly the lieutenant. After he calmed down he said to me, "I think if a few of us go out here across this field and stay low to the ground, we won't be seen, and we could out flank the machine gun."

I didn't like his idea, and I countered with one of my own. I said, "If we go out across the open field like you suggest and are spotted by the enemy, we'll have no place to hide when they start shooting at us. I think there is another way we could flank attack the machine gun that is safer. We can't walk on the road, but there is a drain ditch about four feet deep that comes off the swamp and runs alongside the road. It's muddy, but we should be able to walk in it safely. I think it will bring us close enough to the machine gun, and maybe we'll be able to flank attack it. If we can't flank it, we'll try something else."

The lieutenant agreed with my plan, and ordered all twenty or so of us to walk in a single file in the ditch that ran alongside the road. What we didn't know was that we were heading in the general direction of the Douve River. This time I took the rear of the line. As we walked we came to the spot where the men I was with a few minutes earlier had been gunned down. It was a gruesome sight to see those eight men who, just a few minutes earlier were alive and well, were now dead and sprawled out all over the road, lying in their own blood.

We continued walking in the ditch. When I got up to the Douve River with the rest of the men I saw that they were all bunched up around the lieutenant. Being trained as a Ranger, I immediately thought how just one grenade could injure all of us. I said to the lieutenant, "We shouldn't be bunched-up like this. One grenade thrown in among us and we're all dead!" He said to me, "I just want to see where we are." I said, "Go ahead, but order your men to spread out along the river." He did.

I started surveying the ground and taking stock of the situation: the men, what we had to fight with, the unknowns, and, especially, the terrain. What was nice about the situation was that there was no way the Krauts could attack us from the front because of the river, and there was no way they could come at us from behind or flank us from the left because of the swamp. They could only get to us, if they wanted to, from one direction and only one. The terrain and our position were in our favor. I wanted to take advantage of that because we were in no state to do any attacking just yet, not when the Krauts were all built in with mortars and the heavy machine gun, and the only thing we had were rifles and grenades.

I said to the lieutenant, "We're in a relatively safe spot right here. All we need to do now is just spread out a little in the ditch so the machine gun or a grenade or mortar fire can't get us. By staying here we're using the terrain to our advantage, and we can focus on fulfilling your mission of protecting the lock. The Krauts can only get at us from one direction, and if they do attack us, we'll be well protected in this ditch." The lieutenant said to me, "No, soldier, I want to get that machine gun. We're going to walk alongside the river, in the direction of the machine gun, and knock it out of action."

I couldn't blame him for wanting to take out the machine gun, not only for our safety but also since the road was going to undoubtedly be used by the infantry soldiers landing later on Utah Beach to move inland. But the river offered little protection for us if we were to walk along its edge, plus we could easily be spotted by the enemy. I felt there was too much risk involved in trying to get to the machine gun by walking alongside the river.

We'd be better off remaining where we were in the ditch and off the road, and send some scouts out to look for more paratroopers to join us. With a little luck, there was a good chance we'd find a mortar or bazooka crew that could help us knock out the machine gun. With perhaps a little more luck, we'd locate a radio operator or someone who could assist the Navy lieutenant in communicating the coordinates of the machine gun to one of our naval ships that would soon be arriving off of Utah Beach. The ship could then blow the machine gun and Krauts up there off the face of the earth with a barrage of naval artillery fire.

The 501st lieutenant didn't want to hear any of this. Finally I said to him, "Alright, let's try it your way, but I think we're taking a big chance." The lieutenant ordered his men to start walking alongside the river in the direction of the machine gun. He followed near the end of the line, as did the Navy lieutenant, and I followed along at the very end.

Little did the lieutenant realize that he had just ordered himself and his men to their death. During my Ranger training, the Commandos taught that if you're in enemy territory and a flare goes up you hit the ground immediately and lie flat. It was written in their training manual. But the American G.I. training manual says if you're in enemy territory and a flare goes up remain standing and stay motionless until the flare burns itself out, and the enemy will think you're trees or fence posts. Big difference in these two sets of instructions as what to do under the same circumstance. The lieutenant and his men began to walk along the river, when suddenly a flare went up and illuminated the whole area as if there were a night ball game going on. Instinctively, I hit the ground, just as the British Commando training manual said. The other men immediately stood motionless, just as the American training manual said to do.

All of a sudden the heavy machine gun opened up on us. It roared like a lion as it sprayed bullets all over the place. I laid on the ground and watched in horror as about twenty guys just a few feet in front of me get shot to pieces and knocked all over the place as if they were bowling pins. As the bullets ripped their way through their human targets, they took with them the lives of some fine young Americans—men I had known for only a few hours, but who have forever remained in my memory. I can still hear the roar of the machine gun and the cries of the men as they were mercilessly shot, and feel the dirt hitting my face from the bullets that passed through the men and penetrated the ground. What saved me was the fact that I hit the ground immediately as soon as I saw that flare go up. Another factor may have been the men that had fallen dead in front of me absorbed any machine gun bullets that otherwise would have hit me. The slaughter was over in a matter of seconds.

The Commando training manual says when a flare goes up you hit the ground, but also says when that flare goes out you get up and move. I didn't want to hang around in the area where the flare went up, so as soon as it burned out I got up and got the hell out of there. I headed back in the direction from where we came. Since we had moved safely to the river, I figured I probably could go back safely. Aside from myself, Moehle, one other paratrooper, and the Navy lieutenant survived the assault from the machine gun, and they followed me as I ran back.

Each of us was quite shaken by the assault. I had my M-1 carbine, and Moehle had one, but the other paratrooper and the Navy man did not have any rifles. So all we had were two M-1 carbines among us four soldiers—not much to fight with. I asked the paratrooper who didn't have a rifle to carry my backpack for me, which he did. My backpack contained food rations, dry clothes, socks and other important items.

The four of us ran back on the road that we had just come down. It was now about an hour or two before daylight. Just off the road there was the beginning of a little strip of woods, and alongside the woods was a rather large wheat field. Being trained as a Commando, I figured if the Krauts were going to come looking for me, it would be more difficult to find me if I'm hiding in a large wheat field as opposed to being on a road, or hiding in a small strip of woods. I stopped running and began to walk towards the wheat field. The Navy lieutenant said, "What am I supposed to do?" I said to him, "I don't give a God damn what you do, but I'm going into the wheat field." Moehle followed me as I headed towards the field. The other paratrooper and the Navy lieutenant went into the woods. I never saw them again.

I was just about to enter the wheat field with Moehle, when I noticed a wounded paratrooper lying on the ground in pain just outside the woods. He had a broken leg. When he jumped he was carrying a bundle on his leg that had a roll of wire in it, and he wasn't able to let it go before he hit the ground. The leg bundle had somehow interfered with his landing, and caused him to break his leg.

This wounded paratrooper was of the absurd impression that a medic and an ambulance were going to come along any minute and take him back to the rear and patch him up. During our pre-invasion briefing we were told this is what would happen if we got hit, but most of us didn't believe it. We were in enemy territory, and I knew that there was, at best, only a slim chance that a medic was going to come around any time soon to help him. I said to him, "Try to stay calm, and if I come across a medic out here I'll tell him to come over to you." What actually happened is that when daybreak came some Krauts found him and killed him and other wounded paratroopers they found.

Moehle and I went into the wheat field to hide and observe the situation around us. When it became daylight I got on my knees and carefully lifted my head just high enough to peek over the top of the growing wheat to see what was going on around me. The sun was out all day on June 6th, 1944, at least where we were. I had a good view of the high ground and where the enemy was positioned with the machine gun. It was in a red house. By the following day the same red house and the machine gun were completely destroyed by cannon rounds fired from one of the Allied warships positioned off Utah Beach.

This is when I saw my first real live Kraut. He came out from where they were positioned on the high ground to look at the dead paratroopers who were gunned down earlier by the machine-gun fire. These were the same paratroopers that I got out of the swamp. I wanted to shoot him, but he was too far away for me to get him with my M-1 carbine. I carefully moved out of the wheat field to get closer to the Kraut, but the ones on the high ground must have seen me because they opened up on me with the machine gun. I literally ran for my life back into the wheat field, dove on to the ground, crawled a ways, and then laid flat and motionless on the ground until I no longer heard the machine gun firing. It was a horrifying experience, and I still don't how I survived it.

After awhile I got back on my knees and carefully lifted my head just enough to look over the top of the growing wheat to see what was going on. By this time it was just before noon on D-Day. I must have looked like a turkey hanging out in that wheat field, and the Krauts on the high ground must have seen me, because this time the bastards fired a mortar round at me. The round exploded about five feet away but, miraculously, didn't injure me. I must admit it was a pretty damn good shot. It damned near killed me, and I'm sure that the Krauts thought that it had. The reason it didn't is because I was on my knees and, by the grace of God, the exploding fragments from it went right over my head, about two feet above me. If I had been standing it would have definitely killed me.

I was completely covered in black soot from the explosion, but aside from a few tiny fragments that hit my left arm I was amazingly unscathed. To this day on the left sleeve of the combat jacket I wore I can still see traces of black soot as well as some small round holes from the mortar round. The explosion shook me up quite a bit, both physically and emotionally. The impact of the round made a small crater in the ground and later in the day, to spite the Krauts, I took a crap in the crater!

I stayed put in the wheat field for the remainder of the afternoon of D-Day. It got hot in that field. I hadn't slept in over 24 hours, hadn't eaten in awhile, or changed my clothes after having been in that swamp, and having had several close encounters with death, I had become physically exhausted and emotionally drained. Around 5 or 6 o'clock that evening I looked to my rear and saw, about a mile or so in the distance, what appeared to be a bunch of paratroopers walking. Moehle and I crawled out of the wheat field and into the ditch that ran alongside the road and started heading for them.

We were in the ditch walking, when all of a sudden machine-gun fire came at us from the direction of, but beyond, the small woods near us. We started running in the ditch to get the woods between us and the machine gun. As I ran, to my astonishment I saw my musette bag on the ground, just lying on the side of the road. The paratrooper I had given it to must have left the woods and thrown it away. I instantly picked it up and kept running. Despite the machine-gun fire, I felt pretty good about getting my pack back. Not getting hit by all the Kraut fire, and now getting my pack back, I figured God must have been looking out for me.

We continued running toward the men we had seen in the distance. As we got closer we could see they were paratroopers. There were about a dozen or so, and there was a captain among them, as well as a medic. They were from the 501st PIR. I said to the captain, "Stay the hell off that road, Sir, because it's covered with machine guns and mortars about a mile or so up." He said, "I was about to go up that road; how do you know the Krauts have it covered with machine guns and mortars up ahead?" I shouted sarcastically, "Because a heavy machine gun fired on my ass during the night and today, as did a mortar, and just now, as I was running to you, we were under machine-gun fire! The machine-gun fire covering the road has killed a lot of men, and it'll kill you and your men too if you aren't careful!"

We headed back in the direction that Moehle and I had just come from but, upon my recommendation, we walked in the ditch instead of on the road. By this time it had been about eighteen hours since we jumped into Normandy, and I had become anxious because I figured we might be able to go far enough to see how successful the invasion had been. I also wanted to bring the medic to the paratrooper with the broken leg I had found earlier. I wanted to check on him to keep my promise that if I came across a medic I would bring him over.

As we headed along the road in the ditch, we saw a small French farmhouse about a hundred yards off the road. I hadn't noticed it earlier when I was in the same ditch heading in the opposite direction, since I had been running for my life. We heard some gunfire. It wasn't at us but it had come from nearby. It was hard to tell where it had come from because we were hearing gunfire all over the area, but it seemed like it had come from the farmhouse.

We approached the house carefully. No one shot at us. When we got kind of close to it an old man came out of the front door shouting with delight "Americana!, Americana!" and motioned us to come inside. Moehle and I cautiously approached and entered the house while the rest of the men waited outside behind some trees. In one of the rooms there was an unusually large barrel of wine. The barrel was so large it occupied at least one-fourth of the area on the first floor.

The old man couldn't speak English, but he was acting quite friendly toward us—too friendly. He was smiling at me and, motioning with his hands, "invited" me and Moehle to go to the area upstairs, which was little more than a single room or small attic. That's when I knew something was wrong, and I wasn't about to go up the stairs. I couldn't speak French, so I motioned with my hand for him to go up first. He wouldn't move. He just stood there, pretending not to have understood my hand gesture.

I looked in his eyes, and I saw fear—he was afraid to go upstairs. I pointed my rifle at his head and, with a cold stern look on my face, motioned him to go upstairs. He then nervously walked up the steps, and as soon as his head got just above the top of the stairs I heard a rifle shot and the old man tumbled down the stairs, dead as a door nail.

There were Krauts up in that attic. I immediately grabbed one of my hand grenades, pulled out its safety pin and threw it up the stairwell into the attic. After it exploded I went up there and found two dead Krauts. They would have killed Moehle and me if we had done what the old Frenchman wanted us to do. I learned from this experience that during war trust no one, including civilians who you would ordinarily expect you could trust.

I searched the house for booby-traps and more Krauts. I didn't find either, so I waved to the captain to come on into the house. I explained to him what had happened. He decided that he was going to use the farm-house and the surrounding property as a command post and an area to take care of wounded soldiers. He also wanted to establish a defensive line of men to protect the road and help thwart a Kraut offensive maneuver toward the beach.

Keep in mind that the overall purpose of the 101st Airborne Division on D-Day was to secure the roadways that originated from Utah Beach, thereby facilitating the inland movement of infantry soldiers that already had, or were going to come ashore on Utah. The captain knew that the road near the farmhouse would be needed by the Allied forces to move inland, and it would be wise to set up a defensive line near it. But the prob-lem was he only had about a dozen men or so. He needed more men to establish any kind of a meaningful defensive position.

We carried the bodies of the old man and the two Krauts outside and left them in the rear of the property. At this time it was just starting to get dark. I said to the captain, "Sir, I know of a wounded man up a ways on the road, near a small wooded area. He's got a broken leg, and I'd like to bring a medic to him." He said to me, "I want you to go the rear and find the colonel,* and tell him where I am, what you've seen thus far, and what you know, and that I need more men to reinforce our line." I said, "Yes, Sir." I started out to look for the colonel and suddenly, again, a Heavenly voice said to me, "Don't go out onto that road." I wasn't about to argue with the "voice." Instead of walking on the road or even in the drainage ditch, I walked through some thick brush that was adjacent to the road. Shortly after I heard a machine gun open up on the road. I don't know why it did, but if I had been out there I would have been cut to pieces.

I continued walking through the brush and I came to a point where there was a fork in the road. The right fork led in the general direction of the English Channel, whereas the left one ran perpendicular to the Douve River. This fork would become known as "Hell's Corner" because of all the intense fighting that would take place there the following day.

---

*The captain may have been referring to Colonel Howard R. Johnson of the 101st Airborne Division's 501st PIR. The mission of the 1st Battalion of the 501st PIR on D-Day was to seize the lock on the Douve River at La Barquette. The mission of the 2nd Battalion was to destroy the Douve River bridges on the main road from St. Come-du-Mont to Carentan.

Just as I began to walk through the brush in the direction of the right fork, I heard some moaning coming from nearby. I looked around a little and found a wounded paratrooper covered underneath his parachute. I kicked his parachute off and away from him, and asked, "What the hell are you doing?" He said, "I've been hit. A medic stopped by earlier, and told me he would come back to get me and bring me to a field hospital. He hasn't come back yet." It was now about 7:00 pm in the evening of D-Day, and I said to him "How long have you been lying here?" He said "I've been here since 12 noon." The poor chap had been lying there for a good seven hours, unattended. I told him that I was on a little errand, but that I knew of a field hospital that was being established on the grounds of the farmhouse nearby, and that once I got there I would send a medic out to get him.

As I continued on my journey to find the colonel, I managed to find a rather large package of chocolate bars. In addition to dropping paratroopers the Allied forces also dropped a variety of packages that contained different supplies. The contents of a package could be easily identified by the color of the parachute that was used to drop it. That way soldiers wouldn't have to open them to find out what was inside. I opened the package of chocolate bars, ate a few, and carried the rest with me so that when I returned to the farmhouse the wounded men could have a little treat.

I never did find the colonel. But, in addition to the chocolate bars, I found something else—something that the captain needed: men to reinforce his defensive position. While looking for the colonel I came across a very long and wide drainage ditch. The ditch appeared to be ultimately coming out of the swamp that I had originally landed in, and headed over to the Douve River. The ditch was essentially perpendicular to the swamp and river and had to be at least a mile long. This ditch was undoubtedly another of German Field Marshall Erwin Rommel's means of providing a defense against an Allied invasion. He must have ordered this and other such ditches to be dug so that in the event of an invasion he could use them to flood the area and slow the inland movement of Allied soldiers.

I jumped into the ditch and walked a bit, and I found that it was loaded with paratroopers of the 101st Airborne Division, all lined up in force. I figured it wasn't necessary to have all of these men here in the rear. It was a waste of resources, actually. It would be better if at least some of them could move up to the farmhouse where they'd be closer to the enemy's line. I climbed out of the ditch and, while looking down at the men, I said in a very commanding voice, "I'm from Regimental Headquarters of the 506th, are there any 506 men among you?" About two dozen men from the 506th PIR came up to me as if I were an officer. I didn't recognize any of them. I said, again in a commanding voice, I need you guys from the 506 to come with me." They all assumed I was going to bring them to a 506 outfit, because they all followed me back to the farmhouse. While we were heading back I stopped and checked on the wounded man that I had found near the fork in the road. We carried him back to the farmhouse to be treated.

When we arrived I found the captain and said, "Sir, I didn't find the colonel, but I got some more men for you to place on the defensive line. These guys are carrying a lot of different types of weapons, and they'll be able to help strengthen your line quite a bit." The captain was delighted to get more men. He smiled and said to me, "Good work, soldier. Go and position them."

The farmhouse was located between the swamp and the river, which meant the Krauts couldn't flank attack us from either direction. It was possible for them to attack us from only two directions, so I positioned all the 506th PIR men that I just brought back along with the other dozen or so men that were with the captain when I first met him in defensive lines close to the farmhouse and facing the directions from which Krauts could attack. It was good that the captain had the foresight to see the need for a defensive line at our position, and fortuitous that I was able to get a bunch of guys to man the line, as on the following day the Krauts would attack our position.

I reminded the captain of the wounded man I had found earlier in the day— the paratrooper who had broken his leg and who was up ahead, closer to the enemy line in the small woods waiting for a medic. The captain said, "Alright, go find the medic and tell him that I said that he is to go with you to the wounded man." By this time I was completely exhausted and my nerves were on edge. I was in dire need of some sleep. I hadn't had any sleep since the night of June 4th. I replied to the captain, "Sir, I don't need to go back out there anymore. I can just tell the medic where to find the wounded paratrooper. I've been running all around out there all day with all those Krauts shooting at me. I'm getting nervous about going out again, being exhausted as I am and with all of those Krauts out there. I'm extremely tired, and I need to get a little rest." The captain ordered me to go with the medic, so I did.

The medic and I headed out to get the paratrooper with the broken leg. It was now dark. We avoided the road because it was covered by Kraut machine guns, and we had to cross one of the defensive lines I had just set-up. I told the paratroopers manning the line that the medic and I were going out to bring back a wounded paratrooper who was about a half mile or so ahead, and when we returned to be careful not to mistake us for Krauts and shoot us. As we were on our way to the wounded man, we entered a wooded area and came across an 8-foot wide drain ditch. In order to continue on, we had to either cross this ditch or walk over to the road. I said to the medic "To hell with the road. It's too risky." I dropped back about 15 yards, and then I ran as fast as I could and jumped over the ditch without difficulty.

I waited for the medic to join me, but he didn't. I jumped back over the ditch to look for him, and I found him on the ground crawling around in circles. He was scared half to death from all the gun, cannon and mortar fire going on all around us. I said, "What the hell are you doing crawling around? We don't have time to crawl our way around out here! We've got to get that wounded man. Now get up off of your hands and knees and let's get going!" I finally got him to cross the ditch with me, but he was too scared to walk any further. He was petrified. I told him to go back to the farmhouse, and I continued on without him.

I walked by myself through the darkness of night to the small woods. As I made my way through the woods to get to the other side where I had last seen the paratrooper with the broken leg, I noticed dead American paratroopers all over the place. There were many of them, just lying there on the ground stone-cold dead. A skirmish with the Krauts must have taken place in the small woods sometime during the day. It was quite eerie walking among those dead paratroopers in the darkness. To ease my nerves, I imagined that all those men lying there dead weren't there at all, they were somewhere else. When I got about halfway through the woods I came across some more paratroopers, only these were live ones. They were lying on the ground, taking cover behind trees.

As I made my way through the woods, I came across a paratrooper who was badly wounded. He had been shot in the leg and arm, and was covered in blood. He asked me to help him, and I told him that I couldn't just yet because I was looking for another wounded man nearby who I had found earlier in the day and promised that I would help him. When I got to the edge of the woods, in the area where I had left the paratrooper with the broken leg earlier in the day, I met another guy taking cover behind a tree. I said to him, "Have you seen a paratrooper with a broken leg around here? I found him earlier, and I promised I would help him." The paratrooper said to me, "Yeah, I know the guy you're talking about. He's dead. The Krauts shot him." I figured the Krauts were going to kill all wounded G.I.s, and that I had better get back to that other wounded man I had just seen before the Krauts got to him.

I went back to other wounded paratrooper and said, "Well soldier, today is your lucky day. I'm going to take you to a field hospital." I lifted him up and put him over my right shoulder and proceeded to carry him back to the farmhouse, which was about half a mile or so away. He was bleeding quite profusely. The blood that oozed from his leg wound was as thick as molasses and got all over my right hand and clothing as I carried him. Suddenly, to my surprise, one-by-one the paratroopers that were in that woods lying low behind the trees got up and followed me out of the woods. There had to have been at least twenty of them. I guess they figured since I was carrying a wounded man, that I must have known of a safer location, and that it would be in their best interest to follow me and get them the hell out of the woods.

As I made my way back to the farmhouse carrying the wounded man with the other twenty or so paratroopers behind me, I came to the ditch that I had to jump over earlier, the one where I had left the medic. I knew I had to get the wounded man across that ditch, but I also knew that I couldn't jump over it with him on my back. One of the paratroopers behind me had some cord, so we tied one end around the wounded man's chest, and we lowered him down into the ditch. I asked a few of the other paratroopers to jump over the ditch, which they did, and then I threw the other end of the cord over to them.

They started dragging the wounded man across the bottom of the ditch, and my plan to get him to the other side seemed to be going smoothly until he let out this very loud scream. I don't know what caused him to scream so loudly, but the Krauts must have heard him because all of a sudden a flare went up into the open ground next to the woods we were in. The paratroopers there with me froze like fence posts. I said to the soldiers "Forget about the flare. We're in the shadows of the woods, we can move about without being seen. The flare is out in the open ground, and that's where the Krauts are looking for us with that heavy machine gun. They can't see us in these woods. Let's keep pulling him across the ditch so we can get the hell out of here."

At first they ignored me and remained motionless, but as they saw me moving about without drawing fire from the Krauts they too continued on with what we'd been doing. We crossed the ditch, and I continued on with carrying the wounded man back to the farmhouse. When we arrived I told the captain that I got about twenty more men to reinforce his lines. He couldn't believe it. He told me to position the men along with the others that I had put on the lines earlier, and then get some rest. In total, I single-handedly found well over forty paratroopers to add to his dozen or so men to reinforce his lines. He was quite pleased with what I had done.

I dug a foxhole near one of the defensive lines and crawled into it. D-Day had finally come to an end, and what a day it was. Despite the years of planning and all our many months of rigorous and intense training, little had gone as planned, at least for the paratroopers. Casualties within the Allied attack forces were quite high. Of the nearly 7,000 paratroopers of the 101st Airborne Division that jumped into France during the early hours of June 6, 1944, at best only 2,500 or so were fighting in some organized unit by the end of the day. Some were just scattered and the rest had either been wounded, killed, or taken prisoner. Many more would become casualties during the days that followed.

Yet despite all the confusion, the mishaps, and all the plans that had gone awry, somehow the paratroopers and the rest of the Allied forces that attacked Normandy on June 6, 1944 had accomplished much of what was expected of them. As I rested in the dirt of Normandy, I stared up at the night sky and thanked God that I, unlike many of my fellow Screaming Eagles, had miraculously survived the day. A feeling of accomplishment descended upon me and, despite all the gunfire going on around the area, I was able to doze off and get a few hours of badly needed sleep.

25.

D-DAY PLUS ONE

I awoke just before daybreak on June 7th, 1944. I went to the farmhouse to check on the wounded man I had brought back the previous evening. He was still alive and the medic believed that he was going to survive. Hearing that made me feel real good. A little later the captain saw me and said, "You've done a good job, Womer. I asked Moehle about you, and he told me all about how you got a bunch of men out of a swamp yesterday morning when we jumped. You've saved the lives of some wounded men, and you've done a lot to reinforce our line. I'm going to write all that you've done in my report so that your commanding officer will know what you did and that you'll get proper credit. I'm also going to see about getting you into the 501, with my outfit. I need men like you."

Of course, I was delighted by what he said. I figured he'd get me transferred into his outfit, and then he'd make me a sergeant, and maybe eventually I'd become a second lieutenant. But none of this would happen because about an hour after the captain spoke with me he left the farmhouse to meet with another officer, and while en route he was shot dead by a Kraut sniper! I don't think he ever had the chance to record what I had done in his official report before he was killed. He was replaced by another officer in the 501st PIR.

Later that morning I decided to do some sniping myself. There was a tall tree nearby that we were using as a lookout post to watch the enemy on the high ground in the distance. Some of the limbs had been cut away to better enable observation. I got rid of my M-1 Carbine and found an M-1 Garand, climbed the tree and positioned myself in it in such a way so that I could spot and shoot Krauts. Not long after I perched myself I spotted a Kraut in a nearby field among some cows. He was big and fat and, strangely, was wearing a heavy overcoat despite the intense June heat.

I aimed my rifle at him and, just as I lined him up in my sights and was about to pull the trigger, an 88mm cannon round came flying right through the tree where the limbs had been cut and whizzed right by me, no more than a foot or two away from where I was perched. The cannon round was fired by the Krauts over on the high ground south of our position. The only reason it didn't explode is because it miraculously passed through where the limbs had been cut. A couple of feet higher or lower it would have almost certainly hit a limb and exploded and killed me. I don't think the Krauts fired their 88mm cannon at me, I think they were trying to get the paratroopers hiding in some of the ditches behind me.

I immediately jumped down from my perch, angry and shaking like a leaf on a tree during a windstorm. This incident shook me up quite a bit. It was yet another tantalizingly close encounter with death, and I had only been in combat little more than a day! I'll be dead in no time I thought to myself. A lieutenant of the 501st PIR saw how terrified and angry I was. In an attempt to calm me down he said, "Take it easy, soldier, the 506th is going to relieve us soon." I said to him, "For Christ sake if I keep going on like this I'm going to get killed before we're relieved!"

Throughout the rest of the morning and into the afternoon the invasion chaos and fighting continued. It's a good thing that I'd found those more than forty paratroopers to reinforce our lines near the farmhouse, because we skirmished with the Krauts several times throughout the day. They'd shoot at us and kill or wound some of us, and we'd shoot back and kill or wound some of them. Then the shooting would stop for awhile, and then start again. By the end of the day most of the Krauts had retreated further inland.

During one of the skirmishes on June 7th, some Krauts got so close to us they were able to throw a grenade into our line, not too far from where I was positioned. When the grenade exploded it killed a couple of men and wounded a couple of others. Those of us who weren't hit from the blast began cursing and firing back at the Krauts with a vengeance. We shot and killed a bunch of them, and the rest pulled back out of rifle range.

After the Krauts pulled back an officer in the 501st PIR came over to me and ordered me to find the colonel to tell him that we were being attacked and needed more men to reinforce our line. This was the second time that I, a paratrooper in the 506th PIR, was being ordered by an officer of the 501st PIR to find a 501st PIR colonel. I've always felt that the reason why I, instead of a paratrooper in the 501st, was given such an order was that the officers didn't want one of their own men to get killed. They thought a guy from the 506th PIR was more expendable.

I told the lieutenant that I had no idea where to find the colonel, and that I didn't even know what he looked like. The lieutenant gave me a specific location as to where he was, and flat out ordered me to go and find him. I didn't want to go looking for him, as there was a good chance I'd get killed doing so. But we'd lost a number of men, and our position needed to be reinforced, so I nervously left our line, amidst all the Kraut snipers and other Kraut soldiers out in the surrounding fields and woods.

When I got to the location where the lieutenant told me I could find the colonel, I was told by another 501st lieutenant that the colonel had left! I told the lieutenant about our situation, and that we needed more men, and he told me he couldn't spare any. So much for getting help. I nervously and cautiously headed back to my line. Just as I was approaching it I heard the sound of a child crying from the area where the Krauts had been a little earlier when we skirmished with them. I didn't hear or see any fighting between our line and the enemy, so I went over to see if I could find the crying child.

There were LOTS of dead Krauts out there. And lying there with the dead, to my disbelief, was a boy who looked no more than 12 years old dressed in a Kraut uniform, badly wounded and crying and writhing in pain. He was an enemy soldier, but he was also just a boy, and I couldn't help but feel sorry for him. I picked him up and carried him across our line to the farmhouse where other wounded soldiers were being treated. As I carried him the paratroopers that were dug into our line were furious at me because my actions to save the life of the kid could have drawn fire from the Krauts still on the high ground. They had a valid point, but I wasn't about to let that boy die. It also turned out my actions didn't draw any fire from the enemy.

HELL'S CORNER

At some point in the morning or early afternoon of June 7th a battalion of

German paratroopers* left their position north of us and headed south in the direction of Carentan. Also at some point during that morning the 501st PIR had set up a position of machine guns, mortars and rifleman facing north at the intersection that a little later in the day would become known as "Hell's Corner," the place where I had found a wounded man the day before. The Kraut paratroopers headed in the direction of the 501st PIR at the intersection. The guys with me were out of rifle range of the Krauts so we couldn't shoot at them, but we could see them.

Once the Krauts were a few hundred yards or so north of Hell's Corner, the American paratroopers opened up and began to cut down the Krauts like a lawn mower on grass. Kraut paratroopers that were taking cover or wounded and lying on the ground reached up and tried to motion with their arms to the guys behind them to retreat, but the American paratroopers shot their arms off as fast as they could raise them. The Krauts fought back, but it was a futile effort on their part. I could actually hear American officers shouting to their men "Cease fire! Cease fire!" but the American paratroopers kept on firing and killed or wounded more Krauts.

Eventually the firing stopped and the remaining Kraut paratroopers surrendered. There were about 350 of them taken prisoner. About two dozen or so American paratroopers lined up the Krauts along one of the roads at Hell's Corner and stood guard over them. The Krauts on the high ground in Carentan that were manning heavy machine guns, mortars and other artillery weapons spotted the line of Kraut prisoners and, mistaking them for a line of American soldiers, opened up on them. When the carnage ended most of the 350 or so Kraut prisoners were either dead or wounded.

I walked over to the area to get a closer look at the enemy paratroopers.

---

*In May 1944, the German Parachute Infantry Regiment 6 (Fallschirmjäger Regiment 6) of the German 2nd Fallschirmjäger Division was assigned to the 91st Luftlande Division stationed in the Cotenin Pennisula. Fallschirmjäger Regiment 6 was commanded by Colonel Friedrich von der Heydte. On the morning of June 7th, portions of the 1st Battalion of FJR 6 retreated south of their position near St. Marie du Mont in the direction of Carentan in order to reunite with the regiment's other two battalions holding the town. While trying to reach Carentan, FJR 6's 1st Battalion was nearly destroyed after encountering U.S. paratroopers in the vicinity of the intersection known as "Hell's Corner."

Thinking about how those American paratroopers that I had led out of the swamp had been unmercifully chopped to pieces by the Kraut heavy machine gun in the early hours of D-Day, it made me feel good to see all of those dead and wounded Krauts. The Krauts had been wearing camouflaged paratrooper suits, which they were ordered to remove when they were taken prisoner. But underneath their camouflage suits they wore brand new blue army uniforms. They were beautiful uniforms. I must admit I was a little envious.

26.

NO TIME TO CRY

June 14, 1944

Dear Mother:

I know you are worrying your head off, but I guess you have a right to. I'm in the best of health and I hope to stay that way. I had a few close starts, but I wasn't alone.... That Commando training that I had sure came in handy.... What happened over here is once in a life-time with a person. It's wonderful yet very sad. I can tell you this much, when this thing is over with I will cry for a week or two, but until then I will hold back.

I miss you all, more than I can say.

Your son, Jack

It isn't as easy as some may think to shoot and kill an enemy soldier. Any combat veteran who says otherwise is either lying or is mentally deranged. As with most soldiers, at first I found it difficult to shoot an enemy solider, but after awhile I got used to it. After witnessing death, destruction and comrades being killed, it doesn't take too long to become hardened to killing the enemy. Killing becomes a way of life for a combat soldier. No one that I knew liked to kill, but we had to do it and we accepted it as part of our job. The most difficult part about killing is living the rest of your life with the knowledge of lives you've taken.

One part about killing that I could never get used to was seeing the eyes of an enemy soldier just as I shot him. It bothered me to observe the pain, fear and horror in a man's eyes immediately after being shot and about to die. This is another reason why I preferred to use an M-1 Garand rifle rather than an M-1 Carbine. The killing distance of a bullet fired from a Garand is much greater than that from a Carbine. I much preferred shooting an enemy soldier from a distance rather than close-up because then I wouldn't be able to see the expression in his eyes.

As the first week of the Allied invasion of France came to an end the 101st Airborne Division had successfully completed most of its invasion missions. But the areas inland of Utah Beach into which thousands upon thousands of Allied soldiers had descended and battled on D-Day and the days that followed were fearful. Moans, groans and death cries rose all around, as did the sounds of machine gun fire, rifles, exploding grenades, mortars and artillery. The fields were trampled down, filled with dead men, and soaked with blood. The field hospitals were full of maimed, wounded and dying men.

The grounds were littered with headless and limbless torsos of both American and German soldiers, and unrecognizable pieces of human bodies. The streams and drain ditches were clogged with corpses. Dead and wounded were everywhere. Many had been shot by machine gun or rifle fire, others had been blown apart by artillery, mortar rounds or grenades. There was nothing but death, ruin and destruction all around. The stench of decaying human flesh that filled the hot summer air was sickening and inescapable. Such were the battlefields in Normandy, France on June 6th, 1944 and the days that followed.

The stress of being a combat solider can be unbearable. By the end of the first week after D-Day I had seen so many dead American and German soldiers, so much destruction, and had so many near-death experiences myself, that I just assumed it was only a matter of time before I too would get knocked off. To me it seemed that it wasn't a question of if I was going to get hit, it was only a matter of when. That's how combat soldiers begin to feel after a while. You start living day to day. Each morning your primary objective is not to get killed or wounded on that day, and you will find yourself doing whatever it takes to achieve this objective. You don't think of tomorrow, since it's not important. Only today is important. As this survival instinct takes over, changes in a soldier's behavior emerge. During war soldiers will steal, destroy, disobey laws, be disrespectful to civilians, and do other things that they would never even think of doing if they weren't soldiers in a foreign country.

It was at about this time, about a week after D-Day, when I reconnected with the Filthy Thirteen. I met up with Joe Oleskiewicz, Jake McNiece, and Lieutenant Shrable Williams, the leader of one of the other sections in our demolition platoon. Up until this time I'd been separated from the 506th PIR and fought with the 501st. I'd had absolutely no idea what had happened to the Filthy Thirteen. When I asked what had happened to the guys Joe told me what he knew, including that a couple of my closest pals had been killed and a couple of other guys in the section were missing.

Although it was nice to see Joe, Jake and other guys from the demolitions platoon, at about this point the reality of the war began to get to me. I wanted to pause for a moment to just sit down and have a good cry. I wanted to shed tears of joy over the success of the invasion, tears of sadness over the loss of my dear buddies and all the Allied soldiers who had been killed or seriously wounded during the invasion, and tears for myself, for while I had done my duty as a soldier, I knew that I would never be the same person that I was before D-Day.

I was sure proud of myself, and proud to be a Womer, but I knew then that I would never quite get over the war. The only thing I could hope for was that I would learn to live with it. I wanted to cry, but there was no time, as I was preoccupied with keeping myself alive. I figured it would better to wait until after the war, if I survived that long, and then I would sit down and cry for a week or more.

27.

GOO-GOO AND PEEPNUTS ARE KILLED

July 22, 1944

To My Darling Theresa:
Since I have been here I feel like crying all of the time. You see darling, I lost two of my best pals. We always went [everywhere] together, so you see wherever I go I kind of have them with me in thought. Theresa, I just don't laugh enough anymore. I get along with the fellows fine, but since I lost my two friends I stay mostly to myself.

Love, Jack

When I met up with Joe Oleskiewicz and Jake McNiece about a week after D-Day, Joe explained to me what he had done since our jump into Normandy, and I told him what happened to me and what I had done with the 501st PIR. He said that he too had landed in a swamp, and went on to tell me what he knew regarding the whereabouts of the guys in the Filthy Thirteen.

Joe knew that I was especially close to Goo-Goo (George Radecka) and Peepnuts (John Hale), and it broke my heart when he told me that both had been killed. Apparently, Goo-Goo had landed together with Joe and Peepnuts in the same swamp. Goo-Goo had come out of the swamp with Joe, and said he was going to go up to the small woods, the same small woods where I had been on D-Day just before I went into the wheat field. Joe didn't go with Goo-Goo, and never saw him again, but somehow he learned that Goo-Goo had been killed by the machine gun fire.

I asked Joe about Peepnuts. Joe said, "Jack, Peepnuts landed in the swamp with Goo-Goo and I, and got shot in the head on D-Day by a sniper. He laid there dead with his head down in his helmet for two or three days before they got him out of the swamp." The news that Goo-Goo and Peepnuts had been killed upset me quite a bit, as I was quite fond of both of them.

Peepnuts was one of two children in his family, along with an older sister. His life's dream was to become a medical doctor, a surgeon. At the time he entered military service he was in college, and had only one more year of pre-med classes to complete before he could apply for medical school. He was a devout Catholic, as were his parents and sister. At the time of his death Peepnuts was just two months shy of his twenty-third birthday. The only personal items found on his body were two letters from home, a pen and pencil, some photographs of his parents and sister, two religious medals, and 7 dollars and 68 cents. I was very fond of Peepnuts and spent a lot of time palling around with him because he was a real nice guy. Everyone liked him.*

I was concerned that Peepnuts' and Goo-Goo's bodies would never be found or buried, and would just lie out there and rot in the hot summer sun. I wanted to go find them and remove one of their two dogtags and report their locations so that they would be properly identified and buried.

---

*Some of the details mentioned here were obtained from a letter Kathryn Hale (Peepnuts' mother) wrote to Jack Womer's mother on January 21, 1945 (see next page). In the book *The Filthy Thirteen*, by Jake McNiece and Richard Killblane (pp. 211–12), McNiece describes a visit he had with Peepnuts' parents, Kathryn and John Hale at their residence in Poulsbo, Washington in 1947. According to McNiece, during this visit, Mrs. Hale told him that her son used to ride to and from school in a school bus, and every morning at eight thirty the family dog (a Collie) would walk with John up to the gate in the family's front yard and see him off as he rode to school on the bus. At three thirty every afternoon the dog waited at the gate for John to return home from school. According to Jake, Mrs. Hale went on to say that this behavior of the family dog went on for years, while John went to school and continued on even after he entered the military; but on June 6th, 1944, the dog stopped going to the gate to wait for John. When Mrs. Hale noticed the dog's change in behavior on D-Day she felt that something "bad" had happened to her son. According to McNiece, she went on to say that "about ten days later [which would be about June 16th, 1944] we were notified that he had been killed in action," and that the dog never again went back to the gate in the family's front yard. See page 300 for additional details.

Poulsbo Washington.
January 21st 1945.

Dear Mrs Womer:-

I am writing you this letter,although you are not
acquainted with me!; Your son Jack was a buddy of my son John R.Hale,
in the Filthy Thirteen mission,and I thought,as devoted and close to
each other as our sons were,in that history making brave mission;it
would be nice to contact these buddies homes,if possible,and I might
have knowlege of some of the achievements you had not recieved,or
you may know something I have not heard of our sons bravery.
I hope and pray you were spared the news we recieved-Our only son,and
baby was killed June 20th-2 months before his 23 birthday;to the day.
We recieved a telegram June 17th that Bob was wounded the 9th Of June,
then no further news until August 1st we recieved a telegram stating
Son was killed June 20th.in Normandy France.
It just about killed us at first,but time has helped in this grief.
We had a very comforting letter fro Bobs Colonel Sink,he told us Bob
was a soldier of excellent record,and that he had the rights of his
church at graveside,and a high mass was sid as soon as it could be
arranged.He is buried in Saint Mere Eglisse France.in Govt.cemetary.
I hope your son survived,but if he did not my deep
est sympathy and prayers are with you in your grief.
We recieved the PurpleHeart and the Presidents citation and Merit of
Honor Posthomously for son,and at first I couldnt stand to look at
the merits,but now time has helped a lot,and I am very proud of all3.
I work in Keyport Torpedo station,(helping make torpedo
the station is just 3 miles from our surburban home here,and Mr Hale
works in the Puget Sound Navy Yard in Bremerton,15 miles from us here.
We are 22 miles from Seattle.
Bob was taking premedics and had one more year of
college before entering medical college-and we all planned so for his
dream to come true,to be a good surgeon-but guess it just was not to
be.
We have a daughter,26 years old married 3 years-her husband is a
major in the aircorps,stationed now at Grand Island Nebraska-her hubby
is to go overseas around the 1st of February.
She will return home for a little while.
We had a nice letter from a buddy of Bobs,Keith Carpente
and he wrote from Holland,and enclosed the Dec,4th clipping of the
Filthy Thirteen mission on D day-did you see that,I have 2 clippings
of this,and would share the i with you if you have not seen it.
It was from this clipping I got your incomplete address,and I am so
in hopes the postmaster will help me get in touch with you.
We did not recieve many of Bobs posessions-just 2 letter
his pen and pencil,some kodack snaps of us,and 2 religious medals.
and $7.66 cents taken off his body-I dont know what they done with his
other things,maybe later we will recieve them.
I have been trying since the 1st of January,to get these
letters all written,and the first ones I got off have been answered.
Mrs Leech wrote from San Francisco that James is a prisoner of war.
Mrs Green wrote her James is too a prisoner of war,working in a sugar
factory over in Germany,Their home is Norwood Ohio.
Mrs Darnell wrote her son is a prisoner of war too-she lives in
Cartersville Georgia-and Mrs Faroda wrote from Johnstown Pa.her
brother Henry Maran was wounded badly by shrapnel in his head,was

Peepnuts' mother's letter to the
mother of Jack Womer, providing
all her news and also requesting for
more about how their boys were
doing. *Letter: Kathyrn I. Hale,
from the Womer family."*

2/
in the hospital some time before he was returned to his outfir-he now
is in Holland.
May God bless you and yours,and if you will,I would love to
hear from you if you recieve this letter.
If your son lives,and I pray he does,maybe he can tell me something of
my son Bob,as Colonel Sink told me his buddies were near by when he
met his death,but he could tell me no more.
My last letter I recieved from Bob was May 15th-I know
he wrote me later than that,but so many of his letters and gifts were
never recieved.
We did not get his xmas gift he sent,and he sent me an Easter gift,and
I never recieved it either-the ship must gone down.
We sent him a nice expensive ring,and he never recieved that either.
Well I must close,
Sincerely I am
Kathyrn I Hale(Mrs John F.Hale.
mother of Corporal John F.Hale.

Route 3 Box 686
Poulsbo-Washington.

From-
Mrs John F.Hale
Route 3 Box 686
Poulsbo-Wn.

Mr and Mrs Womer
(Parents of Jack N Womer,Paratrooper)
Postmaster
Dundalk
Maryland.

Joe and some other guys told me not to worry about it, as there were crews assigned to find the dead, identify them and bury them properly. Learning of these crews made me feel a little better, but I still wanted to find them to pay my respects. I didn't know where I could find Peepnuts' body, and Joe wasn't sure either. But I at least knew where I could find Goo-Goo's and went up to the small woods to look for him.

By this time most of the Krauts had withdrawn from the area, so there was no longer much threat of getting shot. There were a lot of dead U.S. paratroopers lying all over the place in the woods. I examined every one but none of them was Goo-Goo. I then went into the wheat field and again came across a lot of dead paratroopers, most of whom were in groups where they had been killed by the heavy machine gun or mortar fire, but I didn't recognize any of them.

I continued walking out there in the field, and came across the body of a paratrooper. The body was badly shot up, almost to the point where it was mangled, but the head was intact. I took a close look at the face, and saw that it was Goo-Goo. It was definitely him. Goo-Goo must have made it through the small woods, but for some reason he decided to go into the open field, and the machine gun cut him to pieces.

28.

CARENTAN—A RED ROSE FOR A SOLDIER

June 19, 1944

Dear Theresa:

I'm hoping to get a letter from you today . . .

The only thing I got for my birthday was a rose and a drink of some kind, given to me by some French people. The lady said I should send a piece of the rose to you. I will, so take good care of it for me.

I love you.

Jack

The significance of the French city of Carentan was that it had to be taken in order for the Allied forces to take control of the Cotenin Peninsula. Carentan is where the 4th Infantry Division from Utah Beach was to join forces with the 29th and 1st Infantry Divisions from Omaha. Once the forces from the two U.S. beachheads were united, the three divisions would then take the rest of the Cotenin Peninsula from the Krauts to establish a solid foothold on the coast of France. A primary objective of the 101st Airborne Division was to secure Carentan from the enemy to allow the infantry divisions to join together. The Krauts were well aware of the importance of the crossroads town, and they would fight like rats to keep control of it.

Attempts by the 101st Airborne Division to take control of Carentan began on June 8th. It would take six full days of hard fighting before the Allied forces, for all practical purposes, took control of the city. On June 8th, me and the 501st PIR men I was with were about two miles north of

Carentan when we began to fight our way south toward the city. We arrived at its outskirts just before daybreak on June 11th, and soon got into one hell of a battle with the Krauts that lasted another day and a half.

The fighting was ferocious. It would stop for awhile, and then start up again. We ran into more Kraut paratroopers, who must have been the best men they had. There were other Kraut units too, and then we began to encounter SS troops. During this time Carentan was set ablaze from Allied ground artillery and naval guns to try and flush the enemy out. Our fighter planes would also swoop in to drop bombs and strafe the city. We shot and killed practically every Kraut that we saw, but no matter how many we killed the ones that survived kept on fighting.

At one point, after two days and nights of nearly constant fighting, the group I was with went from about 60 men down to just 18. We had no sleep or rest of any kind, and were completely exhausted, yet we continued fighting, just the few of us. Eventually our line was reinforced with additional men, and we fought for two more days with little or no rest. The fighting didn't let up until our tanks from the 2nd Armored Division moved in, and that's when most of the Krauts finally pulled out.

It took about six days to take the town from the Krauts. But for days after we took control of Carentan there still remained throughout the city pockets of German machine gun nests and snipers, and those Kraut pockets launched counterattacks and would temporarily regain control of portions of the city. The fighting to take and maintain control of that place was brutal.

TAKING PRISONERS

We were able to capture a few Krauts, regular army soldiers, and hold them as prisoners. Just as the men who served in the U.S. regular army to fight against the Krauts were for the most part drafted, for the most part the Germans were drafted by the Nazis to fight against Allies. They were just average soldiers who, like us, would have preferred if the war had never started and would much rather be back home. Many of the prisoners we took were convinced that Germany would lose the war by the fall of 1944.

The other type of German soldier was the *Waffen Schutstaffel*, or SS. Soldiers of the SS were hand-picked by the Nazi party, and their selection was based on racial purity and absolute loyalty to Hitler. SS soldiers underwent more rigorous training than the regular German army, and had their own uniforms. They viewed themselves as extraordinary soldiers, and took great pride in being viciously brutal against civilians and prisoners of war, and even German army soldiers if they suspected any degree of disloyalty.

To put it bluntly, SS soldiers were sick bastards who were fanatically in favor of Hitler's intent to rule the world. Even the German regular army soldiers despised them. We captured a few SS men at Carentan. Many of the paratroopers that captured SS soldiers never took them prisoners. They were told that they were being taken as prisoners, but instead they were taken off somewhere and shot to death.

We made the regular army Krauts we took as prisoners in Carentan work for us. We had them do all sorts of menial tasks. I will say that the Krauts worked just as hard as prisoners as they fought as soldiers—they really threw themselves into it. Once I was assigned to guard about eight Kraut prisoners with a couple of other paratroopers, one of whom spoke fluent German. We needed them to move a large stack of crates.

A couple of the prisoners were bitter about having been captured and were purposely moving slowly and being lazy about moving the crates. The two guards with me couldn't get the lazy prisoners to work harder, so they asked me if I could do something about it. I thought for a moment, and remembered when I was training to be an Army Ranger the British Commando instructors told us that Krauts are deathly afraid of being sent to Russia, and if we ever take prisoners and they become uncooperative to threaten to send them to Russia. I told the paratrooper who spoke German to sternly tell the two lazy POWs that if they didn't work harder we were going to send them to the east, and they could work under Russian soldiers instead. He told them, and the two Krauts immediately began working as hard as they could for us.

A RED ROSE FOR A SOLDIER

On the morning of June 17th, 1944, the day before my 27th birthday, I said to myself, "I will not allow myself to get knocked off until after my birthday," and resolved to survive that day no matter what. As fate would have it, I found out after the war that two of my dear friends in the 29th Infantry Division, Harry Hendricks and John Polyniak, got hit on June 17th while their division was fighting its way to the key town of St. Lo.

John Polyniak of Company C, 116th Infantry Regiment, was shot in the waist by a Kraut sniper. He survived the wound but could not return to duty because, despite extensive rehabilitation, his wound caused him to be partially but permanently crippled from the waist down. My childhood buddy Harry Hendricks, of Company C, 175th Infantry Regiment, wasn't so "lucky," as he was killed. He was 25 years old.

For me, June 17th, 1944 started out uneventful. I had been back with the Filthy Thirteen for a few days. We were on patrol in Carentan, and everything seemed under control. But things changed quickly when out of nowhere Krauts attacked us. A machine gun opened up on us while we were walking down a street. I instantly dove into someone's front yard vegetable garden and laid flat on my belly. Bullets sprayed back and forth right over my head, just missing me by inches. I said to myself, "Christ I'm not going to make it to my birthday." We fought back and our artillery positioned outside of Carentan fired phosphorus shells into the city. These rounds set a lot of the buildings on fire, and it appeared that the whole city was ablaze.

Finally the Krauts suddenly stopped shooting—why, I don't know, but they did. Our officers shouted "Advance now!" We began to move forward, as ordered, but we cursed back at them and at each other because we didn't know if the Krauts were still around and if they were going to cut us all down when we started to advance.

We cautiously walked up one of the streets of Carentan, and to my surprise I saw an elderly French woman in her garden. She was picking roses, of all things, and seemed to be completely oblivious about the town being on fire or the fighting between us and the Krauts. As I approached her she stopped gardening, stood up and smiled at me. Her face was wrinkled from age and the stress of war, but her eyes were kind and sincere. She greeted me in broken English. I said hello and, not knowing what else to say, I told her that my birthday was June 18th, the next day, and that I was hoping to get a letter from Theresa, my fiancée who was back home in the United States. She again smiled, wished me a happy birthday with her accented English, and gave me a red rose as a birthday present.

She carefully inserted the stem portion of the rose into one of my top pockets, such that the petals were showing. She said that I should send a piece of the rose to the "woman I love." All of this seemed quite strange and surreal to me, but I felt that her giving me the rose was a good omen and that it would bring me luck. I took the old lady's advice, and on the day after my birthday I sent Theresa three petals from the rose and asked her to take good care of them for me, which she did. What I didn't know, was that rose was going to save a man's life.

A few days later, while we were back at our position on the outskirts of Carentan, Jake McNiece said to me, "Hey Jack let's go into town and get haircuts." We went into Carentan and, low and behold, we see General Taylor of the 101st Airborne standing on a reviewing stand giving out medals to some of the division's paratroopers. As Jake and I observed the ceremony, somebody in that town decided to notify the Krauts, who were now positioned about five to six miles south of Carentan, about the fact that General Taylor and many other high-level officers were there bunched together in the town square. That "someone" in the town fired a flare to enable the Krauts to determine the range of the town square and sight it in as a target. Moments later, 88mm artillery rounds start flying in on us. The town square became as dark as night from the smoke from the exploding 88s.

Us paratroopers wanted to get the hell out of there and take cover. McNiece was able to run out of the area, but there were so many of us bunched together that most of us couldn't run and ended up piling on top of one another. Despite the Kraut artillery fire, General Taylor continued to stand on the reviewing platform, while holding onto the hand railing of the platform hollering, "At ease!" Underneath me was a colonel also shouting "At ease!" "At ease!" because that's what he heard General Taylor doing. I figured if that son-of-a-bitch can say it, I can say it too, so I start shouting "At ease!" "At ease!" Sure enough, some of the guys on top of me climbed off, and the next thing I know I'd grabbed my rifle and was up on my feet running the hell out of there.

Army trucks raced around all over the place picking up G.I.s and getting them out of town. I ran down a nearby road, along some grass, and about a block in front of me was a person standing still and pointing to a house and shouting to me: "That's the house where the flare was shot up!" I ran over to the house and just as I got there a civilian family came running out. Among them was a man, a civilian, wearing German military boots. In those boots he looked just like a Kraut. The G.I.s on the trucks going by saw me with my rifle and shouted "Kill that son-of-a-bitch!" I stopped the guy, and he showed me identification papers saying that he'd been cleared to live and work in the town. (Civilians were required to have such clearance.) I thought to myself, "This guy looks like a Kraut to me. I'll bet he's the son-of-a-bitch who fired the flare."

"Shoot him!" I said to myself. Under the circumstances, it seemed like the appropriate thing for me to do, but I didn't because I wasn't absolutely sure whether he was innocent or had something to do with setting off the flare. I knocked the papers out of his hand and ignored everything that he was saying to me. I ordered him to turn around and put his hands above his head, and I began hitting him with the butt of my rifle. I figured if he were guilty of setting off the flare I could get him to confess by beating it out of him. The U.S. soldiers in trucks on the road kept on shouting "Kill the bastard! Kill the bastard!" Instead, I kept beating him. I repeatedly kicked him and hit him all over with my rifle butt. Blood came out of his back and head.

The G.I.s kept shouting "Kill him! Kill him!" He hadn't confessed, and by this point I was about to go ahead and shoot him when all of a sudden the elderly woman who gave me the red rose a few days prior came running down the road toward me. She was crying her eyes out, waving her arms and screaming at the top of her lungs, "Stop! Stop! Please no kill! No kill!" When she got to where I was she began telling me as best as she could, in broken English, that this man had nothing to do with the flare. Apparently she knew him. I don't know how she knew him, or whether they were related, but she impressed me as being sincere, and just seeing the old woman calmed me down quite a bit. I settled down and spared the man's life.

The guys on the trucks kept on shouting "Kill the bastard! Kill the bastard!", but I did not and would not because the old lady who gave me the red rose for my birthday pleaded for me not to. She told me that the man I had beaten was not a German, nor was he a traitor. I believed her, but I still didn't know who this guy was and why he was wearing Kraut military boots. I tried calling some MPs who were near by but they were too busy tending to other issues. By this time a colonel had come by, and he ordered me to take the guy over to an MP station and have him checked out.

Over the next week or so I couldn't get this incident out of my mind. I kept wondering whether the man I had come so close to killing had in fact set off the flare that enabled the Krauts to target us, or if he was just an innocent bystander who was wrongly accused and unjustly beaten by me. After a couple of weeks my curiosity became unbearable, so I went into Carentan to the MP station and asked them if that guy that I had turned over to them was a Kraut sympathizer or not. The MPs told me they had investigated him and confirmed that he was an innocent man.

Thank God I hadn't killed him! If I had I never would have forgiven myself. The old lady who gave me the red rose for my birthday saved the man's life. Even now, decades after the war, I frequently reflect on this incident in Carentan, and how strange it was. What were the odds of me meeting the old lady the first time when she gave me the rose, and then meeting up with her again under those circumstances? If I had not previously met her, I would probably have paid no attention to her when she was pleading for me to spare the man's life.

The taking of Carentan was the last significant combat action of the 101st Airborne Division during the Normandy campaign. By the end of June 1944, the 101st had completed its invasion missions and was sent back toward the English Channel, closer to Utah Beach and in the vicinity of St. Mere Eglise. Here we would rest and await our return to England. For the first time in about three weeks, we were finally able to get hot meals, take hot showers, and sleep without being awoken every twenty minutes by gunfire. Many of us used this time to collect German military artifacts. I took insignia, medals, fountain pens, knives and a couple of Walther P38 pistols (lugers) off of some dead Krauts and sent them to my parents' home in Dundalk as souvenirs of D-Day. I even found a couple of American parachutes, and sent one back to my father and one to Theresa.

Newspapers across the country publicized the success of the Allied invasion of France, and many papers gave special mention to the contributions made by U.S. paratroopers. As far as I know I was the only paratrooper from Dundalk, so when the local papers wrote stories on the invasion of France they would often mention me by name as being one of the first to jump into France on D-Day. I soon became a bit of a local hero, and my father strutted around town as proud as a peacock.

My father even went as far as loaning Mr. Sax, who owned and operated a grocery store in Dundalk, the parachute and other invasion-related artifacts that I sent home. Mr Sax prominently displayed the parachute and the other invasion-related stuff in his storefront window along with a photograph of me in uniform, as well as a brief description of what each artifact was and what I and the rest of the 101st Airborne did during the Normandy invasion.

My father also loaned Mr. Gutman, another Dundalk merchant, some of the artifacts I sent home. When in town going about their business, people would frequently stop in front of Mr. Sax's and Mr. Gutman's stores to view the artifacts and discuss them with the store owners and other townspeople. I had become a local hero.

As nice as these accolades were, they could not clear the sadness that I and the rest of the Filthy Thirteen felt in our hearts and minds over the loss of our comrades. Casualties within our section, as well as the rest of the 101st Airborne Division, were high. Only six of the twelve members of the Filthy Thirteen that jumped into France on D-Day would return to England.

Of the Filthy Thirteen that were not returning to England, three had been killed, and three had been captured and taken prisoner by the Krauts. Those killed were Corporal John Hale, George Radecka, and Roland Baribeau. Also killed was Charles Mellen, the second lieutenant of our demolitions platoon. Those captured and taken prisoner were Charles Darnell, Robert Cone, and James Green. Also taken prisoner was James Leech, who jumped into Normandy with the Filthy Thirteen from the same plane, but was not a member of the section. We would eventually get replacements for our lost comrades.

29.

BACK TO ENGLAND

The Normandy invasion had been a success and the Allied forces were making slow but steady headway into France. While the war was far from over and the Krauts continued to put up a good fight, they were outnumbered and outgunned, and were gradually being pushed back. By July of 1944 it was apparent that Adolf Hitler's master plan was coming unraveled. Even some of Hitler's own military commanders tried to assassinate him in July of 1944.

Having completed its D-Day missions, in mid-July of 1944 the 101st Airborne Division was sent back, by boat, to England for rest and relaxation. The Filthy Thirteen, or what was left of it, went back to its Quonset hut on the manor estate of Sir Ernest and Lady Wills in Littlecote. Every paratrooper was issued new clothes, received back pay, and given a seven-day pass to go wherever he wanted.

MARY EDWARDS AND HITLER'S BUZZ BOMBS

Practically every paratrooper, including myself, had a girlfriend in London. Most of us immediately put on our new clothes, stuffed our back pay into our wallets, and hopped on a London-bound train to spend our time and money on our girlfriends. We needed to get away from the war for a while, as our nerves had been shattered from our participation in the invasion. Not only did the seven-day pass help us to unwind, it also kept us from going insane.

I went to London to visit my girlfriend, Mary Edwards. By this time Hitler had begun firing his infamous V-1 missiles, or "buzz bombs" as they were called, from France into England. He didn't launch any buzz bombs prior to or during the Normandy invasion because they had not yet been fully developed. I did, however, see V-1 launchers while I was in France during the invasion. Naturally, we destroyed whatever launchers we saw.

Buzz bombs were 25-foot-long rockets with wings that carried over two thousand pounds of explosive material. They flew over 300 miles per hour until their engines cut out and the bomb crashed and exploded. It was difficult to predict where a buzz bomb was going to crash, but when an incoming one stopped "buzzing" that meant it was about to crash and explode, and you had better run for cover.

The impact of an exploding buzz bomb could be quite devastating. I've personally witnessed them destroy buildings and homes within areas in London up to three or four city blocks, and shatter every glass window within a mile of the impact. The buzz bombs were more often launched during the night than the day. Consequently, many of the people in London often routinely slept in underground shelters to avoid being killed while sleeping at night in their home, or because their homes had already been destroyed by one.

Buckingham Palace was a primary target of the buzz bombs. When I went to London in July 1944 to meet Mary Edwards, I met her as she came out of work across from Buckingham Palace, and we immediately took a bus heading out of town to get away from the threat of buzz bombs. We rented a room in Hammersmith, which is in the western suburbs of London. That evening we had a nice dinner in a local restaurant and went back to our room. Our plan was to rent the room for the entire duration I would be on leave so we could spend some quality time together and so she would be able to sleep soundly and peacefully by not having the constant threat of an incoming buzz bomb. She would then return to London every morning to work and travel back to Hammersmith in the evening.

I had a locket that I wore around my neck with a photo of Theresa, my fiancée, in it. When I had last spent time with Mary, just before D-Day, she decided that she would like to have a photo of herself in the locket. So she gave me one, and I put it in the locket on top of Theresa's photo. Mary was impressed that I had put her photo on top of Theresa's. Sometime after D-Day, while I was still in France, I reversed the photos: I put Theresa's back on top of the photo of Mary, but I had since forgotten that I had done so.

So now it is mid-July, 1944. Mary and I are stark-assed naked in bed together in our rented room in Hammersmith. The only thing I was wearing was the chain around my neck holding the locket and my dogtags. We had finished our "festivities" and were just lying in bed holding hands and relaxing. Mary noticed the locket around my neck. She gently lifted it off my chest and opened it, only to find that I had placed Theresa's photo on top of hers. Very touching! She kneed me in my balls and yelled "I figured as much!" Boy was she angry.

Mary wouldn't talk to me for the rest of the evening. There was absolutely nothing I could say that would make her feel better toward me, so I just laid in bed with her and didn't say a word. During the night, to our surprise, we heard a buzz bomb come in and explode, right there in Hammersmith! Then we heard another, and another. While I was a bit frightened, I acted calm and, figuring Mary was frightened too, I used the threat of the incoming buzz bombs as an excuse to snuggle up to her and protect her. To my amazement, she wasn't the least bit afraid of the buzz bombs, and she started speaking to me again.

After the V-1's stopped coming in I said to Mary, "I'd like to see a buzz bomb come in during the day." She said calmly, "Well that's no problem, Jack. Come to London with me tomorrow, and we'll go down to Tower Bridge. If we wait a while on that bridge we should get a pretty good look at a buzz bomb coming in over the Thames." I said "Great, let's do it!" The following morning we hopped on a bus and went to London.

During Mary's lunch break we walked out onto the Tower Bridge and stood there holding hands and waiting patiently for a buzz bomb to come by. Suddenly, Mary squeezed my hand, and said "Jack! We're in luck!" I said "Why is that Mary?" She said "The siren alarm that buzz bombs are coming in just sounded. So there's at least one coming!" A short while later a buzz bomb came flying in right over where we were standing on the Tower Bridge, not more than thirty feet above us. I could have hit it with a stone! Mary wasn't the least bit scared. I was quite impressed with her bravery.

She had lived through dozens of bombing raids. She'd been in the military since 1941, and was quite used to air attacks. I've asked many women in the United States if they could have done what Mary Edwards did and all of them emphatically say "No!" They usually tell me that Mary must have really loved me to do something like that with me.

During my stay with Mary that July I learned the behavior of incoming buzz bombs. There are four different ways an incoming buzz bomb could act. The first way is that you hear it coming in, but then it runs out of fuel, causing the motor to cut off and the "buzzing" sound to stop. Within a minute it silently glides into the earth or a structure, and when it hits it could knock out two or three blocks of houses. The second way a buzz bomb acts is that it comes in the same way only the motor doesn't cut off. The bomb crashes into something while the motor was still running and "buzzing."

The third way a buzz bomb acts is that it comes in and you hear the buzzing sound getting louder and louder, meaning that it's heading in your direction. You pray to God that it goes past you, and it does pass you, and you breathe a sigh of relief, but then it makes a U-turn and comes back toward you. When that happens you're really upset.

The fourth is the worst way. Here, the buzz bomb comes in but the motor cuts off before you ever hear it buzzing, and it glides toward you and you have no idea it's coming your way. If you are lucky, the buzz bomb hits something and explodes far enough away that you are not injured by it. All at once you hear a loud explosion out of nowhere. It scares the hell out of you, but at least you are not hurt by it. The people who are not so lucky don't hear anything, they just get killed or injured from the explosion.

The week I spent with Mary Edwards that July served to provide just as much mental therapy as it did rest and relaxation. After having spent most of June in battle and experiencing the horrors of war for the first time, I, as with most of my fellow paratroopers, had become edgy and uptight. As a woman, Mary provided me with gentle companionship. As a person who was living through the war and helped fight it, she provided me with emotional comfort. She spent many hours listening to me describe what I had been through and how I was feeling inside. With her kind, understanding nature and patient ear she kept me from falling apart that summer. In return, I provided her with much needed male companionship and emotional support.

Mary was in love with me, and I was in love with her. The problem was that I was also in love with and engaged to Theresa Cook. If I survived the war, I would have to choose either Mary or Theresa to be my wife. Fate had brought Mary and me together to provide one another the support each of us needed to get through the war. Once the war was over, such companionship and emotional support would no longer be needed. It broke my heart when I told Mary during that week in July 1944, that I if I survived the war I would marry Theresa. She told me she understood why, and I believe she did. Mary and I remained very good friends for the rest of the war. We never had any contact afterward. But I have often thought of her and wondered about her.

ANOTHER COMBAT JUMP (ALMOST!)

Since Mary worked in the intelligence headquarters of General Eisenhower, she was privy to a lot of secret information and knew more than I about what the 101st Airborne Division and other Allied units were doing or going to do. While I was with her in July she asked me, "You're going to jump again aren't you?" I said, "I haven't heard anything about another combat jump," which was, in fact, the truth. She said, "But a paratrooper unit is going to make another jump in France, and I think it's the 101st Airborne Division."

I didn't know it at the time, but what Mary was referring to was the jump that the 101st Airborne Division was supposed to make on August 17th, 1944 near Falaise, France to help other Allied forces encircle the Krauts that were retreating southeastwardly from Normandy.

I told Mary she was mistaken, as not only had the paratroopers not been told about such a jump, we hadn't undergone any specific training for a combat mission. If we were to go back into action sometime soon surely we would have begun to train for it—or so I thought. But what Mary told me was correct! During the first week of August, after I returned to Littlecote from my seven-day pass to London, we were told that the 101st Airborne Division was going to make another combat jump, and that we would make it soon.

When we heard the news about another jump we began to get real nervous, and for good reason. First of all, we had received new men to replace the guys who had been killed, wounded or captured during the Normandy invasion. These new recruits were quite young and quite green.

None of them had been in combat. We didn't know how the new recruits would behave when we got into action—would they listen to us and fight along with us combat experienced paratroopers, or would they run and hide like scared rabbits when the shooting started?

Second, each of us veterans of the Normandy invasion had narrowly escaped death at least once—would we be so lucky on another jump? Third, we would have little, if any, time to train for our mission. We spent months training for our mission in Normandy, and even after all that, much had gone wrong. One could only assume that much more would go wrong during a mission that involved considerably less preparation.

The news that we were to make another combat jump really began to work on our nerves. During the second week of August we were sent to airfields that were sealed off and at which we could have no communication with anyone outside. We were told that we were to jump near Falaise, France and were given our specific missions. On August 17th, the day we were to fly, we packed our gear and supplies and boarded our planes. As we sat in the planes with the engines running and the propellers spinning about to take off, we were told that our jump was cancelled! Apparently, U.S. General George Patton's army had gotten to Falaise so quickly that there was no longer a need for the 101st Airborne to assist. With Patton on one side and the British and Canadians on the other, the German pocket had already been crushed. We got off the planes, unpacked our gear and returned to our camps. We cracked like eggs.

THE MINISTER'S DAUGHTER

One day in the early part of September, just before we were to be sent off to prepare for our jump into Holland, I went for a walk on the grounds of Sir Will's manor estate. I walked over to the pond to see if I could spot some fish, and when I got there I noticed a beautiful young woman wearing a bathing suit and lying on a blanket, sunning herself. Her five-year-old son was also there, playing near the pond. I later learned that she was the daughter of the minister who preached in the chapel in Sir Will's manor house. I was unaware that the minister had a daughter, and this was the first time I had laid eyes on this woman or her young son.

I tried a couple of times to start a conversation with her but she completely ignored me. I was about to walk away when all of a sudden the boy fell into a deep part of the pond and was drowning. Apparently, he had crawled onto the limb of a tree that extended over the pond, and fell in. He splashed frantically and went underwater. As a true Commando, and without any waiting or indecisiveness, I instinctively jumped into the pond and swam under the water to where I thought the boy was. I found him and pulled him to the surface, getting his head above water. He started screaming his head off as I swam out of the pond carrying him under one arm and onto dry land. He wasn't injured, but he was pretty shaken up.

Upon seeing how I had saved her son, the boy's mother completely reversed her attitude toward me. She ran over and thanked me profusely for saving her son. I tried to walk away, but she grabbed my arm to keep me from leaving and talked to me as if we were long lost friends. While I stood there soaking wet, she asked me all sorts of questions, such as my name, how long I was staying at the manor estate, if I had ever been to London. The 101st Airborne Division was about to jump into Holland to participate in Operation Market-Garden, but of course I couldn't tell her that, as it was confidential information.

I mentioned to her that I was going to leave for a while, without giving her any specific details as to where and why. She said, "How long will you be gone?" I told her I'll probably be away for the coming weekend, as a minimum. She said "Well I'll tell you what, when you return from your trip, I want to take you to London to some very exquisite nightclubs. They're really great clubs, but you can't wear your uniform because they don't allow American soldiers into them. You can wear my husband's civilian clothes to disguise yourself as an Englishman, since my husband doesn't need them now as he's in the English army, in Africa."

I thought to myself: "Here I am in England as an American soldier having just come back from Normandy where I wore an American uniform while putting my ass on the line trying to save the English people from Hitler, and I just saved her son's life wearing my American uniform, and she wants to show me her gratitude by taking me to places in London where American soldiers are neither welcomed or allowed!" As beautiful as she was, I was quite angered by her offer, and it was all I could do to control my voice. I said to her, "Thank you, but don't worry about repaying me because this little safari that I'm going on is probably going to be a long one." I never saw her again.

30.

OPERATION MARKET-GARDEN: THE BATTLE FOR HOLLAND

Dear Mom and Dad,
After we came back from France there were only eight of us. When we jumped in Holland there were seven of us, but only four of us came back.* I guess one more jump and there won't be any of us left, but of course I hope this is not the case.

Cpl. Jack Womer (December 17, 1944)

The invasion that began on D-Day was a major success for the Allied forces. After nearly two months of grueling battle they finally broke through the German defenses in Normandy and advanced quickly across France and into Belgium. By September, the Allies had a battlefront that extended over three hundred miles and that was relatively close to the western border of Germany, from the Schelde Estuary in the north through Belgium and eastern France to the Swiss border. Their ultimate objective was to penetrate into Germany's Rhine-Ruhr industrial heartland, which would effectively bring the war with the Third Reich to an end.

---

*The four that came back from Holland were: Jake McNiece, Jack Womer, Jack Agnew, and Charles Plauda. Regarding the Filthy Thirteeners remaining after the invasion of France, Jack was probably referring to those who were still alive, i.e. either had returned to England or had been captured. This would imply that four of the twelve who jumped into France had died. Jack knew that George Radecka, John Hale, and Roland Baribeau were killed, and at the time he wrote this letter he was of the impression that James Green also had died. Jack would find out a few months later that Green had, in fact, survived and was a prisoner of war.

Although the Allied forces made good headway toward Germany, the further they advanced the more difficult it became to provide them with adequate and timely supplies. This was due to two reasons. First, was the limited number of functional roads and railways available for transit. Prior to the Normandy invasion the Allied air forces had destroyed many railroads, bridges and roadways within France as a means to keep the German military from deploying additional troops and weapons to Normandy during the invasion. While this measure was quite effective in helping to thwart German counterattacks, it presented the Allies the same problem with movement as they advanced in the other direction.

Second, even into September 1944, despite the strong presence of Allied forces in France and Belgium, the Nazis still controlled major ports in the coastal towns of LeHarve, Boulogne, Calais and Dunkirk, and at the mouth of the Schelde estuary. This forced the Allies to ship supplies and equipment to other ports or beaches that were further away from their spearheads at the front.

The lack of functional roadways, railways and bridges within France, along with the Germans holding on to key ports, created problems for the Allied command in its ability to provide the armies with supplies. As a result, the further inland Allied forces progressed, the more difficult it became for fuel, ammunition and other deliveries to keep up. Patton's Third Army, which had advanced farthest from the beachhead, found it most difficult to get supplies. Courtney Hodges' First Army was hardly in better shape. By early September this problem had progressed to the point where the movement of the Allied forces toward Germany had practically come to a halt.

THE PLAN

British Field Marshall Bernard Montgomery, commanding the 21st Army Group at the northern end of the Allied front, felt that if available resources could be diverted to him he could cross the Rhine River in Holland and outflank the Germans' Siegfried Line. The proposed plan was to have the British Second Army, positioned in Belgium near the Meuse-Escaut Canal, advance rapidly northward on Highway 69 through the Dutch cities of Eindhoven, Son, Veghel, Orave, Nijmegen and Osterbeek to Arnhem—a stretch of about 100 miles. Once north of Arnhem, through which the

Rhine flowed, British Second Army could then turn right and head south-eastward about 40 miles, putting them directly into the heart of Germany's Rhine-Ruhr region.

In order for Montgomery's plan to be successful, it was imperative that Second Army move quickly, so as not to allow the Krauts positioned in Holland or near the German border enough time to plan and execute counteroffensives that could slow or even stop the advance. The problem for the Allies was that the Germans controlled both the towns and the river bridges that ran through these cities, and had positions in various places along the highway.

Other problems were that Highway 69 was a narrow road, and was the only one British Second Army could use to move northward through Holland in order to accomplish the mission. Rapid deployment of tens of thousands of troops and thousands of tanks and trucks packed with supplies and equipment on a single narrow road would be a challenge in itself, let alone having to do it in the presence of enemy forces.

To help ensure rapid movement of Second Army through Holland, Montgomery's plan, code named "Operation Market-Garden," called for an initial, massive dropping of paratroopers along a 40-mile section of Highway 69 that ran through Eindhoven, Son, Veghel, Orave, Nijmegen, Osterbeek, and Arnhem. The airborne assault would be initiated just before the ground advance of Second Army into Holland.

The paratroopers were given the responsibility of seizing and holding these cities and securing the main bridges on Highway 69. As British Second Army passed through a city, the paratroopers that had secured the locale would link up and advance with them. The "Market" portion of Operation Market-Garden pertained to the airborne assault, whereas the "Garden" portion pertained to the ground advance of Second Army, led by the tanks of Brian Horrocks' XXX Corps.

The paratroopers of the Allied forces would be from the U.S. 101st and 82nd Airborne Divisions, the British 1st British Airborne Division and the 1st Polish Parachute Brigade. The 101st Airborne was to jump near the town of Son, seize the town and its bridge, and then head south and take Eindhoven. They were to then head back north through Son and secure the bridges located between Eindhoven and Veghel, and the stretch of Highway 69 that ran between the two cities. Soldiers of the 101st

Airborne would name this stretch of road "Hell's Highway" because of the intense fighting that took place there.

The 82nd Airborne was assigned to take and hold Nijmegen, and secure the bridges and portion of Highway 69 from Grave to Nijmegen and the Groesbeek Heights. The British 1st Airborne, followed by the 1st Polish Parachute Brigade, were assigned to land outside Arnhem, advance to the city and seize its large highway bridge over the Rhine. This was the farthest of the airborne penetrations into Holland, and prompted one British planner to wonder if they might be going "a bridge too far," a phrase which later became the title of a bestselling book.

Over 20,000 paratroopers were landed in Holland during Operation Market-Garden. Almost an equal number of troops were flown in by glider, along with thousands of tons of equipment. It was, and remains, the largest airborne drop in world history. The amount of soldiers, equipment, supplies and weapons brought in via air transport during Operation Market-Garden was so large that it required several days.

Supreme Allied Commander General Eisenhower approved Operation Market-Garden on Sunday, September 10th, 1944. The operation began on Sunday, September 17th, leaving essentially no time for any of the Allied forces to prepare for the mission. By September 20th, after only four days into the battle, it was clear to the Allied command that the Market-Garden plan had failed, and that the war against Germany would not be over by the end of 1944, as hoped. By September 26th, after 10 days of fighting, Operation Market-Garden was over, and had accomplished little for the Allied forces.

The 82nd Airborne Division would remain in Holland until November 13th, and the 101st Airborne would remain until November 27th, to fend off Kraut counterattacks and maintain control of any ground that had been won. During this time, from September 26th to mid-November 1944, both airborne divisions took more casualties than they did during September 17th–25th, Operation Market-Garden itself. The men of the 101st Airborne were among the first soldiers to enter Holland during the offensive, and would be the last to leave as a result.

Conceptually, Operation Market-Garden had a lot of merit. In implementation it failed. The reasons for the failure and the extent to which it fell short have been the subject of controversy ever since it took place. A major factor was that the Germans turned out to be more resilient after their defeat in France than the Allies expected. They improvised with a conglomeration of units who all hit back hard. The British 1st Airborne was especially unlucky in that—unknown to Allied intelligence—two SS Panzer divisions happened to be resting near Arnhem at the time of the attack, and the British division was nearly wiped out. With the front suddenly closer to Germany the Krauts were also able to reinforce and supply their side more easily than in Normandy, and there was also the reputed tendency of British soldiers in Second Army to advance and act slowly, relative to the Americans. Rather than speculate on or add to the countless number of theories of why Operation Market-Garden failed, I prefer to just describe my experiences in Holland from September 17th through November 27th of 1944.

THE MISSION OF THE 101ST AIRBORNE DIVISION

The 101st Airborne Division was to drop a few miles north of Eindhoven in the vicinity of the towns of Son, Veghel, and St Oedenrode, along Highway 69, or Hell's Highway as we called it. The Division's objectives by nightfall of the first day of the attack were to capture the bridges intact over the River Aa and the Willems Canal at Heeswijk and Veghel (assigned to the 501st PIR); the River Dommel at St Oedenrode (assigned to the 502nd PIR); and the Wilhelmina Canal at Son (assigned to the 506th PIR), and then go onto capture Eindhoven and the three bridges over the Dommel River just south and east of there.

The 101st Airborne would jump into Holland in the afternoon of September 17th, the first day of the attack, which meant that we would have only a few hours to secure all of the above bridges and capture Eindhoven by nightfall of that day. The Filthy Thirteen section of the 506th PIR's Demolitions Platoon was assigned to support the regiment's 1st Battalion. The task of the 1st and 2nd Battalions of the 506th PIR was to take the bridge over the Wilhelmina Canal at Son intact, then join the 3rd Battalion in attacking Eindhoven, where it would hold the city and its bridges until the British armored columns arrived.

We learned about the operation less than a week before we were to participate in it. A day or two later we were sent to an airfield with our equipment and gear in preparation for the jump. We were restricted to the airfield, and couldn't communicate with anyone outside of it. Tents had been set up with sand-table displays of the areas in Holland where the Allied forces would attack. These were used as aids to help inform us of our mission. Here we learned that we would jump into Holland during daylight hours. The main reason for the daytime jump was to avoid a lot of the mishaps and confusion that happened at Normandy, plus it was assumed that German anti-aircraft defenses in the Dutch countryside wouldn't be nearly as formidable as along the French coast.

Before we learned of the specific details of Operation Market-Garden us seasoned paratroopers were already quite nervous about it. Not knowing whether this jump would be cancelled at the last minute as our Falaise jump had been, nor having any time to train for our mission, and having to go into battle with a bunch of green replacements, while remembering the high casualties following our jump into Normandy, stirred a great deal of anxiety within us. We were scared.

Hearing that we would jump into Holland and that we would do so during the day added to our anxiety. Unlike Normandy, the section of Holland where we would jump and fight was within 40 miles of Germany, the enemy's homeland. That we would jump during the day meant that we would have no cover from the darkness and would be in full view of any enemy soldiers in the area. Most of us Normandy veterans were certain we were going to get killed this time around. Many of us were.

31.

THE JUMP INTO HOLLAND

Janey, you ask me about some of my friends?

Well, when I went to France on D-Day, after we came back, I left most of my friends in France. They were just unlucky I guess. So you see Jane, it's best not to have good friends because it's hard to take after they go."

Sgt. Jack Womer
(to his sister Jane on January 7, 1945)

In the morning of Sunday, September 17th, 1944 we assembled on the airfield with our gear and prepared for our flight from England to Holland. There were a lot of C-47s at the airbase, and a lot of paratroopers nervously standing around waiting to board. I knew that we were going to fly over the English Channel into enemy-occupied territory, and I recalled that many paratroopers drowned in the early morning hours on D-Day because their pilots turned on the green jump light while still over the Channel.

Either the pilots were too frightened to fly further into France for fear of being shot down, or they became disoriented in the darkness and lost their bearings. Either way, many a paratrooper jumped right into the English Channel and drowned because that's where the pilots turned on the green light to jump. After the men jumped out of the planes to their deaths, the pilots turned around and went back to the airbase in England.

I was nervous that something similar could happen to us while on our way to jump in Holland. The name of the plane the Filthy Thirteen would board was "Ridge Runner." Before I boarded the Ridge Runner I said to the pilot "Are you sure you know where our drop zone is? I don't want you to make the same mistake that pilots made on D-Day. I don't want me or the other men on this plane to get killed because of a mistake on your part." The pilot replied, "Don't worry. I'm damn sure of where I'm supposed to take you. We too heard about what happened on D-Day, and General Eisenhower told us pilots that if we make the same mistake we're going to be shot." I didn't know that Eisenhower had made such a statement to the pilots. But I did know that he was the kind of a guy who would do so, and follow through on it too. I felt quite relieved by what the pilot of our plane said to me. We took off from England and, escorted by P-38s that flew above us, crossed the Channel to Belgium to get to Holland.

Jake McNiece had made me the number three man in the stick, which is the most important person in the stick as he is responsible for coordinating with the pilot precisely when the men are to begin to jump from the plane. When a plane full of paratroopers approaches its drop zone, the pilot turns on the red jump light to alert them to get ready. The jump door is opened and each paratrooper is to stand, get into formation, and connect the cloth hook-up line of his main parachute to the metal anchor line that runs down the length of the plane's ceiling.

The green and red lights are located in such a way that the third man has the best view of them and the paratrooper stick. When the plane reaches the drop zone and the pilot turns on the green light, the third man in the stick will see it and at that point he gives the order for the men to start jumping from the plane.

Soon after we entered Dutch airspace the Krauts opened up on us with antiaircraft fire—lots of it—which made us even more nervous. Eventually the red light in our plane was turned on. I ordered everyone to stand and prepare to jump. The doorway was opened and I looked outside to see hundreds of our paratrooper-filled C-47s flying side-by-side and very close to one another. I could see that paratrooper sticks in some of the planes ahead of us had started to jump, so I knew we were getting close to our drop zone and that I had better keep a close watch for the green light to come on.

JUMPING WHILE THE JUMP LIGHT IS STILL RED

As I stood looking at the planes outside while waiting for the green light,

I saw the plane flying next to ours get hit by antiaircraft fire. The plane lost control, and started to drift dangerously close to us. Realizing that their plane was going to crash, the men in it began to jump from the aircraft. As the men jumped, their hit plane continued to drift toward us and some of the paratroopers were jumping dangerously close to the propellers of our plane.

It was obvious that one of two things was going to happen. Either the plane that was hit would crash into our plane and kill us all, or the paratroopers who were jumping into the propellers of our plane would cause us to crash. In either event, it was as plain as day that we were all going to get killed unless we got the hell out of our plane immediately. I gave the order to jump, despite the fact the red light in our plane was still on and that we were not yet over our drop zone.

Except for Chuck Plauda, all of us paratroopers got the hell out of our plane in the blink of an eye. Plauda's reserve parachute opened inside the plane, which prevented him from jumping. I'm convinced he became frightened from the antiaircraft fire coming up at us and was too scared to jump, so he deliberately pulled the cord on his reserve chute in order to get out of having to jump. I was so mad at him I could have shot him. He stayed on the plane with the pilot, co-pilot and the jump-stick man (the man that stands by the door and kicks you out in case you freeze.)

Afterwards I assumed the other plane, the one that had been hit, had collided with our plane and caused it to crash, killing Plauda, the pilot, co-pilot and the jump-stick man. Apparently our plane survived, as did Plauda and the other three guys. Plauda eventually met up with us in Holland, and he told me that after we jumped our pilot was able to swiftly maneuver our plane safely away from the other plane, which did in fact crash. Naturally, Plauda was on my shit list for not jumping with us, but I didn't want to confront him with it while we were in Holland. Plauda was a little crazy, and I knew he would get back at me if I got on his ass about opening his reserve parachute to avoid having to jump. He may have gone as far as to shoot me while we were in combat, doing it in such a way as to give the impression I was killed by enemy fire.

But I eventually got on Plauda's ass about opening his chute in the plane. When we left Holland in late November 1944 we were sent to Mourmelon le Grand, France, a small town just outside the city of Reims, for rest and relaxation. Soon after we arrived in France I confronted Plauda about the stunt he pulled in the plane. We got into one hell of a brawl. I beat the shit out of him—I nearly killed him with my bare hands. Shortly afterwards Plauda left the 506th's demolition platoon. I don't know whether he was kicked out or requested to be transferred. All I know is that he was gone. I never saw him again.*

SON

We parachuted into a field just outside of Son that turned out to be close to our intended drop zone. We were only about 200 yards from Highway 69, the main road that goes into Eindhoven. There were few if any Krauts around, and we weren't confronted with any enemy resistance. In another hour gliders carrying artillery and other equipment were going to land in the same field. Our immediate job was to collect our equipment and get off the field to our designated areas before the gliders came in. We had just about cleared the field as the glider planes came into view.

We ran towards a nearby wooded area to get out of the way of the incoming gliders. Certain men from each unit had gone directly to the woods to set off colored smoke flares. This was done to help the paratroopers in the field re-unite with their specific units. Each unit had its own specific colored smoke for identification purposes. When the paratroopers in the fields headed towards the woods they would look for the colored smoke that pertained to their unit.

I ran as fast as I could towards the woods in the direction of the smoke of the 506th PIR's demolitions platoon. As I ran through the field I noticed two gliders coming in right at me. They were only about fifty feet or so above the ground, and were dangerously close to each other, and dangerously close to me. Just as one of the gliders was about 10 feet above my head, one of the wings of the other one hit into the glider above me. I immediately ducked to avoid getting hit by pieces of the planes, as well as the men or equipment inside them. Both planes flipped tail-over-head, split in half and crashed upside down right where I was.

*Charles Plauda stayed in the army after WWII and did a tour of duty in Korea. In 1950 he was killed in a motorcycle accident in Japan and is buried in the Fort Snelling National Cemetery, Minneapolis. (Personal communication with Richard Killblane, September, 2011.)

I was absolutely certain that I was going to get killed.

Miraculously, the crash missed me by inches. Once again, my guardian angel protected me from certain death. The only injury I received was a cut across my nose. I ducked so hard and fast that it caused my helmet to slam into my face and cut me across the nose. It was a bad cut, but just a cut; actually it was the worst injury I sustained throughout the entire war. My first lieutenant, R.E. Haley, wanted to nominate me for a Purple Heart medal but I told him not to. I didn't want the medal because I didn't think I was worthy of it. To me, getting a Purple Heart for cutting your head on your helmet was disrespectful to the men who were wounded by the enemy. I also felt that if I received the Purple Heart under these circumstances it would bring me bad luck. I refused it.

We headed south through the woods and then on Highway 69 toward Son, to fulfill the 506th PIR's mission of capturing the town and securing the Son Bridge, which traversed the Wilhelmina Canal. As we entered Son its civilians were all lined up on Highway 69, cheering us on as if we were in a Fourth of July parade. As we passed through the town people gave us food and drink, the young women jumped all over us, the children waved and danced, the old women hugged and kissed us, and the old men shook our hands—it was a wonderful and totally unexpected greeting. The Dutch civilians were genuinely delighted to see us, and were happy to share what little they had.

As we made our way toward the Wilhelmina Canal the Krauts opened up on us with 88mm cannons and heavy machine guns they had positioned along the canal. They knocked the hell out of us and caused a lot of casualties, but we eventually were able to neutralize the 88's and machine guns with bazooka and mortar fire. Just as we got close to the Son Bridge and were about to take it, with a huge roar the wooden structure blew up into the sky and fell to earth as splinters. The Krauts had placed explosives on the bridge to destroy it in case of an Allied attack. They really waited till the last minute before blowing it up.

With the Son Bridge gone, the 506th PIR had no quick and easy way to cross the Wilhelmina Canal and continue heading south on Highway 69 to Eindhoven. Makeshift bridges were made from anything that could float. The guys used these improvised rafts and bridges to cross the canal, but they enabled only a few men to cross at a time, and then only slowly.

It would take hours for all the men in the 506th to cross. It was already beginning to get dark, and there was no way for the 506th PIR to cross the Wilhelmina Canal, march to Eindhoven, and take the city and its three bridges by nightfall as originally assigned to do. Here we were, just a few hours in Holland, and already Operation Market-Garden was beginning to fall apart. We crossed over to the other side of the Wilhelmina Canal on the makeshift bridges and spent the night on the outskirts of Son.

32.

EINDHOVEN

On the morning of the second day of Market-Garden, September 18th, the 506th PIR headed south on Highway 69 for Eindhoven, just five or so miles away. We reached the town's outskirts by about mid morning. We got into some fighting with Krauts along the way, and in the town itself, but there were fewer than we expected and we didn't have too much difficulty in taking Eindhoven or its three bridges.

The biggest problem we had when we entered Eindhoven was not with the Krauts but with the town's citizens. Just as in Son, as we entered Eindhoven its citizens filled the city's streets to celebrate our arrival. They shouted cheers at us, hugged us, kissed us, and gave us food and drink. The streets were packed with people. It was like being at Times Square in New York City on New Year's Eve. We could hardly move through the city. The people were so happy to see us that they slowed us down in accomplishing our objectives. But by mid-afternoon we had secured the three bridges that crossed the Dommel River just south and east of the town. We still had not seen any of the British Second Army, even though according to the original Market-Garden plan we should have. They finally arrived late in the afternoon that day.

Everything had been going reasonably well for us until the evening of Tuesday, September 19th. During the day, the Krauts had made a series of counterattacks on the Allied troops positioned in Arnhem and at other places along Highway 69 between Arnhem and Eindhoven, but not on Eindhoven itself. The Krauts didn't attempt any counterattacks in Eindhoven during the day because there were British Spitfires and U.S. P-38's

circling the city most of the day to help cover us. When night came, however, the Spitfires and P-38s left, and in came Kraut bombers. They were
going to level the town.

The hundreds of British convoy trucks that had come into Eindhoven
the day before were loaded with ammunition, guns, grenades, and other
explosives and equipment, and were jammed bumper-to-bumper in the
streets in the middle of the city. The Kraut bombers flew over Eindhoven
and dropped incendiary bombs, which set the whole city on fire. Not only
did the bombs destroy buildings and kill or wound a lot of civilians and
Allied troops, they also set the British convoy trucks on fire, causing the
explosive materials and ammunition to detonate, which caused more casualties and a tremendous loss of badly needed supplies and equipment.
When you think about it, keeping the British convoy trucks jammed in
the streets of Eindhoven was pretty stupid.

The Filthy Thirteen and the other two sections of the 506th PIR
demolitions platoon were guarding the three bridges in Eindhoven when
the bombing started. Close to each bridge was an air raid shelter. I was
positioned at the third bridge, about eight feet away from the door to the
shelter. Everyone except me who was near the third bridge had run into
the air raid shelter when the bombing began. I was outside and all alone,
just watching the Kraut planes bomb the city. I don't remember anyone
firing back at the Kraut bombers with anti aircraft weapons.

I got so infuriated at the Kraut bombers and what they were doing to
us, and that no one on the ground was firing back, that I starting firing
my M-1 Garand at the planes. I provided the only anti-aircraft fire in the
area of the third bridge! I fired 19 clips of ammunition, a total of 152 bullet
rounds, at the bombers. I just had to fight back, I was that disgusted. I
don't know whether I hit any of the Kraut bombers, but I needed to do
something, and firing my M-1 at the bombers made me feel a lot better.

After I had shot off all of my ammunition at the bombers I went inside
the air raid shelter. There was a young lieutenant in there shaking like a
leaf on a tree. I didn't know who he was, but he obviously had never been
in combat. He was scared half to death. He said to me after I stepped
inside, "Did the 50-caliber machine gun that was shooting out there get
hit? I don't hear it anymore." He thought he heard someone firing a 50-
caliber machine gun, when it was really just me firing my 30-caliber M-1

Garand. When you're in an air raid shelter and there's a gun going off outside, the gun often sounds a lot louder on the inside of the shelter than it does on the outside because of an echo that can be produced in the room.

I replied: "Lieutenant, there was no 50-caliber out there firing. I was the only one out there doing any shooting, and I was firing my M-1. I stopped firing when I ran out of ammunition." Embarrassed, the young lieutenant said, "I heard a 50-caliber out there, now what happened to it?" I said "Sir, I was the only one out there firing back at the Krauts. There was no 50-caliber machine gun out there firing at them. If you think I'm wrong, you should go outside and see for yourself." "Never mind," he snapped. The lieutenant was too scared to move from his spot in the shelter with all the bombing going on outside.

During the same bombing attack my former first sergeant William Myers and second lieutenant Eugene Dance from my days with the 29th Ranger Battalion were wounded. Like me, they had joined the 101st Airborne's 506th Parachute Infantry Regiment after the 29th Rangers had disbanded. By the time of Operation Market-Garden Dance was a first lieutenant, and Myers was one of his sergeants. Myers died from his wounds. A piece of shrapnel went through his belt and into him. He clung to life for three days, in agony, and then he died. Dance was taken away by some medics and treated. He was able to return to the 506th PIR.

33.

THE KILLING OF CORPORAL JOSEPH J. OLESKIEWICZ

On September 20th, 1944 and the days that followed, the Krauts continued launching counterattacks on Son, Veghel, Udall, Nijmegen, Arnhem and other towns north of Eindhoven. The 506th PIR demolitions platoon and the other elements of the regiment that had been in Eindhoven were ordered to head north on Hell's Highway to join the rest of the 101st Airborne Division.

Veghel had been taken from the Krauts by the 501st PIR when Operation Market-Garden began on September 17th. When we arrived there on or about September 20th it was under attack and already partially reoccupied by the Krauts. A lot of British troops as well as American paratroopers were in Veghel when we got there. There were German tanks and British tanks all over the place. For days we and the other Allied troops fought like hell to keep control of the town, and the Krauts fought like hell to take it from us. A lot of shooting and killing took place while we were there.

By this time the Filthy Thirteen, as did the rest of the demolitions platoon, had taken a lot of casualties. Two of the Filthy Thirteeners had been killed, and others were wounded. Jake McNiece, Joe Oleskiewicz, Jack Agnew and I were the only guys left from the Filthy Thirteen who hadn't been hit. Jake was the buck sergeant of the Filthy Thirteen, Joe was the only remaining corporal, and Agnew and I were the only remaining privates. We four were all that were left of the Filthy Thirteen since our jump into Holland. Chuck Plauda, who was supposed to jump with us but chickened-out while in the plane, had not yet arrived in Holland.

A HEADLESS PARATROOPER

One day while we were in Veghel, Jake and Joe and I walked down a road in a direction heading out of town to see what was going on out there. When we got to the edge of the town and were about to head out into open ground where the 501st PIR position started, we stopped in front of a house to survey the situation in front of us. Several hundred yards ahead of us and to the right was a Kraut tank, just sitting there. To our left was a British tank, also several hundred yards away, and directly opposite the Kraut tank.

A lieutenant from the 501st PIR came over to us and said to Jake: "I want you and your two men to follow me and my men on this road, into the open area. We're going to try and outflank that Kraut tank over there and knock it out of action." The lieutenant was in a front line company in the 501st PIR, and us three were in the regimental headquarters demolition platoon of the 506th PIR, but when you're in battle it doesn't matter what unit you are with; you do whatever a higher ranking officer tells you. Jake told the lieutenant that he couldn't go because he had men back in town, which wasn't true at all. The only guy he had back in town was Jack Agnew. The lieutenant ordered Jake to go back into the town to his "men," and Joe Oleskiewicz and I to stay with him to take out the Kraut tank. Jake got himself off the hook in trying to take out the Kraut tank, as he was the sergeant, and left Joe and I in the hands of a lieutenant that we didn't know.

Jake headed back into town, and Joe and I and the 501st lieutenant continued on the road into the open field, where the Kraut tank was watching us. We couldn't have gone more than 20 yards when the tank opened up on us with its 88mm cannon. The three of us ran for cover. I don't know where Joe went, but the lieutenant and I dove down into a ditch that ran adjacent to the left side of the road. I landed right on top of a paratrooper who had had his head blown off. The tank had hit him right in the head with a cannon round.

The Krauts in the tank were using their 88 like it was a sniper rifle, which is a very unusual thing to do with an 88mm cannon. They were eyeballing the road looking for soldiers going into or out of the town and, using their cannon were picking off anyone they saw. We were the only guys on the road at the time, so they had definitely fired at us. I don't know what the hell the British tank was doing, all I know is it wasn't firing back at all.

The Kraut tank fired its 88 some more at us but the rounds flew right over our heads. I remained motionless in the ditch, on top of the paratrooper with no head. I had landed on the dead paratrooper in such a way that I was facing him and my head lined-up about where his head would have been if it hadn't been blown off. I could tell he hadn't been dead very long. As I laid on him I could smell his flesh and blood as it oozed from what little remained of his neck, and I could feel an occasional twitch and hear sounds from his body. After a while, being on top of this headless torso began to bother me to the point where I could no longer remain there. I shouted to the 501st lieutenant, "I landed on top of a dead man with no head. Can I go over him and go somewhere else?" The lieutenant shouted back, "I don't give a God damn where you go!"

I didn't know where Joe Oleskiewicz had gone. The Krauts in the tank were still shooting their 88mm cannon. I didn't know who they were firing at, but they were firing at someone. I noticed that the Krauts had not fired at the house that we had stopped in front of a short while ago. I figured the house would be a safer place, so I decided to get in there to protect myself. I crawled over the dead man and out onto the road, and ran like hell to the house. Once inside I thought I had better get into the cellar because if the Krauts turned the gun on the house I'd be safer in the cellar. I opened the cellar door and saw that it was packed wall-to-wall with paratroopers from the 501st PIR. There was absolutely no way I could get down into that cellar. I couldn't even get down the steps.

I yelled out in a commanding voice to them: "If you hear shooting out in the back, you better get the hell out of this cellar!" since shooting out back would mean the Krauts were there. They said back to me, as if I were an officer, "Yes, Sir." I felt a little better knowing all of those paratroopers were down there, that I wasn't alone. I had temporarily joined up with the 501st in Normandy, and knew they were a damn good outfit. It felt reassuring to see them there. I went to the upstairs floor of the house, broke a darkened window and looked outside. The whole backyard of the house was loaded with paratroopers.

I was worried about the paratroopers hiding in the basement. The Krauts were still firing their 88mm cannon, and I figured if the tank should see any of the guys in the backyard they would open up on them and the rounds would hit the house. The house would then collapse on all of those men down in the cellar. There would be no way for them to get out, as there were just too many of them. I went downstairs to the first floor, stopped where I was, and got on my knees and started praying. All of a sudden the Kraut tank stopped firing its cannon. It had moved somewhere else. I thought it had withdrawn from the area entirely, but I realized a little while later that it relocated to another position nearby, and was still watching us.

JOE OLESKIEWICZ GETS KILLED

Once everything appeared to have settled down I came back out of the house, unaware of the fact that the Kraut tank was still somewhere out there. I found out from some guys in the 501st PIR that we had received orders to move back into town. I hollered for Joe, and out of nowhere he showed up and was standing next to me. We began heading into town on the same road we had walked down earlier.

The 501st lieutenant who had previously ordered us to go with him was nearby and said to us, "Which of you guys can shoot a bazooka?" There was a bazooka lying on the ground, near where the lieutenant was. Both Joe and I knew how to shoot a bazooka. Joe was a corporal, and I was only a private, and I don't remember whether the lieutenant told Joe to pick up the bazooka because he had a higher rank than me, or he volunteered to pick it up. All I know is that Joe got the bazooka, not realizing the Kraut tank was still out there watching us.

We now had a bazooka, but we didn't have any rounds for it. Another officer from the 501st who was about 20 or 30 yards away from us shouted, "Hey you two, I've got three bazooka rounds." He motioned for us to come over and get them. I went over and Joe continued heading into town. Just as the officer handed me the three bazooka rounds the Kraut tank fired its cannon. The officer and I hit the ground immediately.

I remained flat on the ground, and after a few minutes when I felt it was safe I got up and continued walking, crouched over at a fast pace, into town. I was also looking around for Joe, but since I didn't see him I figured he had taken cover somewhere like I had when the Kraut tank fired. I stopped and shouted "Joe" as loud as I could. He didn't yell back and he didn't come out from anywhere. I shouted his name a few more times, but still no word or sign.

I continued walking down the road into town. After I had gone just a few more yards, on the ground on the side of the road I came across a large, mangled chunk of a freshly killed U.S. soldier. It was what was left of Joe. I knew it was him because I recognized the shoulder holster he had been wearing to carry his 45-caliber model 1911 pistol. Joe had taken a direct hit from the 88mm round fired from the Kraut tank. It had blown him in half. He was messed up pretty badly. It broke my heart to see him like that. Even after all of these years it is hard for me to talk about Joe getting killed.

The Krauts in the tank must have seen Joe carrying the bazooka and that's why they gave him the "honor" of shooting their cannon at him. The only thing that saved me is that I had gone over to get the bazooka rounds. If the officer had not called me over at the precise moment that he did, or if I had been carrying the bazooka instead of Joe, it would have been my mangled body lying on the ground. Again, I had narrowly escaped certain death. As I stared at what was left of Joe I wondered how much longer my luck would last.

A couple of hours after Joe was killed the Krauts that were in the tank abandoned it and withdrew from the area. Why they withdrew and left the tank behind I don't know, but they did. I went over to the tank because I wanted to see this evil thing that had killed Joe. Next to the tank I saw a dead Kraut and about two dozen shell casings of German 88mm rounds. That's how many of those shells those bastards fired at us. They had fired that 88mm cannon as if it were a rifle.

The English tank that was a couple of hundred yards away hadn't fired one shot at the Kraut tank, even though the English were supposed to be our back-up. I went over to the English tank to ask the soldiers why they hadn't fired at the Kraut tank. When I got there I saw a bunch of English soldiers sitting around it, chit-chatting and drinking tea. I was so disgusted I didn't even bother to ask what the hell they were doing while the Kraut tank was firing at us. I could see for myself what they had been doing. I turned around and walked back into town.

In the book *The Filthy Thirteen* Jake McNiece claims that he was in the immediate area when Joe went "missing," but didn't realize Joe had been killed until almost a year later, in the summer of 1945, after the war had ended. Jake states that he and Sergeant Leonard Johnson, a former platoon sergeant of Jake's, had been drinking one day that summer, and after the two became drunk that Johnson opened up and told Jake that Joe had been killed and explained how it happened.

According to Jake, Johnson said that he and Joe and another paratrooper named Stanley Spiewack were in Veghel running from German tanks that were just yards away from them. The three of them ran shoulder-to-shoulder towards a foxhole that could only hold two people, and that himself and Spiewack jumped into the foxhole, leaving Joe out. Johnson then claimed, according to Jake, that Joe then stood up to run for a ditch, and one of the tanks that was just ten or twelve yards away shot Joe with an 88mm cannon round. Jake then claims that Johnson said he never told Jake about what had happened to Joe because he was afraid Jake would think it was his fault. Jake says that Johnson confessed that Joe's getting killed the way that he did bothered him quite a lot.

Jake also claimed that he too was there running away from the tanks but didn't witness Joe's death. He claims that he saw the mangled remains, but did not know they were Joe's. Jake claims that ever since he found out from Johnson that the remains were those of Joe, that he has nightmares about seeing what was left of Joe's body.

I was with Joe Oleskiewicz when he was killed. I can say with absolute certainty that Jake wasn't with Joe or I, nor was Sergeant Leonard Johnson or Stanely Spiewack. Nor were there German tanks ten or twelve yards away from Joe when he got killed. What Sergeant Johnson supposedly told Jake in the summer of 1945 about Joe Oleskiewicz is simply not true.

Jake implies in his book that while we were still in Holland he asked me if I knew what happened to Joe, and that I had said no. I don't know why Jake would state this in his book, because when I got back into town shortly after Joe was killed I met up with Jake and Lieutenant Haley and told them exactly what had happened to Joe. I told them that Joe had taken a direct hit from an 88mm round fired from the Kraut tank that was out in that field. Jake knew what had happened to Joe the very day that it happened.

Why Jake has claimed that he never knew what happened to Joe until after the war is beyond me. I suspect he carries some guilt about having lied to the lieutenant from the 501st PIR to get out of the order to help outflank the German tank, leaving Joe and I in the hands of an officer none of us knew, and that Joe was later killed by the tank. Perhaps by making up a story as to how Joe was killed to cover up what really happened is Jake's way of dealing with any guilt that he feels—that he is trying to convince himself he's not to blame.*

*One possible explanation that reconciles some of the large differences between Jack Womer's recollection and Jake McNiece's is that McNiece later returned to the battle area where he had left Womer and Joe Oleskiewicz, after the latter had been killed. By this time Womer may have left the area and went back into town, and more German tanks moved in. This would explain why Womer doesn't recall seeing Jake McNiece, Sergeant Leonard Johnson, Stanely Spiewack or Herb Pierce, or the many German tanks that Jake McNiece claims were in the area. This does not explain, however, why McNiece claims he did not find out how Joe Oleskiewicz got killed until a year later.

34.

LIFE IN HOLLAND

Putting the war aside, life in Holland wasn't too bad. The Dutch people were very nice to us. They didn't have much food, but they were willing to share it with us. They were genuinely glad we had arrived and they supported us. Many of the people wore wooden shoes, which reminded me of when I would sometimes wear wooden shoes when I worked in the steel mills.

TEACHING NUNS TO MAKE PANCAKES

Most of the Dutch people are Catholic, and Holland is loaded with many magnificent churches. The Catholic churches in Holland are the most beautiful ones I have ever seen, in any country. One morning, after we had been in Holland for a week or so, I was near a convent and I met up with about a dozen Catholic nuns. They were glad the American G.I.s were in Holland, and they wanted to make me breakfast. They couldn't speak English very well, but one of them was able to ask what I would like to eat. "Pancakes," I said. "Vas is das?" they said back to me. "Pancakes. . . . You know, flap-jacks," I answered. "Vas is puncake? Flap-jack?" they said back to me. I said: "Take me to your kitchen." "Ya, kitchen," they replied.

They took me to their kitchen. It was quite large. It had a big old cast iron stove that had a fire burning inside it. They all stood and watched as I took some eggs, flour, milk, and butter and whipped up a large batch of pancake batter. I poured portions of the batter into a large cast-iron frying pan on the stove to make the pancakes. As I watched the batter cook into pancakes, I realized I needed a spatula to flip them. "Saptula?" I asked. The nuns looked confused, so I pretended to hold a spatula in my hand and made a flipping motion with my wrist. "Spatula," I repeated. "Ya, spatula, spatula," they replied. One of them walked away for a moment, came back with a large meat cleaver, handed it to me and said "Spatula." I had to flip the pancakes with a meat cleaver!

I stood over the stove and cooked about fifty pancakes, and then we sat down at a large table and ate them. "Puncake goot, ya," I heard many of them say. The nuns loved them! Instead of the nuns making me breakfast, I had taught them how to make pancakes. To show their appreciation they gave me a set of wooden Rosary beads.

GETTING A NAZI FLAG

Since D-Day my father had been writing to me and asking me to get him a Nazi flag, the type that had a swastika on it. He wanted one as a souvenir. During the time I was in France after D-Day I looked all over for a Nazi flag but never found any. They were hard to come by because they were a highly sought-after souvenir among G.I.s. Around the end of September, while we were in Eindhoven, we came across a Dutch soldier who spoke perfect German and who hated the Krauts. He had a motorcycle, so we asked him to serve as a messenger and as an interpreter for us, so we could deliver important information and communicate with any Krauts that we captured as prisoners.

I asked the Dutch soldier if he knew where I could get a Nazi swastika flag. He said, "Well, I know where there may be one. There's a very fancy house, a short distance from here, where a very nice wealthy family once lived. When the Krauts took control of Eindhoven some big-shot Kraut who was a general in the SS liked the house so much that he decided he was going to live in it and use it as his headquarters. He shot the father and threw the family out on the street and moved into their house. While he stayed there he hung a large Nazi flag out of one of the upstairs windows to let everyone know the house was his. The Krauts are now gone, but the flag may still be inside there. Get on my motorcycle and I'll take you to the house so you can look for it."

We rode to the house, and tried to get inside but couldn't because it was locked up. There were no flags hanging from it. I searched the front door for booby traps, and kicked it in and went inside. It was a magnificent home. The townspeople had stripped it of its furniture and other belongings after the Krauts pulled out of Eindhoven, but it was still a magnificent home. I went upstairs, and there were three bedrooms up there. Each had its own private bathroom, which in those days was very unusual. I searched each bedroom, but didn't find any flags.

I went up into the attic and, to my delight, there was a neatly folded Nazi flag with a swastika on it. I searched it for booby traps, and unfolded it on the floor. It was in perfect condition, exactly what my father wanted! I ran my bayonet through the center of the flag, to "kill it." Then I folded it and stuffed it in my shirt and got to hell out of there. I hid the flag from the other guys until I was able to mail it to my father back in the United States.

MY "GIFT" TO GERMANY

One day during the first week or so of October, I looked up to the sky and saw about 1,500 American B-17 bombers fly into Germany. When you see a sight such as this there is no doubt as to which side is destined to win the war. The ultimate objective of Operation Market-Garden was to achieve the inevitable Allied victory over Germany sooner rather than later. It was never intended to decide if the Allied forces would win the war, but rather when they would. Even though Operation Market-Garden did not work out the way Field Marshal Montgomery had planned, it didn't change the fact that Allied forces were pushing in the Germans on every sector. By this time many of us were more concerned with our disposition after we had achieved victory in Europe, assuming we would live to see it. We wondered if we would be sent home, or instead sent to the Pacific Theater to fight the Japanese.

On the same day I saw the bombers I walked across the Dutch border and entered Germany for a while, just to be able to say that I had, in fact, been there. When I crossed the border and was standing on German soil I was so amused by it all that I felt that I had to leave something behind, just to let the German people know that an American soldier was there. So I did leave something behind—I took a nice huge crap right on German soil! When I had finished I walked back into Holland and felt proud. I often wonder if I was the first American G.I. to shit on German soil during World War II.

PROMOTED TO CORPORAL

During the middle of October 1944 I was promoted to corporal to replace Joe Oleskiewicz. The promotion came with a $16 per month pay increase. By this time the Filthy Thirteen had been given replacements for those who had been wounded or killed. Four men were assigned to me. None of them were over twenty-one years old, and all of them were as green as green could be. One of them followed me around like a puppy dog, and did everything I did. It drove me crazy.

At the time I became a corporal we were living in a farm house that had been damaged quite a bit by the fighting that had been going on. The outside walls looked like Swiss cheese from all of the shell holes in it. The windows had been blown out, and only about half of the roof remained. We may have been better off sleeping outside. In back of the house was a small barn that had a chicken with one leg missing, some skinny pigs, and a couple cows that were sick and provided milk that made us ill. The farm had a large garden that had just about every vegetable known growing in it, so we ate a lot of vegetables. The new recruits had a rough time adapting to our living conditions.

POEM BY AN UNKNOWN PARATROOPER

By the end of October, 1944 we had moved from the farm house and were living in an old red barn. The barn was home to three dairy cows, and contained loads of hay. The living conditions in the barn were actually better than those of the house from which we had come. Cows are quiet and easy going. We didn't mind living with the cows, and they didn't seem to mind sharing their home with us. Besides, they provided us with fresh milk.

The nicest thing about living in this barn is that it was the only building in town that had a functioning electric light in it. On Sundays the 506th PIR regimental chaplain held his church services there because of the light. During these services the whole barn would fill up with soldiers, and unless you got there well in advance you wouldn't be able to get in. I always had a good seat for Sunday services because I lived in the barn.

During one particular Sunday service in late October or early November, our chaplain read the most touching poem I've ever heard. It's the best description I am aware of that expresses a paratrooper's feelings just before jumping into battle. The poem was written by a paratrooper in the 101st Airborne prior to the division's jump into Holland on September 17th,

1944 during Operation Market-Garden. The identity of the paratrooper is unknown, but it is likely that he was in the 506th Parachute Infantry Regiment.* The poem is as follows:

> Look God, I have never spoken to You,
> But now I want to say, How do You do?
> You see God, they told me You didn't exist,
> and, like a fool, I believed all this.
>
> Last night from a shell hole, I saw Your sky,
> and figured right then they told me a lie.
> Had I taken the time to see the things You made,
> I'd have known they weren't calling a spade a spade.
>
> I wonder, God, if You'd shake my hand,
> Somehow I feel, You would understand.
> Funny, I had to come to this hellish place,
> before I had time to see Your face.
>
> Well I guess there isn't much more to say,
> But I'm sure glad, God, I met You today.
> I guess the zero hour will soon be here.
> But I'm not afraid, since I know You're near.
>
> The signal! Well God, I have to go,
> I like You a lot, this I want You to know.
>
> Look now, this will be a horrible fight.
> Who knows, I may come to Your home tonight.
> Though I wasn't friendly to You before,
> I wonder, God, if You will wait at Your door?
>
> Look, I'm crying! Me, shedding tears!
> I wish I had known You all those years.
> Well God, I have to go now, so goodbye.
> Strange, since I met You, I'm not afraid to die.

---

*The chaplain was most likely Father John S. Maloney, a catholic priest and chaplain in the 506th PIR. Cpl. Womer mailed his hand-written transcription of the poem to his father, Walk Womer, in Dundalk, Maryland in a letter dated November 6, 1944.

Sadly, the paratrooper was killed in action in Holland. His prophetic poem was found in his pocket when his remains were recovered. I felt a connection to the paratrooper, as I had lost three of my best buddies, George Radecka, John Hale, and Joe Oleskiewicz, after having jumped into combat with them in Normandy and Holland. I was so deeply moved by the poem that I asked the chaplain if I could copy it by hand. He permitted me to do so and, for safe keeping, I mailed my hand-written transcription of the poem to my father back home in Maryland.

When I came home from the war in 1945, I asked my father for the letter that contained my transcription of the poem. He didn't know where it was, and told me he didn't know what had happened to it. I looked all over but I couldn't find it. I was quite upset about it. For the next sixty-three years I thought that it had been lost, until one day, October 24th, 2007, just about sixty-three years to the day that I had first heard the poem, it was found while searching for background materials for this book. The envelope containing the poem that I mailed to my father turned up in an old suitcase that had in it many of my other letters that I sent home during the war. Sitting at my kitchen table, I read the poem over and over again for about ten minutes. It brought me right back to Holland, 1944, and made me realize just how blessed I was for having survived the war.

PEACHES THE CAT

One day while on patrol along the Rhine River in late October of 1944 I came across a homeless cat wandering around the riverbank. The poor thing was skin and bone. He hadn't eaten in a long time. He followed me as I walked along the bank. He seemed to be quite friendly toward me, but not toward the other guys I was walking with. The weather had become chilly, and I knew the cat was cold and hungry. I felt sorry for him, so I picked him up and carried him inside of my coat. I named him Peaches because he had orange and white fur.

At the time the guys in my demolitions platoon were still living in the big old red barn with three dairy cows that provided us with fresh milk. When we got back to the barn after our patrol duty I gave Peaches some meat and poured fresh cow's milk into my helmet and placed it on the floor. Boy did he love filling his belly with fresh milk. He knew he was going to have it good living with us demolitions guys.

The only problem was that my first lieutenant, R.E. Haley, had a military dog with him most of the time. The dog had jumped with us using his very own parachute when we jumped into Holland on September 17th. I'm not sure why Lieutenant Haley had the dog, but wherever he went the dog went with him. When Lieutenant Haley would come into our barn, which was about two or three times a day, he'd bring his dog along. The dog would see Peaches and go after him to try to kill him. I knew I had to protect Peaches from the lieutenant's dog, so I made him a little house from an old apple crate. I put a piece of cloth on the bottom of it and covered its open side with a plank so that the dog couldn't get to Peaches.

I kept the apple crate in the area where I slept, next to where my head would rest. During the day, whenever I couldn't carry Peaches around with me, I kept him in the crate with the plank on top to keep him from getting out or Lieutenant Haley's dog from getting in. I also kept him in the crate during the night while I slept. When Peaches had to go to the "toilet" during the night, he'd get up and poke one of his little paws through a space in the crate and tap me on the head. That was his way of telling me he needed to go outside and relieve himself. He was a smart cat.

I had Peaches for a little over a month. When we left Holland in late November, we were sent to Mourmelon le Grand, near the French city of Reims, for rest and relaxation. One evening I went into Reims and carried Peaches with me, inside of my coat. While I was walking down a street a nearby dog spotted Peaches, ran to where we were and barked furiously at us. Peaches became frightened and began to squirm. I lost my grip on him and he ran down an alley way. The dog ran after Peaches but didn't get him. I chased the dog away and looked all over for Peaches, but couldn't find him.

The next day I went back into the city to look for Peaches. I came across a trash can in the alley that he had run down. Inside of it I saw Peaches' orange and white hide which had been neatly removed from his body, and his guts, head, and his skeletal remains. Some French people had found Peaches, killed him, cooked him, and ate him for dinner.

35.

GOODBYE TO HOLLAND

Before we jumped into Holland in September, we were told that we would be there no more than a month. After a month went by we were still in Holland. Just about every day for weeks afterward we heard that any day soon we would pull out and be sent to France for rest and relaxation. Then November rolled in and we were still in Holland, and still living with animals in an old barn. After having been in Holland on the front lines for nearly two months we had become quite anxious to leave the country.

To make matters worse, we hadn't been paid in three months. None of us had any money. I had more than 300 dollars coming to me in back pay, but not one cent in my pocket. Then, when it seemed as if things couldn't get any worse, we learned that President Franklin D. Roosevelt had beat Governor of New York Thomas E. Dewey in the presidential election of November 1944. Roosevelt was re-elected as the president of the United States for a fourth term. Many of us were mad that Roosevelt had been re-elected. We blamed him for getting us into the war, and felt that under his leadership the war would continue on longer than if Dewey had been elected. The morale among us was quite low.

The morale among the Krauts was just as low as ours, if not lower. They knew that we were going to win the war, it was just a matter of time. They were running out of men, territory, supplies and equipment, and even the will to fight. We had captured some German soldiers and they told us what it was like for them behind their own lines. They were given only three days' worth of food rations per week. The other four days they would have to find their own food or go hungry. They knew that Germany had lost the war, but their officers forced them to fight. Their officers told them that if any soldiers were caught not fighting or deliberately surrendering, their families back home would be killed. I believe that this was true. We told our Kraut prisoners that we too were tired of the war and that we wanted it to end and to go home just as much as they did. In some respects the Kraut soldiers were no different than us.

JAKE MCNIECE AND I ALMOST GET KILLED

On or about November 10th, the Filthy Thirteen were assigned to go to the Rhine River to do some reconnaissance on the Kraut positions on the other side. Our orders were to report any enemy positions and movement to our own artillery units. Our artillery guys wanted the information from us so they could aim their eighteen 105mm cannons at specific Kraut positions and knock them out.

It was a clear night, and we made our way the half-mile distance or so to the Rhine without any difficulty. We stopped in an apple orchard to check out the lay of the land and go over some details regarding our mission. From our position the Rhine was about 100 yards wide. Lieutenant Haley was concerned about the possibility of Kraut patrols being on our side of the river. He broke about half of us up into groups of two to three men per group to go to different spots along the Rhine to observe for enemy activity on the opposite side. Using radios, the groups were to report any activity to our artillery units positioned about a thousand yards behind us. Haley and the rest of the guys remained behind in the apple orchard to look out for Kraut patrols.

Jake McNiece and I were one of the groups that Lieutenant Haley sent out. We took a radio and binoculars with us and, using the light from the night stars, we moved quietly through the apple orchard along the banks of the Rhine. We came to a hill that was near a dike and that overlooked the river. We made our way up to near the top of the hill and saw that we had a great view of the Rhine and the opposite side. We got down on the ground and observed for any signs of the enemy. At first we didn't see or hear anything, but after a while we heard trucks starting up on the other side. That meant that there was a road over there and that there were Krauts around. Using a map and the sound from the trucks, I estimated the coordinates of their location.

Jack Womer in February 1944, shortly after he earned his paratrooper wings. Unlike most paratroopers, Jack was given only about ten days to earn his wings instead of the usual thirty. Being in tip-top physical condition from his Ranger training, Jack had no problem becoming a Screaming Eagle, and, judging from the photo, appears quite happy to be a member of the notorious Filthy Thirteen.
Photo: the Womer family

The famous demonstration jump that took place on March 23, 1944 in England. Womer is one of the paratroopers in the sky, and on the reviewing stand are Prime Minister Winston Churchill, General Maxwell Taylor of the 101st Airborne Division, and Supreme Allied Commander Dwight Eisenhower.
Photo: U.S. National Archives

A cartoon sketch of Jack Womer having a midnight snack. Jack wrote on the bottom "I guess this is cake from home and I'm hiding under my covers. The fellow drew this picture and put my name at the bottom of it. Ha Ha." The sketch is believed to have been made by Mike Marquez while the Filthy Thirteen were staying at the estate of Sir Ernest and Lady Wills in Littlecote, Wiltshire.
Photo: the Womer family

Corporal John "Peepnuts" Hale, Jack Womer's best friend. This photo was taken the afternoon of June 5th, 1944 at Exeter Airfield, just hours before the 101st Airborne Division jumped into Normandy. Hale was killed in Normandy, probably within hours after this photo was taken.
Photo: U.S. National Archives

Ross A. Moehle, another member of the 101st Airborne Division's 506th Regimental Headquarters Company. Jack and Moehle spent most of D-Day with each other fighting German soldiers. Moehle survived the war and returned to Litchfield, Illinois, though he never attended any reunions. He spoke little of his war experiences, although he did on occasion talk briefly about D-Day and being with a soldier named "Jack," but only when in the company of close friends who were also WWII veterans. Moehle died in 1988 at the age of 72. *Photo: Maggie Moehle Gilbert*

Sgt Jack Womer, on a seven-day pass to Nice, France in June 1945. The war in Europe was now over, and Jack was certainly entitled to a little rest and relaxation. *Photo: the Womer family*

Jack Womer (sitting with back against the wall), in Normandy, France shortly after D-Day. Jack got separated from the rest of the Filthy Thirteen when they jumped into Normandy and hooked up with men of the 501st PIR for about a week. Jack believes that this photo was taken while he was with the 501st. It may have been taken at the first farm below the Angoville au Plain, as the current owner of the farm, Maurice Leonard, claims he recognizes the courtyard. *Photo: Lt. John Reeder via M. Bando*

Jake got on the radio and told our artillery units that we heard trucks starting up across the Rhine and gave them the coordinates. He then told them to fire for range. A few seconds later, one of our 105mm cannons fired a single round. It went right over our heads and exploded on the other side of the Rhine, exactly where we thought the trucks were located.

Seeing that it was a perfect shot, Jake then told our artillery units to fire for effect. Within seconds we heard our eighteen artillery cannons begin to fire volleys. But instead of flying over our heads and into enemy lines, the rounds landed right where WE were located. The exploding rounds made the ground shake as if we were in the middle of an earthquake. Somehow our artillery unit made an error with the coordinates, and were now firing at Jake and I instead of the Krauts! Jake got back on the radio and shouted "Hold your fire! Hold your fire! You're shooting at us! Hold fire!" but our own artillery rounds kept pouring in on us.

To protect ourselves we got up and ran over the top of the hill and on to the side that faced the Rhine and the Kraut positions. Jake kept shouting "Hold your fire! Hold your fire!" Finally, after what seemed like an eternity, but was probably no more than 30 seconds, the artillery stopped. We reissued the same coordinates and our artillery resumed its fire. This time the rounds landed on their intended target. Again, I had narrowly escaped death.

SO LONG, HOLLAND

While we were in Holland we were issued daily rations, but most of the time we ate whatever food we could get our hands on. We never went without food, as there were plenty of vegetable gardens and all sorts of animals running around over there. If we wanted meat we'd kill an animal, clean it, cook it and eat it. There were no turkeys in Holland, at least none that we ever saw, so on Thanksgiving Day, November 23rd, we ate boiled pig.

We left Holland on November 27th, and by December 2nd, 1944 we were in Mourmelon le Grand, France, for rest. Casualties within the 101st Airborne Division during our time in Holland were high, about 65 percent. Of the eleven men in the Filthy Thirteen I had jumped with less than six months earlier in Normandy, three had been killed and three were taken prisoner while in Normandy. Of those of us who returned to England and were sent together to Holland, only four of us came back: Jake McNiece,

Jack Agnew, Chuck Plauda, and myself. I figured at this rate of turnover, one more combat jump and there wouldn't be any of us original guys left. But by this time many of us believed by what we had seen for ourselves, and by what we had been reading in the *Stars and Stripes*, that there would be no more fighting, that Germany was finished, and that the war was as good as over. This belief of ours made us feel real good.

We got a nice rest while we were in Mourmelon le Grand. Shortly after we arrived Jake McNiece and Jack Agnew transferred from the Filthy Thirteen to the Ninth Troop Carrier Command Pathfinders unit. At about the same time Plauda also left the Filthy Thirteen, after I beat the hell out of him for the stunt he pulled in the plane when we were sent to Holland.

I almost got approved to go back home, to Maryland, on a 30-day furlough. Only two men out of a few thousand were allowed to go back home, and my officers tried real hard to get me the furlough but couldn't. I just missed being picked by the skin of my teeth. I lost out to a guy who had been wounded while in Holland whose father died about a month earlier. Plus his wife had had a baby while he was overseas, and he had not yet seen his child. He was more entitled to get the furlough than I was. As much as I would have loved to have gone home for a month, I didn't mind losing out to him.

When the Christmas season was upon us we heard that we were going to get passes to go to Paris the week before Christmas. We were all excited about this. On the evening of December 17th, 1944, we washed up and packed some clothes in preparation for our trip to Paris the following day. I was assigned Charge of Quarters duty that day. It was a 24-hour duty that extended from December 17th into the 18th. This meant that I had to stay awake all night and keep an eye on things, and wake everyone if an emergency came up.

After the men had gone to bed on that night I sat down and wrote letters to my fiancée Theresa and my parents. After I completed my letters I looked closely at the men in the Filthy Thirteen as they slept. There were a lot of new faces since I had joined the group about a year earlier. It dawned on me that of the men in the Filthy Thirteen that I had jumped with less than six months earlier in Normandy on D-Day, I was the only one remaining. The rest were either dead, wounded, taken prisoner or had left. I thought about how very lucky I had been up to this point. I worried that if we went into combat again my luck was going to run out, given the high casualty rates within the 101st Airborne Division following the Normandy invasion and Operation Market-Garden.

But what was there to worry about? Tomorrow we were leaving for Paris for the Christmas holiday. From all accounts it seemed Germany was about to surrender any day, and we were probably going to be sent home by the end of February 1945. What could be better?

36.

ON TO BASTOGNE: THE BATTLE OF THE BULGE

Janey, you ask if I do any trading with the Germans?
Well, in a way I do, but all of them are now dead Germans, so you see
  I always make out on the deal.

                                        Sgt. Jack Womer
                                        (to his sister, Jane, January 7, 1945)

Things couldn't have been any worse. While we were preparing to go to
Paris for Christmas and expecting to hear any day that the Germans
had surrendered, on December 16th they launched a massive counteroffensive against the American line in the Ardennes, a region of extensive forests
and rolling hills, located primarily in Belgium and Luxembourg.

The primary objective of Hitler's surprise attack was to split the Allied
front by assaulting across the Meuse River and turning north to seize
Antwerp, a critical port city in Belgium. This would split the Allied in front
in two, isolating the British army group and American Ninth Army in the
north. It was a long shot on their part, but if the Krauts were successful in
severing the Allied front it was conceivable they could win the war in
Europe. As a minimum, their success would prolong the war, allowing
them time to bring more modern weapons on line, like their new jet fighters and V-2 rockets, or enabling them to negotiate more favorable terms
of surrender.

The Ardennes offensive began with a huge artillery barrage and attacks
by the 5th and 6th SS Panzer Armies and 7th Army against a nearly forty-
mile American front. At the northern shoulder of the attack, the U.S. 99th

Infantry Division, with later assistance from the 1st and 2nd Divisions, was able to stop the Kraut advance, much to their credit. However, attacks by the 5th Panzer Army against the U.S. 106th and 28th Infantry Divisions and 7th Armored just to the south in the area of St. Vith were successful. The Krauts were pushing their way through the Ardennes, forming a "bulge" in the Allied front and beginning to penetrate Belgium.

Speed was now of the essence for the Krauts. In order for their offensive to succeed, they had to move quickly to stay ahead of any Allied counteroffensives. Two railroad lines and all of the main roads in the Ardennes converged on the Belgium town called Bastogne, located about 30 miles southwest of St. Vith. Control of Bastogne was vital for both sides. Allied control of the town before the Krauts arrived would prevent, or at least slow, the German advance. German control of Bastogne before any Allied forces arrived would greatly increase the likelihood of their success.

Elements of Germany's 5th Panzer Army that had broken through the American lines around St. Vith were already heading toward Bastogne. Most of the U.S. 106th Infantry Division had been surrounded and forced to surrender, but the 28th Infantry Division was putting up one hell of a fight to keep the Panzers from reaching Bastogne. General Eisenhower knew he had to get additional Allied troops to the area, and get them there fast. The only reserve units that were available were the 82nd and 101st Airborne Divisions. During the morning of December 17th Eisenhower issued orders for the 101st Airborne to go and reinforce the Allied positions near Bastogne, and the 82nd Airborne to go further northeast to help reinforce the Allied position at St. Vith.

At about two o'clock in the morning on the 18th, while I was in Charge of Quarters I received word about the order for the 101st Airborne Division to head north to Bastogne. "Wake up guys! We have to go up to the front immediately!" I shouted. I woke everyone from a pleasant sleep to inform them that we were not going to Paris after all, that we were going to the front lines to fight, and that we had to hurry and pack our gear and get ready to move out. Everyone was mad at me because I disturbed them from a nice rest to deliver the bad news. Most of the guys thought I was joking and tried to go back to sleep. They soon realized this was no joke.

The biggest problem we had was our lack of equipment. We had turned most of our combat gear in after we left Holland, and now we had nothing. We had little to no winter field clothing, no ammunition, no guns or other supplies because we had just come off the front line and were resting. When distributing equipment, the army naturally gives priority to the guys that are on the front lines or about to go to the front. Guys like us that have just come off the front are given low priority when it comes to receiving supplies. Here we were, about to go back into a decisive battle with the Krauts on only three weeks rest, with little supplies or equipment, and without any details on our mission or the fight that was coming. Try to imagine how we felt.

Once we had heard that we were going to Bastogne I was promoted to buck sergeant to back-fill the vacancy created by Jake McNiece's departure to the Pathfinders. I was given a Thompson submachine gun, the firearm buck sergeants generally carry. The only problem was that I didn't have any ammunition for it.

The entire 101st Airborne Division, about 11,000 men, would travel to Bastogne in trucks, a distance of about 130 miles northeast from where we were in Mourmelon le Grand. It was mid-December and it was cold and we had no winter combat clothing. Most of us had to ride in open trucks since there weren't enough enclosed ones to transport all of us. Worse yet, many of us had to stand in the open trucks because there weren't enough seats. We froze our asses off in those trucks as we made our way to Bastogne.

As we were on the road a lieutenant drove by in a jeep and I said to him, "Sir, I don't have any ammo clips for my Tommy gun." He threw to me a 30-round magazine clip loaded with the standard 45-caliber automatic Colt pistol (ACP) bullets, the type used in a Tommy gun. I had acquired quite a bit of experience with the Thompson submachine gun when I trained to be a Ranger, and I knew how to handle it. I inserted the clip into the gun, and suddenly it fired a burst of about five rounds. To this day I don't know why that gun went off, but it did, and when it did it sounded like a God-damned cannon. The lieutenant chewed me out because if there had been any enemy patrols within a mile they would have heard it. Of all of the men in the 101st Airborne Division, I'm convinced that I was the first to fire a shot during the Battle for Bastogne!

We arrived in the town on the morning of December 19th. Despite being outmanned and outgunned, the 28th Infantry Division with some of the 10th Armored had been able to slow the approach of Hitler's 5th Panzer Army to Bastogne long enough to allow us to arrive just before the Krauts. Once the 101st Airborne reached Bastogne the different regiments and other units were sent to the neighboring villages and woods to form an outer perimeter against the Kraut advance. The Filthy Thirteen along with the 1st Battalion and other components of the 506th PIR were sent to a wooded area a few miles northeast of Bastogne, close to a small village called Noville and near a road that ran through the two towns.

Other U.S. military units that had been in the southern portion of the Ardennes were also pulled in to help defend Bastogne. There were some surviving elements from the 28th Infantry and parts of the 9th and 10th Armored Divisions. The objective of the American forces was to keep the rapidly approaching Germans from taking the city. Our mission was strictly defensive.

NOVILLE

When we arrived at the wooded area near Noville there was already a fight going on between some American tank units and some Kraut tank units. There were tanks all over the place shooting at one another. Many of us had by now received some supplies and equipment, although some men still didn't have rifles or ammunition. We were still short on bazookas, mortars, food and winter clothing.

We got into one hell of a fight with the Kraut tanks and some Kraut infantry almost immediately upon arriving near Noville. We fought for a while and then the Krauts withdrew. They attacked again, and withdrew again. The fighting was fierce throughout the day and well into the next. A lot of men were killed on both sides, but we did our part to fend off the Kraut advance while the rest of the American forces completed their deployment at Bastogne. By the early afternoon of December 19th, about 22,000 American soldiers, half of whom were from the 101st Airborne, had taken up positions around Bastogne and were waiting for the full Kraut advance.

By December 21st, seven German divisions had the American defensive ring completely surrounded and outnumbered, and cut off from its own supply lines. The Krauts occupied a lot of the high ground that was nearby, and the muzzles of their rifles, Panzer cannons, and ground artillery were aiming right down at us. We nonetheless held on and defended our lines.

The thick fog that hung around us most of the time the first few days was a mixed blessing. The Krauts had moved in pretty close to our lines, and the fog helped to hide us from them. But the fog also prevented any of our air support to fly over and drop supplies or bomb the Kraut positions, since the pilots would've been blinded.

There was a lot of fighting taking place along the lines, but there really wasn't much we or the Krauts could do in terms of advancing anywhere until the clouds in the sky left and the fog lifted. Despite the intense fighting we were in and our being outgunned and outnumbered, not one Kraut soldier got through our lines.

FOY

We fought the Krauts and bivouacked in the woods near Noville for about two days, and then moved with the rest of the 1st Battalion of the 506th PIR about a mile south to a wooded area near the small town of Foy. The areas surrounding the village were crawling with Krauts. On the way to Foy we ran into some Krauts positioned in a wooded area near a railroad. Many of them were wearing white sheets and blended in with the snow. We didn't see them until we were very close to their position.

We got into one hell of a gun fight with those Krauts. We killed most of them, and those that weren't killed were wounded. But we had lost a lot more of our men. There were bodies and blood all over the place. In my mind, I can still see the dead and wounded, and the dark red blood as it oozed from their bodies and stained the white snow where they fell.

By this time we had been in the area of Bastogne for nearly three days, and had successfully defended the city. But we were already down a lot of men from our prior two days of fighting in Noville, and now, after what happened on our way to Foy, we had even fewer men to fight with, and less ammunition. We were completely surrounded, and didn't know when or even if we were going to receive more supplies and men. The stress of being in this situation began to work on our nerves.

We settled in a wooded area just outside of Foy and not more than 300 yards from the Kraut lines. The Ardennes is not a nice place to camp. The forest is so thick that sunlight hardly penetrates through the pine trees.

It's a naturally cold, damp and dark forest. It's hard to see anything in those woods. To make matters worse the weather conditions were terrible. Belgium was quite cold that December. Most of the time there were cloudy skies, lots of fog, and plenty of snow. When there was no snow falling it was usually icy rain.

We stayed in foxholes that we had to dig ourselves using our small, army-issued entrenching shovels. The foxholes had to be wide enough to fit two men and deep enough to stand in. Between the ground being frozen solid and full of tree roots and having only trench shovels to work with, digging those foxholes was a real pain in the ass. To make matters worse, just as we got done with digging our foxholes we were occasionally ordered to relocate to another portion of the forest and dig new ones.

The advantage of staying in foxholes was that they helped to protect us against Kraut infantry and artillery attacks. The trees offered good protection against tank and infantry attacks, but they were a soldier's worst nightmare during an artillery attack. When artillery rounds fired into a pine forest explode, they cause the trees to splinter into small sharp fragments or splinters that fly all over the place like spears. Getting hit with these splinters can actually be worse than getting hit with a bullet, as splinters were often more difficult to remove and treat. They were deadly. We came under artillery attack several times while we were in the woods defending Bastogne, and I saw guys that had been hit by pine tree splinters. If had a choice, I'd much prefer to get hit by a bullet.

The living conditions were quite miserable—the worst we experienced throughout the entire war. In addition to the freezing cold and snow, we had little to no winter clothing. Worse yet, we weren't allowed to start fires for warmth because the flames and smoke would reveal our positions to the enemy. While our foxholes provided some protection against Kraut infantry and artillery attacks, they provided no sanctuary from the brutal cold. It would be freezing during the day, and at night it would get even colder.

We seldom ever had a hot meal. We survived mostly on K-rations and a strong will to live. We lost a lot of guys to frostbite, trench foot and pneumonia. I never truly realized or appreciated just how hard it was for George Washington and his men of the Continental Army when they camped in Valley Forge during the winter of 1777 until I was in Bastogne.

37.

A USELESS REPLACEMENT

We lost a lot of men when we fought in Holland, so we received a lot of new replacements while we were resting in Mourmelon le Grand. Most of the replacements were young kids fresh out of boot camp who had never been in combat. Being green, sometimes these kids would naively do things that could get themselves or others killed. One day while we were bivouacked near Foy, Lieutenant Chickos, a 1st lieutenant in the 506th's Regimental Headquarters Company, came over to me with a replacement who was about 18 years old, and said to me: "Sergeant, I want this man to go over and guard the artillery shells we have stacked-up by that hill over there. See to it that he does it." "Yes, Lieutenant," I replied.

There was a lot of snow on the ground, and there was a heavy fog. You couldn't see more than 10 feet in front of you, but you could see footprints in the snow. I was a little concerned that Krauts might have already discovered the artillery shells and might be near them. I said to the kid, "You go on out there and guard the artillery shells like the lieutenant ordered, and I'll try to get relief for you in about two hours. The Krauts won't be able to see you walking over there because of the fog, but look for footprints to or from the direction of the Krauts. If you see any footprints, don't go to the artillery shells. You turn around and follow your own foot-prints right back here to me, and I'll send a patrol over to where the shells are." The kid disappeared into the woods toward where the artillery shells were stacked. They were only about 50 yards away. I waited a few minutes to see whether he was going to come back to me. He didn't return, so I assumed he didn't see any footprints in the snow and was staying there guarding the shells.

He was there alright. After about an hour or so he began to get cold so he started a big fire right near the artillery shells to keep warm. The fire was so large that I could see the flames and smoke fifty yards away, despite the heavy fog and thickness of the forest. The fire disclosed our exact position, and I knew the Krauts would see it and attack us. I was so mad at that kid I could have punched him. Within seconds, before I could get over to him to put out the fire and chew him out, the Krauts were firing 88mm cannon rounds at us. By this point I was ready to kill the kid because if any of those 88 rounds hit the stack of artillery shells there would have been one hell of an explosion that would have killed us all.

The 88mm rounds were hitting trees, exploding and causing steel shrapnel and wood splinters to fly all over the place. Everyone immediately jumped into their foxholes to take cover. Since I was in charge of the kid, I had to go over to where he was, put out the fire, and get him the hell out of there. I couldn't run out to him with those 88-mm rounds coming in, so I got down on my belly and, with my Thompson submachine gun slung over my back, crawled the fifty yard distance through the snow, the exploding 88-mm rounds, and the flying pieces of trees and splinters to get to where he was.

As I crawled all I kept thinking about was how I was going to rip the kid apart once I got to him. But when I got to him he was curled up on the ground crying hysterically and shaking like a leaf on a tree during a hurricane. He was in shock and completely out of his head with combat fatigue. He was finished as a soldier. I quickly put out the fire, and ordered him to crawl back with me to our foxholes. He wouldn't move an inch. He was too petrified with shell shock to move a muscle. I slapped him in his face and shook him a few times to get him out of the shock that he was in. He still wouldn't move. I grabbed my Thompson and pointed it at him and yelled "If you don't crawl back with me immediately I'm going to shoot you right here and now! Now move your ass and let's get the hell out of here!" He crawled back with me.

When we got back to where the rest of the guys were Lieutenant Chickos came over to me and ripped into me for what the kid had done. Even though I had followed Lieutenant Chickos' orders and had nothing to do with the mistake that this kid had made, I was given the blame for it. That's how it goes in the military. Shit flows downstream. It's a chain-of-command thing. After a while the lieutenant calmed down and looked at the kid. He could see he was petrified and in a state of shock. The lieutenant said to me: "Well, there's nothing we can do with him. He's finished. Get him out of here. Send him to the rear." The kid was sent to the rear. I never saw him again.

38.

MIKE MARQUEZ AND THE SCREAMING MEE-MEES

One of the guys in the 506th Regimental Headquarters Company's demolitions platoon was a Mexican named Miguel Marquez. We called him "Mike". Marquez had been in the demolitions platoon from the time the platoon trained in Toccoa, Georgia. By this time he was in the Filthy-Thirteen section of the platoon. Mike's brother, Armando Marquez, was also in the 506th Regimental Headquarters Company, which was very unusual since the military normally doesn't allow two brothers to serve in the same company. I liked Mike a lot. He was quite tough, and a damn good soldier.

One day while we were bivouacked in the woods near Foy, Lieutenant Chickos informed me that our intelligence men had reason to believe that the Krauts intended to attack us very soon. Lieutenant Chickos told me to make sure my men were prepared for an attack and ready to fight. A couple hundred yards beyond the forest that we were in were German Panzer tanks covered with white sheets to blend in with the snow. If they did attack us it wouldn't take them very long to reach our positions. I went around and told the Filthy Thirteeners to be ready for a Kraut Panzer attack, and possibly a Kraut infantry attack.

I'm sure there were guys from our side watching the Krauts, but I didn't know who or where they were, or who they would report to if they saw something. Since the Krauts were already so close to us, I wanted someone that I knew was dependable to keep an eye on them for any movement or other signs of an attack. After what had happened with that young kid we had guard the artillery shells, I didn't want to order a new recruit to watch

242

for Kraut tanks. I wanted someone with experience. Mike Marquez was the only experienced soldier available at the time, and I knew I could depend on him.

I asked one of the new recruits to go find Mike Marquez and tell him to come over to me. After a few minutes Marquez came over to me and said: "Jack, I heard you wanted to see me about something. What do you want?" I said: "Mike, I want you to walk to the edge of the pine tree forest that we're in and keep a close watch on the Krauts on the opposite side of the open area. They may try to attack us sometime soon. If you here the engines of their Panzer tanks turn on or if they start to move, there's a good chance they're going to attack. If their plan is to launch a full scale attack on us they'll most likely have Kraut infantry behind the tanks to make it through the trees, since the tanks can't get through the pine trees. If you see the tanks heading our way, but there are no Kraut foot soldiers behind the tanks, we might not want to get too involved with the attack because the tanks can't get through the trees and get to us. If there are soldiers walking behind the Kraut tanks, well we're in for a hell of a fight. So stay there and keep a close watch. Once you've learned something come back here and let me know."

Mike headed out over to the edge of the woods that faced the Kraut positions a couple of hundred yards away. About an hour later, "screaming mee-mees" start coming in on us. Screaming mee-mees are artillery shells that release hot steel shot that can set trees on fire. They make a characteristic scream-like sound when they come in. They're not intended as antipersonnel rounds, but rather to start fires such as in wooded areas to force soldiers to come out into the open where they can be fired upon. I think they contain sulfur, because when they land in snow they give off a strong odor of rotten eggs. The Krauts were shooting screaming mee-mees over to our positions, to set fire to the pine forest that we were in and force us to come out into the open area that separated us from them so they could shoot us.

All of a sudden Mike Marquez ran through the woods as fast as he could towards me. Now I had no one over at the edge of the woods watching the Krauts, which made me real nervous. Excited, Mike shouted to me "Jack, we're being gassed! We've got to get the hell out of here!" We weren't being gassed. He was being fooled by the sulfur smell created by the screaming mee-mees.

I yelled: "Mike, they're just screaming mee-mees, we're not being gassed. The Krauts are trying to get the trees to catch on fire and force us out in the open. Now if you don't get your ass the hell back to the edge of the woods immediately and watch those Krauts, I'm going to kill you right here and now!" I meant it too, and he knew I meant it. Marquez ran right back to where he was supposed to be. Fortunately, the Kraut tanks and infantry didn't attack us.

Marquez was a good soldier, but in this instance he didn't follow my orders. I needed to say what I said to him, and he knew it too. It was nothing personal. You must understand that when soldiers are in combat and someone messes up there's no apologizing or in-between stuff that follows. It's not like what you see in the war movies in theatres or on television with guys apologizing to one another. It doesn't work that way in real combat. When you're on the front lines and someone makes a mistake or doesn't follow orders to the point where it could have caused you or your own men to get wounded or killed, you don't tell that person "It's alright" or "Don't worry about it." You've got to get on their ass and set them straight. Combat soldiers don't get too many chances. Some don't get any at all. If you want to stay alive you've got to pay close attention to whatever it is you are supposed to be doing.

Mike Marquez and I remained good friends after the war. Sixty years later, during the 2004 Christmas season, I sent him a Christmas card. I wrote: "Mike, do you remember the time when we were in Bastogne and I was going to shoot you?" He sent me a card after he received mine, and in his card he said: "Yes Sergeant Womer, I do remember it. It's a good thing you didn't shoot me, because if you had, we would have probably lost the battle!" I loved it! Mike Marquez passed away in October of 2008.

39.

CHRISTMAS DAY, 1944

On December 22nd, 1944 some Kraut officers approached our lines under a white flag with the intent of offering the Americans an opportunity to surrender honorably. The German officers were brought to the headquarters of Brigadier General Anthony McAuliffe of the 101st Airborne, who at the time was acting as division commander. General Maxwell Taylor, the actual commander of the 101st Airborne, had been summoned to Washington DC before we went to Bastogne, and he was still in the United States at the time.

The Krauts knew that McAuliffe knew they had us completely surrounded and outnumbered. The Krauts also knew that we were running low on ammunition and other supplies. But McAuliffe knew that the Krauts had tried hard several times to penetrate our lines but we were able to hold them back. When the Krauts made the offer to General McAuliffe for us to surrender honorably, McAuliffe replied by laughing in their faces and saying, "Aw nuts." His response has since become famous. The Krauts were disappointed that McAuliffe would not surrender, and they would retaliate.

What we were praying for, and waiting on, was clear weather so that we could get badly needed supplies flown in and dropped down to us. On December 23rd our prayers were answered, as on that day the fog lifted and the sun came out. This allowed a fleet of C-47s to fly over and drop supplies.

On the day before Christmas, the Krauts bombarded us with heavy artillery throughout the afternoon. They stopped for a little while in the

evening, and then taunted us by playing Christmas carols and other popular Christmas songs on loudspeakers. Our lines were only about 300 yards
away from theirs, so we could hear the music loud and clear.

A lot of guys had been hit during the shelling despite the fact they'd
been in their foxholes. Flying pieces of shrapnel would occasionally find
their way into a soldier's body even if he was taking cover. Sometimes
artillery shells landed directly in a foxhole and exploded, and instantly
killed anyone who was in it. A lot of guys were injured from trees that had
been knocked down from exploding artillery. A tree would fall over a foxhole, and the limbs or large branches would drive into the foxhole and
penetrate a man's body.

Whenever the shelling stopped, those of us who weren't wounded
would climb out of our holes to look for wounded soldiers and tend to
their needs. This was actually quite dangerous. The Krauts knew that we
did this, and sometimes they would resume shelling shortly after they had
stopped, to kill or wound the guys who were walking about looking for
wounded men.

The cruelest thing that I witnessed the Krauts do throughout the entire
war occurred on Christmas Eve, 1944. About seven or eight men from the
506th PIR had been severely wounded from the Kraut shelling. They were
in pretty bad shape and needed immediate medical attention if they had
any chance of surviving. Even if they could survive, it was obvious that
they wouldn't be able to return to combat duty. They were finished as far
as the war was concerned.

A few of us helped the ambulance drivers load the wounded into two
ambulances. The ambulance drivers were going to take them back to one
of the 101st Airborne's makeshift aid stations or field hospitals that had
been set up behind our lines. The ambulances took off from our lines on
a dirt road, and we watched from our position as they drove away.

After the ambulances had traveled a few hundred yards we saw them
stop. A bunch of Krauts had forced them to come to a halt, and ordered
the drivers to get out. We watched as the Krauts mercilessly shot and killed
the ambulance drivers and the wounded men, all of whom were unarmed,
and siphon the gasoline out of the ambulances. I don't know whether the
ambulance drivers went the wrong way and inadvertently drove into the
Kraut lines, or had gone in the correct direction and a few Krauts had

penetrated along that dirt road; all I know is that the Krauts killed all of those unarmed men for a few gallons of gasoline.

When a soldier sees his enemy do such things, it creates a desire within him to go out of his way to do the same. Killing is no longer done for purposes of survival or fulfilling a mission, it is done out of vengeance and bitter hatred for the enemy. When we saw this we became filled with rage. We wanted to leave our foxholes with our rifles, grenades and bayonets, and hunt and kill as many Germans as we could find, as if they were wild animals, not for the sake of winning the war, but to get even.

At one point on Christmas Eve the Krauts shelled us with "Christmas cards." These were just propaganda leaflets written to convince us that corporate America and our own military were our real enemy, and that we should join forces with the Krauts and take sides against the United States.

The Krauts placed these leaflets inside of blank artillery shells and fired them at us. They were trying to break our spirit and make us give up. But their attempt at trying to frighten us into surrendering didn't work. None of us gave in to them. They resumed the shelling of our lines with heavy artillery throughout the rest of the evening and until about 2:00 am on Christmas morning. On Christmas day itself they resumed shelling and kept it up for hours. They hit us with some pretty big artillery. When those shells exploded the ground would shake vigorously as if there was an earthquake happening right underneath us. The percussions from the endless stream of exploding rounds rattled every bone and organ in our bodies, and played hell with our nerves.

The artillery barrage shook the hell out of us, both physically and mentally. A lot of men got hit with shrapnel, falling trees or flying splinters from blown-up trees while hiding in their foxholes. They cried out in agony. The rest of us wanted so much to crawl out of our foxholes and help them, but to do so during the artillery barrage would have been sheer suicide.

To endure the shelling, I spent most of Christmas day curled up and face down in the bottom of my foxhole, praying to God that I wouldn't get hit. To help me deal with the stress of the situation I thought of my fiancée Theresa and, in my mind's eye, imagined the life that she and I would have together after the war. I thought of the many lovely Christmas's that Theresa and I would spend together as a couple. (Indeed, we did get married after the war, and we did share many, many Christmas's together —all of them happy!)

Later on Christmas day the weather again cleared, and this allowed our bombers to bomb the hell out of the Kraut positions that had been shelling us. Looking up from our foxholes and seeing our own bombers fly overhead towards the Kraut lines made us feel real good. C-47s also flew overhead and dropped some badly needed supplies on us. I remember many of us collected the parachutes attached to the cartons and cases that were dropped. We cut the parachutes up into long strips and used them as bandaging material for our wounded. We couldn't keep enough bandages on hand, as there were so many wounded soldiers.

It was pretty rough on Christmas day. The only food I ate was a ration can of ham and eggs. On every Christmas day since, I think about what we soldiers experienced on December 25, 1944, and how lucky I was not to have been wounded or killed.

On December 26th, the lead division of General George Patton's Third Army arrived from the south and broke the Kraut line that surrounded us. We were no longer surrounded, and our lines were now reinforced by Patton's first-rate Third Army. Seeing all of those many Third Army tanks and troops sure made us happy. While the battle for Bastogne was far from over, this was the beginning of the end for the Krauts as far as their attempt break through the American front with their offensive.

By the end of December I, like many other front-line combat veterans of Normandy, Holland, and now Bastogne was at wits end with the war. I had been overseas since October of 1942, more than two years, and far longer than anyone else in my platoon with the exception of Eugene Dance. Between Normandy, Holland and Belgium I had spent well over 100 days on the front lines with the enemy. I was tired of shooting people, getting shot at, narrowly escaping death, witnessing people suffer and die, losing close friends, constantly looking over my shoulder and running for cover, sleeping in holes in the ground and blown-out buildings, being away from home…. the whole gamut of being a combat solider. The war had begun to affect me, physically and mentally.

In his book *Band of Brothers*, renowned author Stephen Ambrose and Captain Richard ("Dick") Winters of the 101st Airborne's 506th PIR (who like me was at Normandy, Holland and Bastogne) discuss this point at great length. They describe this condition as a soldier approaching his "breaking point." In *Band of Brothers* there is a quote from an official army report on "Combat Exhaustion" that says:

> . . . psychiatric casualties are as inevitable as gunshot and shrapnel wounds in warfare. . . . Most men were ineffective after 180 days or even 140 days [of combat]. The general consensus was that a man reached his peak of effectiveness in the first 90 days of combat, that after that his efficiency began to fall off, and that he became steadily less valuable thereafter until he was completely useless.

By the end of December the prospect of us soldiers being on the verge of reaching our "breaking points" was becoming a major concern of many of the officers within the 101st Airborne. I and many other guys in the division had, within the past seven months, spent well over 100 days, or over 50% of my time, on the front lines in combat. If the above quoted text is accurate, that meant we were well past our peak of effectiveness and were quickly approaching the 140 day mark at which many of us would be ineffective as soldiers.

I never did reach my breaking point. But there were guys who did, including guys that had spent less time in combat than me. When a guy reached his breaking point he was usually pulled from the front as soon as a replacement could be obtained and sent somewhere where he could, hopefully, calm down. While I didn't "break," by the end of December 1944, I was at wits end with the war. I wanted nothing more than to go home, return to work at the Bethlehem steel mills, marry Theresa, start a family, and put the war completely behind me. I wrote to Theresa constantly expressing exactly how I felt. But I couldn't go home just yet.

40.

STAYING WITH CIVILIANS

By about January 1st, 1945 the Filthy Thirteen and many of the other men in the 506th Regimental Headquarters Company had left their foxholes and begun staying in the homes of civilians in and around Bastogne. The weather was freezing cold while we were there. If we were only planning to remain in a place for a day or two, boarding in civilian homes was a much more appealing alternative to digging into frozen ground and spending nights shivering in an ice-cold foxhole.

Each section of Bastogne had a bürgermeister, who was the head official or leader of his part of the town. When we wanted to stay overnight in the homes of civilians we would check in with the local bürgermeister to help us locate homes to stay in, since he knew everyone and every home in the section. The bürgermeisters also knew that many of us paratroopers were looters and, when it came to the enemy, conquerors. What the bürgermeisters would sometimes do was deliberately send us to lodge with people that were either Kraut civilians living in Bastogne, Nazi sympathizers, or people that he otherwise hated.

There was no running water in the households of Bastogne because of the fighting. All the city pipelines had been shut off because of the battling and the bombings. What little water was available was used for drinking and cooking, not for cleaning or bathing. The citizens of Bastogne were dirty because they were unable to bathe.

Unlike the people of Holland, the Belgium people generally hated us. They wouldn't share any of their food, and they didn't want us staying with them or being around them. They didn't like us, and didn't want us there.

We didn't particularly care to be in Belgium either. There were all kinds of products and goods in Belgium that, when translated into English, had "Made in Germany" written on them. Each time we saw such items our blood boiled.

OUR DAILY EGGS

Although many of the people in the Bastogne area hated us, staying in a Belgium house was better than staying in a Belgium foxhole, especially during winter, and it was indeed cold in Belgium in December of 1944 and January of 1945. We always tried to get permission from the local bürgermeisters to stay in a house that had a barn on the property, because it would contain chickens and cows, from which we could get fresh eggs and milk.

One day, I think it was New Year's Eve, the 506th PIR's Headquarters Company was relocated from the perimeter lines to the city of Bastogne. The Filthy Thirteen had been given permission to stay in two houses in the city, and each had a barn. Six of us, including myself, went to one of the houses, and I sent the remaining half of the Filthy Thirteen to the other which was nearby.

I knocked on the front door of the house, and the most beautiful blonde-haired, blued-eyed woman I have ever seen answered the door. She spoke perfect English. I told her to let us come in because we were going to stay in her house for a few days. "You cannot stay here. Now go away!" she said back to me. I told her that we were there to save Belgium from the Germans. She replied "I am a pure-breed German from Berlin. I don't want to be 'saved' from the Germans, and I don't want any American soldiers in this house!"

Making that insulting comment to me and my men was a big mistake on her part. I asked her how many people lived in the house. She replied: "Five people live in this house, but only four are here right now. The owner is away. Now you must leave immediately." I said back to her: "Well, I'm the one holding the gun. That means I've got the final say as to what happens here. Now I'm telling you that all of us American soldiers are going to stay in this house for a while, whether you like it or not. That means you and the other people here will have to stay in the barn. That's where I want you to go."

She continued to protest, and I said, "I don't have any more time to discuss or argue with you about this. What I'm saying is the law, because I'm the one holding the gun! Now you and your buddies get the hell out of here, and get out of here right NOW or you'll be thrown out!" She and the others packed some things and went to the barn.

There was a chicken coup behind the house next to the barn, with about four dozen hens in it. I left a standing order with the woman that she was to give me and my men six chicken eggs every morning. That way each of us soldiers would get to eat one egg every day for breakfast. Each morning I'd go over to the barn and she'd give me six fresh eggs. We had been in the house for four days and we were being bombed every other night. But we got our six eggs every morning.

The morning of the fifth day I went to the barn to get our eggs. A man that I hadn't seen before came out and said to me: "No eggs. Birds nervous from bombing. Can't lay eggs. No eggs." He was the owner and he had come back the prior evening. I knew he was lying, because the hens had been laying eggs right along throughout the bombing for four days. I said to the owner, "Come with me." I walked over to the chicken coup and noticed that he had put a lock on it. I broke off the lock with the butt of my Thompson, opened the door and chased the hens out of the coup. There were about two dozen eggs in the hens' nests. I said to the owner, "It looks like you lied to me, dad. Now I'm going to take the six eggs that you were supposed to give us, plus six of your hens for lying to me."

One of my men knew how to twist a chicken's head so it would come right off in an instant. I don't know how the hell he did it, but he was quite good at it. I called him over to the coup and, in front of the owner, my man grabbed a hen and, in the blink of an eye, twisted its head off and handed the chicken's head to the owner. He did the same to five others. In addition to six eggs, we had six chickens without heads that were ready to be cleaned, cooked and eaten.

The owner was quite upset with what we had done. But he must have figured that from that point on he'd better come up with six eggs every morning, otherwise we'd kill six more chickens. The next morning I went to the barn and, sure enough, the owner came to the door with six eggs for me. He was more than happy to give them to me too. From then on we had no problem getting our six eggs each day that we stayed in the house.

NO TOILET, NO TOILET PAPER

A few days later I was staying in a different house just outside of Bastogne. It was a two-story house and I was staying on the second floor while an elderly woman lived on the first floor. The woman was covered with dirt from head to toe. She was as black as a mole. She hadn't been able to wash herself in a while because there was no running water.

The Krauts bombed Bastogne just about every other night. If we were bombed while we stayed in a civilian home we usually went into the cellar. The cellars of civilian homes were naturally dark to begin with, and especially at night during an air raid attack when all lights had to be turned off. My concern with this woman being so dirty was that if we had an air raid and we all had to go down into the cellar I wouldn't be able to see her. I might accidentally hurt her or she might hurt me if we bumped into one another. I didn't want to be near this woman if I had to seek shelter in the cellar for any reason. That's how dirty she was.

To prevent an accident, I took the old woman down into the cellar during broad daylight and showed her where I wanted her to stay and where I was going to stay if we had to go down there during an attack. She didn't give me any trouble and was okay with everything I asked her to do. We then went back upstairs, me to my second floor apartment.

I sat at a table in a room that faced the front of the house, and opened up some cans of rations and began to eat. I was looking outside while I was eating, and I saw the old lady walk out to the front of her home. As I was watching, she stopped walking, pulled up her dress, squatted and took a shit right in the front of her house in broad daylight. Her front yard was her toilet! Most of the outhouses in Bastogne were either bombed out or were overflowing with shit. You couldn't get near any of them, so many of the townspeople had to improvise when nature called.

The worst part was that after the old lady finished taking her crap, she started to wipe her ass with some hay out there that was used to put her barn animals' mess on. Seeing what she had done and was doing ruined my whole dinner, so I opened the window and yelled out to her to stop what she was doing. She continued wiping her ass with the hay. I then let go a burst of my Thompson submachine gun to let her know she had upset me. She immediately stopped what she was doing and ran into the house. I never saw her take a crap out there again.

41.

OH THOSE NINETY-DAY WONDERS!

February 8, 1945

Dear Theresa:

Last night I felt your prayers, because I was in a pretty bad spot at the time. I was just lying on a river bank when two enemy flares went up. I just laid still, but shaking because I thought for sure they would open up with machine gun fire right on us. There was an officer with me. I can't tell you why I was on the bank, but it had to be done and we did it."

Sgt. Jack Womer

On January 14th, 1945 the 506th PIR demolitions platoon was ordered to go with the 1st Battalion of the 506th and assist the regiment's 2nd Battalion in the taking of Noville from the Krauts. Noville, Foy, and many of the other small towns and villages around Bastogne had changed hands several times during the Battle of the Bulge. Noville had been retaken by the Krauts sometime after we had left our positions there on December 21st. It seemed ridiculous that we had to go back there and help retake it, but we did.

Afterward we thought we were going to be relieved from duty for a while to get a little rest, but instead we were sent nearly 200 miles south to Alsace, a region in the eastern portion of France located on the Rhine River, along the German border. We were being sent there because the Krauts had attacked, with some success, the American lines along a western portion of the Rhine. General Eisenhower was concerned that unless the American lines were reinforced the attack could escalate into another Bastogne-like battle. The 101st Airborne was given the honors of reinforcing the American lines in Alsace.

The truck ride back to France was just as horrible as the original ride to Belgium. The whole trip was made in freezing cold, snowy or rainy weather. The trucks were open and packed with soldiers, the roads were bumpy, and the ride was quite slow. We arrived in the Haguenau area of Alsace on January 20th, after about two days of riding in trucks, and were put into reserve along the Moder River.

Shortly after we arrived we were issued new clothing, and arrangements were made for us to take hot showers. We hadn't taken a shower or bathed our bodies or washed our clothes for nearly six weeks. We were filthy from head to toe. It felt so good to be able to take a hot shower and put on some nice clean clothing. I have never enjoyed a shower as much as the one I took when we arrived in Haguenau.

A NICE RUSSIAN FAMILY

For the first week I lived in a small farmhouse occupied by a Russian family. The family consisted of a married couple that had an older son and two little children. The older son was a soldier in the Russian army, and was away fighting the Krauts. They hadn't heard from the older son in over a year. I didn't say anything about it, but I feared the poor soul was dead. The family worked six days a week on a farm that was owned by a Frenchman, and was paid $12 per month plus they got to live in the farmhouse. They worked very hard, even the two children.

This Russian family was very good to me. They didn't have much, but what little they had they graciously shared. In return, I gave them whatever rations I was issued or could steal from our company supplies, as well as American cigarettes, which they really liked. The parents thought that I was strange because I was the only American soldier that they knew of that didn't smoke or drink alcohol. Several times I tried to explain why I didn't, but they could never understand.

The two children were just adorable. I felt so sorry for them, having to spend their childhood years in a war zone. Since the 506th PIR was in reserve I had free time on my hands, so I spent most of it playing with the children. They especially loved the ice cream that I made for them. When the owner of the farm wasn't around I'd go into the barn and get some fresh milk from one of the cows, and let it stand in a container to allow the cream to rise to the top. I removed the cream with a ladle and put it in a bowl. I'd stir in the sweetener that was packaged in my ration containers into the bowl, and bring the bowl outside and press it into the snow. I'd stir the mixture a bit, and after a while the coldness from the snow would cause the cream to harden into ice cream. The two kids loved it!

I stayed with this family for at least a week, until near the end of January, when I was issued a five-day pass to go on leave to Paris. It bothered me when it came time for me to say goodbye to the family. I knew I was going to miss them, and that I probably wouldn't see them again. The two children cried, and the parents were sad. I've often wondered whether they survived the war and, if so, how they had made out after it ended.

BACK TO THE FRONT LINE

I returned to Haguenau from my furlough on February 3rd. Shortly after I returned, the 506th PIR was ordered to the front lines in Haguenau to relieve portions of the 79th Infantry Division. The Filthy Thirteen, or rather what was left of us, were sent to a house that was one of an attached row that ran along a road and a canal that branched off of the Moder River. An embankment separated the road from the canal.

The rest of the 506th Headquarters Company's demolitions platoon stayed in houses adjacent to or near ours. Over on the other side of the canal, about 75 yards away from our row of houses, was the same set up with the exception that there were Krauts. That's how close we were to them. I could have hit them with a stone if I threw it hard enough.

We were sent to the frontline to support a company of other guys in the 506th PIR that were positioned in the same row of houses as ours. We had a 50-caliber machine gun set up in one of the upstairs windows that faced the Krauts. We were at a standstill with the Krauts. Neither side was fighting at the moment, but they were holding their side of the canal, while we were holding our side.

THE LEADERSHIP SHORTAGE

A big problem the army was having since D-Day was trying to keep up with the ever- increasing demand to replace the experienced, combat-hardened officers who were being knocked-off at a rapid rate. These experienced officers not only needed to be replaced, they needed to be replaced quickly. Combat-experienced sergeants were often promoted to back-fill the vacancies, but after Operation Market-Garden the supply of experienced sergeants couldn't keep up with the demand.

The army's solution to this problem was to pick men who were book smart and expressed interest in becoming officers, but who may or may not have had any combat experience. These men were rushed through officer training school, and sent to the front line and put in charge of men. Combat-hardened soldiers like me called this type of officer a "90-day wonder."

If I had to choose only one thing that I hated most about the war it would be having to take orders from 90-day wonders. Many of these guys thought they knew it all. But in reality, in combat situations most of them were too afraid to fight, and issued orders that made no sense and only served to get their own men killed and not the enemy.

If you weren't careful you could easily get killed following the orders of a 90-day wonder. A lot of our guys did get killed because of them, sad but true. We learned pretty quickly not to put too much faith in these types. Whenever 90-day wonders would talk the men would pretend to listen but they would usually follow their own instincts or look to their corporal or sergeant for advice and leadership.

A FOOLHARDY MISSION

On February 7th I damned near got killed because of a 90-day wonder in Haguenau. That afternoon, I was in the upstairs room of our row house where the 50-caliber machine gun was set-up. A 90-day wonder came over to me with a captain from the line company that we were supporting.

The green lieutenant said to me: "Sergeant, the captain wants to send a group of his men out on patrol near the canal, but he's worried about an area over there by the embankment that may be mined. Since you guys are demolition experts, he wants some of you to go out there and check for landmines before he sends his own men out. I want you to take some of your men and go out there and look for mines. If you find any, I want you to remove or deactivate them, or at least mark them off so others will know where not to step. When you're finished I want you to report back to the captain and then report back to me."

Being the only trained Ranger in the group, instinctively I began to evaluate the surroundings and weigh things in my mind. I peeked out the window, being careful not to get picked-off by a Kraut sniper, and looked out at the embankment area along the canal. It had been quite cold for a while, and the ground had been frozen solid for weeks. It had also snowed, but most of the snow had melted and the ground was now visible.

Land mines are supposed to be buried a few inches under the surface of the ground. When a person steps on a spot where a land mind is buried the mine explodes. The thought crossed my mind that if the Krauts had wanted to plant mines out there, they would have had a difficult time trying to bury them under the ground since it was frozen solid. They instead would have had to place them above ground, figuring that they would eventually become covered and hidden by snow.

Now that the snow was gone and we could see the ground, I concluded that there couldn't be any mines out there because I couldn't see them sitting on top of the ground. To me it was pretty obvious that there were no mines along that embankment, and sending men out there to look for mines with the Kraut lines so close by was downright foolhardy.

I explained all of this to the line company captain and the 90-day wonder second lieutenant. I told them that it was pretty much a given that there were no mines out there, and if anyone did go out there to look for mines there was a good chance they'd get killed because it was very close to the Krauts' position. The captain and lieutenant wouldn't listen to what I was saying. They still wanted me and some of my men to go out and check for mines.

The real truth was that the captain didn't want to send any of his own men out there because he didn't know whether the Krauts on the other side of the canal would see them and shoot at them. Knowing that the 90-wonder was naïve and gullible, the captain concocted the story about the possibility that mines could be out there, and convinced him that us demolition guys should go out there first. In short, the captain wanted to use me and my men as bait. He was thinking of the safety of his own men, but who was thinking about the safety of Jack Womer and Jack's men! I saw right through what the captain was trying to do, but the 90-day wonder didn't.

This is how war really is. It's not like how you see it in the movies or on television. Not only do you have to watch out for the enemy but you also have to watch out for the men on your own side. Officers will play games with the lives of men in other units to protect themselves and their own men from being killed. If you're not careful, they'll use you and gamble with your life as if you were a card in a poker game.

INTO THE VALLEY OF DEATH

I figured if the captain could play games with the half-assed 90-day wonder so could I. In front of the captain I said to him, "All right, I'll go out there with some of my men, but I think you should come along with us so you can get a firsthand look at how the Krauts are positioned over there on the other side of the canal while me and my guys search for mines. We'll go out once it gets dark." The 90-day wonder agreed.

We knew that the Krauts were positioned just a short distance away, directly across from us on the other side of the canal. We also knew that we had 50-caliber machine guns in the upstairs windows of our row houses that were pointed right at the Kraut positions directly opposite us. What we didn't know, but what we would soon find out, is that the Krauts had 88mm cannons set up downstream from us. The position of these 88s was such that they could shoot at an angle across the canal and along the road right into the area where we were heading to look for mines. Our machine guns were set-up so that they could only shoot straight across the canal, not up or down it, so they couldn't be used against the Krauts' 88mms.

When it got dark, me and two of my men, who were both new recruits, and the 90-day wonder exited our house through the back door. We made our way around to the front of the row houses near the road. We didn't bring our guns because we weren't going out there to fight. The only equipment we brought was our jump knives. There were trees growing along the road. I ordered my two men to go ahead and each to get behind a tree. I told the lieutenant to go ahead and get behind a third tree, and I got behind a fourth. I did this so I could keep an eye on them.

Our plan was to slowly and carefully sneak our way down the road by simultaneously moving from one tree to the next until we reached the area of the embankment where we had to check for mines. We would then head toward the canal on our hands and knees while using our jump knives to probe below the surface of the ground for mines. The ground had been frozen solid, but the melting of the snow over the last couple of days had softened it to the point where, with a little force, we could insert our jump knives into the soil.

We slowly made our way down the road, one tree at a time. But the Krauts must have seen us because all of a sudden 88mm cannon fire started coming in. The 88s must have been close because we could see the flashes from their muzzles as they were fired. The first few rounds went directly over our heads, but they soon began landing all around us. I thought I was going to have a stroke! We ran like hell back to the house from where we had come.

When we got inside I was furious. I threw my helmet against the wall and yelled at the 90-day wonder as if he were a piece of shit and an idiot, which he was. I wanted to shoot the son-of-a-bitch for making us go out there because we all almost got killed. It was a miracle that we hadn't been. A combat soldier doesn't get too many lucky breaks, and I knew that I was already way over my limit.

THE VALLEY OF DEATH REVISITED

After a while the 88mm rounds stopped coming in and I calmed down. The Commando instinct in me told me that we hadn't accomplished our mission to search for mines, and I wanted to go back out there and complete the mission. I know this was foolish of me, but I was determined to finish the job we had started. I went out the back door of the house and looked around for awhile behind the row houses. I removed a log that was blocking a door in an alleyway that led out to the road. I opened the door and noticed that I was standing very close to where we were originally going to look for mines. We didn't need to walk down the road like we had originally done. We could easily go behind the row houses and through that door to get to the area where we had to probe.

I went back into the house, and there was another lieutenant talking to the 90-day wonder that had almost got me killed. I said to the lieutenant, "If you still want me to go out there and check for mines, I'll finish the mission, but I don't want to go with him!" [Meaning the 90-day wonder who almost got me killed.] Thinking of the safety of my own two men, I said, "Lieutenant, we don't need these other two men for what we want to do. You and I can do it ourselves." The lieutenant said to me, "Okay sergeant, you and I will go out and complete the mission." The 90-day wonder lieutenant didn't say a word.

The lieutenant and I went out the back door of the house and took the short-cut I'd found to the area on the embankment where we needed to search for mines. It was pitch dark, and we were on our hands and knees probing the embankment, when all of a sudden the Krauts set off a flare that illuminated the whole area. The whole embankment lit up as if there were a night ball game taking place out there.

I immediately dove flat on the ground as did the lieutenant. The lieutenant was in front of me, and I could feel his boots touching my shoulders as we both laid flat on the ground. I was certain that the Krauts were about to open up on us with machine-gun fire, and our guys would fire back with our 50-calibers in our row houses. The lieutenant and I were about to be right in the middle of one hell of a gun fight, without any weapons of our own, and no place to hide. I felt for certain that I was going to get killed out on that embankment. I thought to myself, "Any second now I'm going to feel bullets hitting me and ripping me to shreds." I hugged the ground as closely as I could, prayed to God to spare me, and wished that I could crawl into my helmet and spend the rest of the war in it.

Surprisingly, not one shot was fired. Lying close to me, the lieutenant whispered, "As soon as that flare goes out, we're going to go right back to the house!" "Okay," I whispered. I wasn't about to argue with him. But as soon as the flare burned out and just as we were about to get up and get the hell out there, the Krauts fired another flare! We remained flat on the ground. I sensed that the lieutenant was about to panic, and I was afraid he was going to make a move or do something that would get us killed. I told him to remain still.

As we remained motionless on the ground, I wondered why the Krauts had not fired at us. They had fired two flares, but they were not firing their weapons. My Commando training told me to surmise what was going through the minds of the Krauts on the other side of the canal. The fact that they had set off two flares and weren't firing at us could only mean that they didn't see us. They must have concluded that no one was out on the embankment, otherwise they'd be shooting at us.

When the second flare went out the lieutenant whispered, "Let's go back to the house." I answered "No! We're going to stay out here and complete our mission, because I don't EVER want to come out here again!" The lieutenant didn't say a word. We both got back on our hands and knees and in the night darkness we probed the embankment for mines all the way to the canal. We didn't find any. We didn't find any mines because there were no mines to be found, as I had originally predicted. We walked back to the house. Mission accomplished.

When we got back I found the line company captain who originally gave the order to search for mines. I said to him: "Sir, there are no mines out there along the embankment. You can send your men out there on patrol." He said back to me: "It's too dangerous to send anyone out there." When he said that I knew for certain I had accomplished the REAL mission. The captain didn't want to know if there were any mines out there, what he really wanted to know is whether the Krauts would shoot at any G.I.s near the canal, and what kind of weaponry they had on hand to protect their side. What he needed was some bait to find out, and Jack Womer was the bait!

42.

TO THE FATHERLAND!

April 4, 1945

Dear Mom and Dad:

We just broke into a safe, and got over $200 each.

I have a lot of fun breaking anything of any use around here in Germany. Not much left of Germany. We've been ordered not to talk to or have anything to do with the Germans.

Your son, Jack

Toward the end of February 1945 the 101st Airborne Division was pulled out of Alsace, and sent west to Mourmelon le Petit, a small French town near Reims, for rest and relaxation. We made the 200-mile trip by railroad, in boxcars. The devastation France had sustained during the war was quite apparent from this trip. Sitting in the boxcars as the train rolled along the French countryside to Mourmelon it was sadly obvious that the towns and villages we passed through or near had been affected by the war. Some had been completely destroyed. Others showed only minor damage. Most were somewhere in-between.

The damage to these towns and villages had left many French citizens homeless. People stood along the railroad tracks, filthy dirty and wearing rags for clothes. As our train rolled by they stretched their arms toward us and begged us to throw them some food. Seeing them half-starved and homeless, we couldn't help but feel sorry for them, especially the children. Many of us tossed our K-rations to them.

When we settled in Mourmelon le Petit things got better for us. The days were gradually getting warmer, birds were singing, the trees were getting buds on them. Life was resuming all around us. After having spent nearly five of the previous six months on the front lines in combat zones in the midst of death and destruction, listening to birds singing instead of rifles firing, and seeing things grow instead of die was a welcome relief. The winter was finally coming to an end, thank God! I wondered if the nice weather and pleasant surroundings was a sign that the war too was coming to an end.

We had a lot of time on our hands while we were there. We received some new recruits, most of whom had just come over from the United States and hadn't seen a lick of action. They were quite young and anxious to get into combat. Some of them were worried that the war would end before they had a chance to fight. They asked us older guys what it was like on D-Day, and at the battles of Holland and Bastogne. They told us how they wished they could have been with us at these battles. We told them our experiences, and how lucky they were that they had NOT been with us.

Our superior officers made us do a lot of exercising and drilling, despite the fact that we were sent to Mourmelon le Petit to rest and relax. This was done to help the new recruits get to know us older guys better, and to keep us all in good shape in case we were needed to go back into action. We trained hard just about every day. In the evenings many of the guys went to a local pub and got drunk.

I never drank alcohol, but whenever I got an evening pass I went out to the nightclubs in Reims, which was close by. On one occasion I met Mickey Rooney, the actor, in a nightclub. He had performed that evening in the club, and afterward some of us got the chance to meet him. He autographed a 500-Franc note for me, but he signed it "John Rooney."

The same day that I met Mickey Rooney the headlines of the *Stars and Stripes* announced that the city of Cologne, Germany, was under control of the Allied forces. Cologne is in the Rhine-Ruhr region of Germany. It was a major industrial city during the war, and the Krauts manufactured a lot of their war materials there. That fact that Cologne fell meant that the Allies were taking control of Germany's industrial heartland, and was a clear sign that the war in Europe was going to end soon. It was very good news.

About a week or so later, in mid-March, the entire 101st Airborne Division received a Presidential Citation for the defense of Bastogne. Allied Supreme Commander Dwight Eisenhower came to Mourmelon le Petit to personally express his gratitude to us and present the award. The weather was getting nicer by the minute, and just about every day we heard news that indicated the war in Europe was going to end soon. Everyone except the new recruits was excited.

DUSSELDORF, GERMANY

The 101st Airborne stayed in Mourmelon le Petit until early April. The division was then sent north by truck to Germany, to an area along the Rhine near Dusseldorf, about 25 miles northwest of Cologne. We were sent there to reinforce the positions in the Ruhr region that the Allied forces now controlled, to help prevent any Kraut counterattacks.

I hadn't stepped foot on German soil since October 1944, when the 101st Airborne was in Holland. Even then I was literally just a few feet into Germany, just over the Dutch border. We were now finally in Germany, the enemy's country, the "Fatherland" as the Krauts called it, to take it from them.

General Eisenhower told us before we went into France and Holland that we were being sent in as liberators. That meant we were sent in to chase the Krauts out and return control of each country to its rightful people. When we received orders to go into Germany, Eisenhower told us that we were being sent in as conquerors. That meant that Germany and anything in it belonged to us and was ours for the taking. You probably won't read the above in any history books on Eisenhower, or see an official memo signed by him that states it as such. But he did tell us this.

By the time we arrived in Dusseldorf the city had been pretty much destroyed by Allied bombers. The same was true for many cities in Germany's Ruhr region. There wasn't much left of them. We were prepared to fight, but we didn't do much. Occasionally we'd mix it up with the Krauts in some minor skirmishing, but nothing much. By this time a lot of German soldiers had either surrendered or were about to.

We restricted the movement of the German people. We kept them off the streets and made them stay in their houses most of the time. We were ordered not to talk to any of the Germans or have anything to do with them unless it was for official business. They hated us, and we hated them, but we talked with one another nonetheless. Most of them were convinced that the war would be over before the end of April.

I spent a lot of time sitting in church steeples looking out over the Rhine-Ruhr region for any signs of enemy movement. The German people were quite religious. Most of them were Catholic, and there were a lot of churches. A church steeple is an ideal spot as an observation post. You can see for miles in each direction. I seldom saw anything suspicious on the part of the enemy, but I did see a lot of destruction. I saw thousands of German soldiers that had surrendered and were marching along roads. I saw a defeated Germany.

When I wasn't looking for the enemy, I, like many of my fellow Screaming Eagles, spent a lot of time destroying things and looting. We were filled with a lot of rage toward Germany for having started the war and being responsible for the deaths and suffering of a lot of innocent people. It was now our chance to get even. So we purposely went out of our way to destroy anything that we came across that was of any use or had any meaning to the German people, and take for ourselves anything we wanted and could carry in our pockets.

Since the Filthy Thirteen were demolition experts, we had access to a lot of explosives. If we wanted to destroy something we'd blow it up. We blew up cars, buses, buildings, sewer lines, monuments of famous German people, and a lot of other things. One night we blew up a safe that contained money. Shortly after we arrived in Dusseldorf, some of us guys in the Filthy Thirteen went into a hotel that had been destroyed by bombing and searched the basement for Kraut soldiers that may have been hiding out. We didn't find any Krauts, but we found a safe hidden behind some shelves. We blew open the safe and discovered that it was loaded with Deutsche Marks, or German money. We divided it up among ourselves and each of us got the equivalent of about 200 U.S. dollars.

But looting and destroying things gets boring real fast. In mid-April I received word from Theresa that two close buddies of mine, John Polyniak and Willard Sparks, were home, in the United States. I grew up with Willard. We were childhood friends, and we were drafted on the same day. We trained together in the 29th Infantry Division. John Polyniak lived just outside of Dundalk, in Baltimore. He and I became Rangers together. Both

Willard and John had been seriously wounded, and were sent home a little earlier than most guys. When I heard they were already home, there was nothing in the world I wanted more than to go home also. To hell with the German loot! I wanted to go home!

On April 12th, 1945 President Franklin D. Roosevelt died. The news was quite shocking and sad. While many of us soldiers didn't care for Roosevelt for sending us off to war, we became quite upset when we heard news that he had passed away. I never liked him, but I respected him. He gave us the best food and the best equipment. I felt especially sorry that we were just weeks, perhaps days, away from winning the war, and he hadn't lived to see it.

43.

LIVING WITH THE ENEMY

hile we were in Dusseldorf we usually stayed in the homes of German civilians instead of sleeping in damaged buildings or outside in tents or foxholes. We'd stay in a home for a few days or a week, until we received orders to go to another area in or near the city, and then we'd stay in another home. We would usually ask the local bürgermeister for homes where we could stay, other times we would find homes on our own and just move in.

GUESTS OF A KRAUT SYMPATHIZER

On one occasion a bürgermeister told us of a three-story house in Dusseldorf that was large enough to accommodate all of the Filthy Thirteen for a few days. He gave us directions to the house and we started walking to it. I took the point as we walked down a street to get to the house. No one but us was out there. The street was lined with houses on each side. As we were walking I noticed someone inside one of the houses hiding behind some curtains, peeking out at us through a window. When the person in the house realized I had spotted him, he quickly ducked behind the curtains. I ordered everyone to stop walking.

An important lesson I had learned during war is to never trust anyone. I don't care who the person is, or what title he has, my advice is not to trust him or her. One of my new recruits came up to me and asked: "What's wrong, Sarge?" "There is someone in that house over there, hiding behind some curtains, spying on us. I feel uneasy about it" I replied. "What are we going to do?" the recruit asked. I said: "We're going to check out that God damn house real carefully, because I don't like what I just saw."

We walked up to the house and knocked on the front door. A man answered. I looked closely at his face and stared into his eyes. He was scared to death. I figured he was scared because there was something in his house that he didn't want us to see. I told him we wanted to come in and look around. He acted as if he didn't understand English, and just stood in the doorway.

When you're in a combat zone in a foreign land dealing with local civilians who can't speak English, you don't need to be able to speak their language in order to communicate effectively so long as you've got a gun in your hands. I positioned the muzzle of my rifle against the man's chest and motioned with my head for him to step aside and get out my way, which he immediately did. We entered the house and I ordered one of my men to stay with the man while the rest of us searched every inch of the house.

The house was well maintained. There were big rooms and nice furniture throughout. It had a large kitchen and stove, and was well stocked with food. We searched the house, and upstairs we found bunk beds where we could tell Kraut soldiers had stayed. We found a stash of Kraut weapons, equipment, and all sorts of stuff that Krauts used, hidden behind fake walls in some of the upstairs rooms. Judging from what we found, it appeared that Kraut soldiers regularly stayed in the house.

It was obvious that the owner, the man who answered the door when we knocked, was a Kraut-sympathizer and had helped the Kraut soldiers. He knew that we now knew he had helped the Krauts, which is why he was so nervous about us being in his home. He had good reason to be nervous. His being a sympathizer and providing assistance to Kraut soldiers meant we could have treated him as if he were an enemy soldier. We could have taken him as a prisoner and sent him off to a POW camp.

His being a Kraut-sympathizer also gave us a good excuse to take over his house and confiscate anything we found in it, eat all of his food and destroy the house when we were done using it. This is exactly what we did, and there was absolutely nothing he could do about it. If he tried to stop us we could have and would have shot him. Everything worked out well for us. We had comfortable bunks to sleep in and plenty of food to eat. When it was time to leave we took any remaining food and anything of his of value that we could carry, and wrecked the interior of his house.

GUESTS OF THE PARENTS OF SS OFFICERS

On another occasion while we were in Dusseldorf my entire demolitions platoon, about forty men, needed lodging for a few a days. The local bürgermeister sent us to a two-story house. I knocked on the front door and an elderly man and woman answered.

I could tell immediately that this couple was well to do. They were both very well dressed and their house was luxurious.

The rooms were large, and fitted with elegant moldings along the ceilings, windows, doorways and floors. The house had a large living room that contained a beautiful grand piano. Each window had custom-made drapes made out of fine material. There was beautiful furniture and carpeting all over the house. Upstairs were three large bedrooms, and each one had its own bathroom, which in those days was quite unusual. The place was magnificent.

What caught my eye the most was that in just about every room of their home were beautifully framed photos of SS officers. The officers in the photos were the sons of the elderly couple. Once we saw the photos we wanted to destroy the house and everything in it. From our point of view, those SS officer sons of the elderly couple were somewhere killing American G.I.s. In situations like this a soldier becomes filled with anger.

We wanted the elderly couple to never forget that they once had Screaming Eagles as "guests" in their home. So we made them watch as we went into each room of their house and took every framed photo of their sons off the walls, throw them onto the floor, and stomp on them until they were completely destroyed.

About half of us soldiers could sleep comfortably upstairs in the house, and the other half could sleep comfortably downstairs. Being a sergeant, I could have slept on a nice comfortable mattress in one of the upstairs bedrooms, but I chose to sleep on the floor in the living room, underneath the grand piano. The rest of the guys thought I was nuts, but the war wasn't over yet and there was always a chance of a Kraut artillery attack. I figured if the Krauts began firing artillery at us during the night while we were sleeping I'd be a lot safer underneath the grand piano than being upstairs. I threw my equipment underneath the piano, and tore down all the long window curtains, folded them into a makeshift mattress and placed it underneath the piano.

After night had set in and just as I was about to crawl underneath the grand piano and sleep, the old man started to speak to me in German. I couldn't understand a word he said. There was a Jewish paratrooper in our platoon who spoke German. I asked the paratrooper to find out what the old man was saying to me. The Jewish paratrooper said: "He wants to know where he is going to sleep, now that you've put your soldiers in all of the bedrooms." I said to the paratrooper: "You tell that son-of-a-bitch that he and is wife can go sleep in the God damn cellar!" The paratrooper told the man and his wife to go to the cellar, and they did.

I was sleeping underneath the grand piano, and at about midnight I heard a knock on the other side of the cellar door. None of the other guys in the platoon bothered to get up and answer it. So I, being the sergeant, got up and answered it. It was the old man. "What's the problem?" I asked him. "Wasser" he said back to me. He wanted a drink of water. "What the hell do you think I am, a God damn waiter? Get back down in that cellar!" I yelled. The old guy just stood there and demanded that I get him "wasser." He wouldn't move. I said to him: "Do you understand 'kaput'? That means death!" "Ya" the old man replied. I said back to him: "Then get the hell back down in that cellar, NOW, or you'll be kaput!" He went back down.

The following day we prepared to move out, but before we parted from the elderly couple we looted their whole house, broke all of the furniture, and smashed every window. We left nothing intact. I know our behavior seems terrible, but you have to keep in mind the tempo of the situation. Looking at the elderly couple, knowing that they were the parents of Kraut SS officers who were killing American soldiers upset us.

THE HOUSE WITH THREE PANTRY CLOSETS

On another occasion the local bürgermeister sent us to another three-story apartment building. The guy that owned it lived on the first floor, and he rented out the apartments on the other two floors. The bürgermeister told us that the owner had helped the Krauts quite a bit, which was music to our ears because now we had a good excuse to take anything of his that was worth taking.

We went to the house and, being gentlemen, we knocked on his door rather than just walk in. The owner opened the door and then we walked in. Since he was a Kraut sympathizer, automatically that meant whatever was in his house was now ours. We immediately began looting the place while he just stood in his foyer, in disbelief. This guy had a lot of good stuff. He had money out on the table, and we took it. He had jewelry in his bedroom and we took it.

There was a side wall off his kitchen. I noticed that there were three rather large pantry closets along the wall. The pantry closets were labeled A, B and C, and each pantry closet door had a lock on it. With the help of the paratrooper in our platoon who was fluent in German, I asked the owner of the house what the pantry closets were all about. Pantry closet labeled A was the closet for the owner, who lived on the first floor. Pantry closet B was the closet that belonged to the occupants, a family, on the second floor, and pantry closet C belonged to the occupant, an old lady who lived by herself, on the third floor.

I didn't like to see locks on doors when I'm a "guest" in the home of a Kraut sympathizer. I tore off the lock of pantry closet C. I opened it up and there was absolutely nothing in it. I broke into pantry closet B and it too was completely empty. I broke into pantry closet A, which belonged to the owner, and as soon as I opened the door goodies started flying right out of the closet. The owner had it packed with eggs, bread, jellies, smoked meats, jarred fruits and vegetables, chocolate—he had everything in there. It was loaded.

The owner then made the mistake of grabbing a loaf of pumpernickel bread from pantry closet A and handing it to me for all of us to eat, as if to say to me, "I'm a nice guy and I'll give you and your men a loaf of bread, and I'll keep the rest of the food." What he didn't realize was that was what HE was going to keep, and that we were going to take the rest.

After we ate his food I looked around for a place to sleep. The other men had already taken most of the good spots. I went upstairs to the second floor and there was a family living up there. One of them was a girl about 14 years old who spoke perfect English. She was very polite and well mannered, and was happy to see us. The girl and her parents were half-starved. It was obvious they hadn't had a good meal in a long time. They seemed like nice people, so I gave them a bunch of the food from the owner's pantry and left them alone.

I went up to the third floor and knocked on the apartment door. An elderly woman opened the door just a crack, and just peeked out at me. I told her to come out, but she wouldn't budge. I pushed the door open and walked into her apartment. "Raus!" (Out!) the old battle ax shouted at me. This old lady was 100% Kraut. She had the map of Germany on her face. She looked as if she could have been Hitler's mother. I paid no attention to her order for me to get out of her apartment. I looked around, and I noticed she had a cot and a bed. I needed something comfortable to sleep on and, since she can't sleep on both of them, I figured I would take the cot, carry it downstairs, and sleep on it.

I grabbed the cot and started carrying it out the door. The old battle ax screamed at me in German. I called the paratrooper who spoke fluent German to come up to the third floor. He came upstairs and I said: "Ask her what her problem is." He asked her in German, she said something in German back to him, and he said to me: "Well, she said she needs both her cot and her bed." I said: "Well you tell her that she knows God damn well that she doesn't need both of them. Tell her she needs to make up her mind NOW as to which one she wants to sleep on, because if she doesn't I'm going to take both of them and then she'll have nothing!" He told her, and she said take the cot.

I carried the cot down to the first floor and slept on it for the two nights we stayed in the house. On the third day we packed our gear and equipment in preparation to move out. As I carried two boxes of machine gun ammunition out of the house, one case under each arm, the old lady happened to be walking by with her dog. She saw me with the ammunition and, realizing I couldn't use my hands or run away, she ordered her dog to attack me, to get back at me for taking her cot.

The dog barked, growled and repeatedly bit my feet. But it was hard for me to do anything about it because my hands were full. I was wearing my paratrooper boots, so I kicked the dog as hard as I could, and after being kicked a couple of times he ran away yelping. I looked over at the old lady with a mean look as if to say: "Lucky for you and that dog that my hands were full, as I would have killed both of you if I hadn't been carrying anything." I know this may seem like a terrible way to treat a lady, but try to understand that when you've been in war for a while and you get into these types of situations you develop a short fuse. You really do.

44.

THE WAR IN EUROPE IS OVER!

May 8, 1945

Dear Jack:

Well the day we've been waiting for has come at last! . . . . We just heard the news that the war in Europe is officially over! . . . . I've waited and waited for this day to come, and often tried to imagine what I'd do. When it finally came I didn't do a thing! I still can hardly believe it. . . . .

The people here are unbelievably happy. Most of them are going to church and listening to the radio. My mother and I went to church downtown and it was so crowded that we could hardly get in the door. We cried so much that my eyes feel as tho' they have a lot of sand in them.

You know, I've been making a Rosary Crusade- that's 54 Rosaries in 54 days succession. Well today is the 54th day and it's the most gratifying thing I've ever done. Of course it may be a coincidence, but it makes me feel good.

I stop every once in a while to pinch myself, I still feel like I'm dreaming."

Always,
Theresa

At the end of April 1945 we received orders to go down to Berchtesgaden, a town in the German Bavarian Alps in the southwestern portion of Bavaria very close to the German-Austrian border. Adolf Hitler had an estate there, the Berghof, which he used as both a residence and headquarters for the Third Reich. Hitler's Berchtesgaden estate included his Kehlsteinhaus (Eagle's Nest), which was his mountain retreat where he entertained guests. A lot of Nazi generals had homes in Berchtesgaden.

Needless to say, a lot of Kraut soldiers, including a major SS presence, had been stationed in Berchtesgaden throughout the war to protect the area. We were sent there to protect against any attempt by Hitler and his remaining armies to retreat to Berchtesgaden and launch a last-ditch counterattack against the Allied forces. In addition to American soldiers, some French troops were sent there as well.

In the latter part of April we boarded a train in Dusseldorf and began our journey to Berchtesgaden by rail. Portions of most of the railroads in Germany had been damaged by Allied bombing, and were in need of repair or replacement. The Allied soldiers dealt with the problem by making German prisoners repair damaged track and lay new ones. As we made our way towards Berchtesgaden we frequently saw groups of German prisoners of war repairing damaged tracks.

At one point on our journey our train had to stop because there was track ahead of us that was badly damaged and was being replaced by German prisoners. While we waited for them to complete their work we were allowed to get off the train and walk around and stretch our legs. There was another set of tracks about ten yards away that ran alongside ours. After a while a train of box cars similar to ours and traveling in the same direction pulled up on the tracks next to us and stopped. I looked over at it and to my surprise the box cars on the train were loaded with black males. Up to this time we had never seen black people while we were on or near the front lines because at the time they were considered unfit for combat and weren't allowed in a combat area. In fact, we had hardly ever seen a black person in Europe. We were completely surprised to see blacks heading closer to the front lines with us.

I walked over to the train and I noticed that many of the blacks were playing cards. They were quite black. I could see that they weren't from the United States, because they had carved their faces and were wearing wire ring jewelry around their necks, in their noses and in their ears. They looked like they had just come from a jungle.

There were French guards over on the train. "Where are you taking these Negroes? Are you taking them into action?" I asked. A French guard replied: "No. No…we're not taking them into action. But we will eventually take them into France. These are French Moroccan blacks. They're from Africa. Notice the bolo knives they're carrying on their legs. You combat guys have captured thousands and thousands of German soldiers as prisoners. We're going to take a lot of the German prisoners off your hands, and bring them to France and make them do manual labor for us. We don't have enough guards to keep watch over the German prisoners, so we're going to have these Negroes help us keep an eye on them. We're going to tell the prisoners that if they don't do as they are told, or if they try to escape or fight back, these Negroes have orders to cut their heads off using bolo knives."

The French guard was quite serious about it. I hadn't been aware that French Moroccan Negroes were being used to guard German prisoners. The real surprise was to observe how frightened the German prisoners were of them. The captured Krauts were petrified of the French Moroccan Negroes, in fear that they may lose their heads to one of them in the blink of an eye and for the slightest reason.

BERCHTESGADEN

In the first week of May we arrived in Berchtesgaden. From this point on army life for us began to get quite easy and, to some extent, enjoyable. We were sent to Berchtesgaden to protect against any last-ditch Nazi stand, but none of that would happen. By the time we arrived in Berchtesgaden the newspapers were saying that Hitler was dead and that the war in Europe would be over in a week.

The first thing one notices when arriving in Berchtesgaden is how naturally beautiful it is. The snow-capped Bavarian Alps and landscape that surround it is absolutely breathtaking. I could see why Hitler had set up residence and retreat estates there. The weather was warm, but it snowed quite a bit in Berchtesgaden in May 1945. The snow quickly melted and, overall, the weather was quite nice. That's how it is in the Bavarian Alps in May.

The 506th's Demolitions Platoon was assigned to stay in a very lovely hotel in Berchtesgaden. I and another sergeant shared a honeymoon suite which had very nice rooms. We slept in beds that were quite large and very, very comfortable. Up until then we had been moving around quite a bit, so it was nice to settle down for awhile in a luxury hotel.

With the war about to end at anytime, we figured we'd better get while the getting was good. We looted the whole town, especially the homes that had belonged to Kraut officers. We broke just about everything that was of any use to the German people, and stole anything that was of value. I stole a lot of very lovely jewelry for Theresa. I stole a lot of men's rings and a solid gold pocket watch for myself. We had a free-for-all in Berchtesgaden.

THE KRAUTS SURRENDER

Prior to our arrival in Bavaria we had been hearing for months from the German citizens as well as from our own military people that the war in Europe would soon end. From what we read in the *Stars and Stripes* and saw happening around us, these rumors appeared to have merit. The Allied forces had entered Germany and were taking control of its cities. German soldiers were surrendering by the tens of thousands. Hitler was reportedly dead. It seemed to be just a matter of days, perhaps hours, before the German military, or what was left of it, would surrender.

On May 7th, 1945 we received word that the war in Europe was officially over. I was eating in a restaurant in Berchtesgaden when I heard the news. Even though we were expecting the news, we were still a little stunned by it. So the war was finally over! When I heard the news I felt a little nervous and couldn't finish my meal. I got up and walked outside. Out in the streets of Berchtesgaden there were lots of French soldiers cheering and singing. Most of us older, war-hardened American soldiers didn't say much or express much emotion. After having served in the military for several years, we learned that most war news was rumor. We were still skeptical, and didn't believe that the war in Europe was, in fact, finally over.

After a while the good news was confirmed, and we became quite happy. But the news made us wonder what would happen to us. Yes, the fighting in Europe was over, but the war wasn't over. The Allied forces were still fighting the Japanese in the Pacific. Were our military commanders going to send us home? Or would they send us to Japan to fight on the Pacific front? In the military anything is possible. We wouldn't find out for weeks whether we would be sent home or to the Pacific to fight the Japanese.

In March, 1945 Theresa had initiated what is known in the Catholic faith as a 54-day Rosary Novena at her church, St. Patrick's Catholic Church in Baltimore. The Rosary is a series of set prayers said in sequence using a set of beads as a guide, followed by meditation. The purpose of Theresa's 54-day Rosary crusade was to petition God to bring an end to the war in Europe. Theresa and other people in her church committed to saying 54 rosaries in 54 days succession at St. Patrick's Church. May 8th, 1945 was the 54th and last day of the Rosary crusade, and on that very day she and the rest of the people in the United States received the news that that war in Europe was officially over. Theresa was a devout Catholic. I'm convinced that the last day of her end-to-war rosary crusade being the same day the people in the United States heard the news that the war in Europe had ended was more than coincidence.

45.

THE LAST PATROL

Even though the war in Europe was over, the fighting between us and the Krauts lingered on a bit. Throughout the Alps around Berchtesgaden and other areas in Germany there were tucked away pockets of German soldiers that either hadn't received the news, or had received it but chose to continue to fight. We received reports of small groups of Krauts ambushing Allied soldiers in some of the areas that surrounded Berchtesgaden.

The day after the war in Europe ended the Filthy Thirteen and some other men from our demolitions platoon were ordered to go on a patrol in the Alps to look for Krauts that might still be hiding out. We headed out from Berchtesgaden on a road that led to the mountains. There were hundreds of German prisoners all along the way, sitting on either side of the road. I walked behind a couple of G.I.s that were carrying a 30-caliber machine gun, and I was carrying two containers filled with ammunition. Our lieutenant was walking a little ahead of me, carrying nothing but a 45-caliber pistol and an M-1 carbine. After a while the two containers of ammunition I was carrying became heavier and heavier, so I ordered two young Kraut prisoners on the side of the road to carry the ammunition for me. I told them I would shoot them if they made any false moves.

After we walked a few miles the road led us into a ravine with mountains all around us. The road weaved in and out along the mountains and there were no longer any Kraut prisoners lining the road, just us. All of a sudden a quad 20mm gun opened up on us. The 20mm was situated on one of the mountains ahead of us, and was shooting down on us. All of us instantly dove for cover along the side of the road. I don't think any of us got hit, but it was a real close call. So much for the war in Europe being over!

We were safe where we were, hiding along the road. But we couldn't move any further forward, and we couldn't go back without getting cut to pieces by the 20mm gun. The Krauts had us pinned down. When they realized they couldn't shoot us with the 20mm while we were hiding, they started firing mortar rounds at us. As the mortar rounds on the mountainsides exploded, rocks began to fall on us. We knew we couldn't remain there much longer without being wounded or killed, but we couldn't get up and run back either without getting mowed down. We were stuck.

We had a mortar with us, but we couldn't use it against the 20mm gun because we weren't sure of its location. It was positioned in the mountain range in such a way that we couldn't see exactly where it was. We only knew about where it was. We were in a jam. There was a rocky hill that was right next to us, rising to about 250 feet. Compared to the other mountains in the area it was small, but it was steep. Its slope must have had an angle of elevation of at least 70 degrees from the base of the road where we were hiding. Some sections of the hill went straight up, close to 90 degrees.

Our lieutenant shouted: "Someone needs to get to the top of the hill next to us, to pinpoint the location of the Krauts so we can knock them out with our mortar. Do any of you think you can climb to the top of the hill?" A few guys volunteered and tried to climb the hill, but they couldn't make it to the top.

The lieutenant was getting frustrated that no one could climb the hill. I had done a lot of cliff and mountain climbing in February 1943, when I trained to become an army Ranger at the British Commando Depot. I knew I could get up there. I shouted back: "Lieutenant, I can climb it." There was another sergeant with us who told the lieutenant that he too could climb the hill. The lieutenant shouted back to us: "Both of you take binoculars and get up to the top of that hill as fast as you can and let us know where the hell that 20mm gun is hiding. We'll knock it out with our mortar."

I slung my Thompson submachine gun over my back, the other sergeant grabbed a pair of binoculars, and we started to scale the hill together.

We had no idea whether there were other Krauts hiding in the other hills and mountains that were near us. If there were, there was a good chance they'd spot us and shoot us. I was quite worried about that. There was a narrow stream that ran down the side of the hill. Naturally, there was more vegetation growing along the stream. I chose to scale the hill along the stream. I figured the vegetation would provide us with some cover from the Krauts, and something to cling to as we climbed.

The other sergeant was right behind me as we started our climb. After I had gone about 20 yards or so, I looked behind me and I saw the other sergeant struggling to make his way up. He had only climbed about 5 yards. I knew he wasn't going to make it to the top. I crawled back down to him, grabbed the binoculars, and continued climbing. As I climbed the Krauts continued firing mortar rounds at our position near the base of the hill.

After a while my arms got tired. My Thompson submachine gun was starting to get quite heavy and too cumbersome to carry along with the binoculars. I left my Thompson on the mountainside, figuring I'd get it on the way down. I continued to climb up the hill. Every few minutes I'd turn to look back at the man who had started the climb with me. He appeared smaller and smaller all the time because he wasn't moving at all. When I was about two-thirds of the way up I took my helmet off because I was getting more tired and I wanted to reduce more weight.

I made it to the top of the hill, exhausted from the climb, without my Tommy gun or helmet. I had no idea what I would find on the top of that hill. I was scared to death that Krauts were up there. If there were, I'd be in a lot of trouble, because the only things I had to fight with were two grenades, a 45-caliber pistol, my trench knife, and my bare hands. I crawled around and, fortunately for me, there was no one else up there.

I crawled to the edge of the hill that was in the general direction of the 20mm gun and, using my binoculars, I looked around at the neighboring hills and mountains and surrounding terrain. I had a birds-eye view of the whole area. I looked specifically for the position of the 20mm gun, as well as any other Kraut positions. I spotted the 20mm right away. It was situated on a mountainside, about 200 yards from our position, exactly at the spot where the road we had been walking on intersected with another road. I counted twelve Krauts, and I could see them firing mortar rounds on our position near the base of the hill I had climbed.

My lieutenant had a map of the area. Using hand signals, I signaled down to the sergeant who had started to climb with me the position of the 20mm gun and mortar, and the number of the Krauts positioned around them. He ran over to our lieutenant and showed him on his map the exact position of the Krauts that I had signaled to him. The lieutenant told our mortar crew where to direct our fire. The first mortar round we fired over-shot the Kraut position by about 30 yards. I signaled down for them to reduce their firing distance by 30 yards. The second mortar round we fired was a direct hit on the Kraut position. I then signaled down for them to continue firing, and to fire for effect.

We fired four more mortar rounds at the Krauts and destroyed their position. I signaled to cease fire, and I climbed down the hill and picked up my helmet and Thompson along the way. While coming down the mountain I almost fell off. If I had fallen I would have landed on solid rock and been killed. I thought to myself, here it is, a day after the war in Europe has ended, and after all the combat I survived during D-Day, Operation Market-Garden, and the Battle of the Bulge, I'm going to get killed by falling off a hill!

We walked over to the Kraut 20mm gun. From our mortar fire, we had killed eight of the twelve Krauts that were there. The others had run away into the woods. W never found them, and they never gave us any more trouble. We blew up the 20mm gun with explosives, and destroyed the mortar. This would be the last time I engaged in combat, and it turned out to be the last patrol of the Filthy Thirteen as a unit.

46.

GOING HOME!

February 16, 1945

Theresa:

During the time I've been overseas, I have [had] many, many friends who are not here now, so the less talk about the past two years the better off it will be with me.

Theresa, you don't quite understand what I have seen over here, but when I come home you will soon learn, I will see that you do.

I will need you more than ever when I come home. You, to me, are the only person I will trust and tell all of my troubles to. I have changed a great deal, but I feel sure you know this by the way my letters come to you.

Jack

A few days after we got the news the war was over the 101st Airborne Division's 506th Parachute Infantry Regiment was sent to Austria. The 506th Demolitions Platoon and other components of the 506th PIR were initially stationed in Wittendorf, a little town way up in the mountains of the Bavarian Alps. After about a week or so we relocated to Saalbach, another mountain town. We had been sent to Austria to keep an eye on the German people. We weren't supposed to talk with Germans unless it was for official business. But we talked to them anyway—what difference would it make, the war was over.

I asked a lot of the local people why they supported Hitler in his attempt to take over the world, and his declaration of war on the United States. I figured I had a right to know, and I wanted to hear the reasons directly from them. They all had the same answer. They would say that they were misled, or that they really liked us and never wanted to fight us, but were forced to do the things they did. They were lying. The truth is they hated our guts.

GERMAN PEOPLE AND BABY FACTORIES

The German people were no good. Many of them believed that Hitler was God. Whenever the Germans were rude or uncooperative with us, we would tell them that unless they start treating us nicely, we would leave and let the Russians take over. When they heard that they changed immediately. Boy, were they afraid of the Russians! They had good reason to be afraid. The Russians wanted to get back at Germany because of what the Krauts had done during their advance into Russia earlier in the war.

Even though I had been fighting the Krauts for years, it wasn't until I was in Austria that I became aware of the extremes that Hitler had resorted to in building his armies and his intent to take over the world. The German boys between 12 and 16 years of age, unlike the German adults, were quite honest with us, and were happy to talk. They were proud to explain to us why, in their opinion, the German people were indeed the master race and superior to everyone else. They were proud to say that they believed in Hitler, and that Germany had a right to conquer the world. They made no bones about telling us these things, as this is how they truly felt. We respected them for their honesty.

The boys had been indoctrinated by Hitler. Prior to, and during the war, when a German boy turned 14 he was sent to a special camp for three hours a day, to train to become a soldier. The training included being brainwashed by a well-educated man who spoke highly about Hitler and his beliefs, the Third Reich, and the supposed superiority of the German people. This was part of the Hitler's indoctrination process. The teenage boys that I met in Germany would have gladly fought to the death.

I witnessed firsthand one of Hitler's infamous "baby" factories. There was a brick building near where we were staying in Austria. I think it was originally a belt factory or a school of some sort prior to the war. One afternoon I walked over to the building and went inside. There were a couple of large rooms that were filled with rows of cribs, and just about every crib had a baby in it. There were at least a hundred babies in the two rooms.

During the war the Krauts had turned the building into a Nazi baby factory. These "factories" were, quite literally, used to "manufacture" pure-breed Nazi babies for the purpose of further populating the German race to support Hitler and the Third Reich. Kraut SS officers would purposely impregnate 100% pure Aryan woman for the intent of building a population of pure-breed Germans that would one day support and fight for Hitler. The pregnant women would go to one of these factories to deliver their babies.

I had heard about these "factories," but I thought it was all rumor, and never believed that they actually existed until I stood in one. What was amazing is how well trained the babies were. When it was feeding time, a nurse would stand in a room and blow into a whistle, and immediately every baby would stand at attention in its crib and wait to be fed. It was an unbelievable sight.

BIDING TIME

By mid-May the days were getting hot, and we were getting impatient as to when we were going to hear word about going home. By this point most of us spent our time playing baseball, swimming, fishing, or just lying out in a field and staring up at the sky, daydreaming about our return to the United States and life after the war. But were we going home? The war in Europe was over, but the war in the Pacific was still being fought. The 101st Airborne Division was a well-trained, experienced fighting unit that had proven itself repeatedly with distinction. These were very good reasons to send us to Japan instead of sending us home.

By about the third week or so of May we began to hear some encouraging news, at least for some of us. The military developed a point system that was based on number of months in service, with extra credit for time in service spent overseas, and the number of commendations a soldier received. A single point was given for every month a solider served in the United States, and two points were given for every month served overseas. Five points were given for every battle or bronze star a soldier was awarded. Men who had the higher number of points would be sent home and discharged, whereas men who had fewer points would remain in the service.

I was inducted into service on April 25th, 1941. I was sent overseas in early October of 1942. It was now almost June 1945. I had been in the service well over four years. I had spent 17 months in the United States, and had been overseas for 33 months. From just my time in service alone I had 83 points. I had received four battle stars, which gave me another 20 points, plus I was about to receive a bronze star, which was another 5 points. The bronze star was issued to all Screaming Eagles who fought at Normandy in June 1944 during the invasion. It was awarded for bravery in action while under enemy fire. This gave me a total of 108 points. I had more points than anyone that I knew in the entire 101st Airborne, with perhaps the exception of Eugene Dance, my former lieutenant, who had about the same amount as me.

In the first week of June I was given a seven day pass to go to Nice for rest and relaxation. Nice is located in the southeast of France, near the Italian border, on the French Riviera, along the Mediterranean Coast. It's absolutely beautiful, I spent five days there, and I don't think I have ever had a better vacation in my entire life. It was fabulous.

Not too long after I returned to Austria from my trip to Nice I heard really good news from General Taylor himself, the commander of the 101st Airborne. He told us that men with over 85 accumulated points would begin their return to the United States on June 28th, which was only a few days away. Of the men with more than 85, those with the most points would be given top priority and get to go home first. I had accumulated 108 points, which guaranteed that I would be among the guys going first. I felt real good about it.

There were a lot of new guys who had come into the 101st Airborne Division to replace those who been knocked-off or wounded. Many of the new guys had been in the service less than a year or two, and didn't have too many points. There was a rumor flying around that they were going to be sent to Japan to fight the Japanese, and they were quite worried about being sent to the Pacific.

Needless to say I was quite excited. I had just turned 28 and had spent the last four years of my life fighting a war. By the grace of God I had survived all the battles I fought in, all of the hundreds of close calls I had with the enemy, and was still in one piece, at least physically. I had beaten the odds.

But I also felt sad when the moment came to leave. I thought that I would be so happy, but I was actually morose because so many of my best friends weren't going home. Peepnuts (John Hale), Goo-Goo (George Radecka), Joe Oleskiewicz, and other buddies of mine were to forever remain on the battlefields or in the military cemeteries of Europe, and it bothered me. If I was going to keep myself together, I needed to forget about them and the war, and get on with my life.

I wanted nothing more than to get home as soon as I could, marry Theresa, get back to work, buy a house, start having children, and put the war behind me. I had it all planned. Theresa and I had already decided that we were going to get married in the Catholic Church. There was a catholic priest who served as one of the chaplains in the 506th PIR. His name was Father John S. Maloney and I was extremely fond of him. All of us were. He said a lot of things to us that comforted us and kept ourselves together whenever the war began to get to us.

I asked Father Maloney to marry Theresa and me, and he said that he'd be honored. By the middle of June Father Maloney had left us. I think he returned to the United States, but before he left he gave me his address in Elmira, New York. He told me to contact him when Theresa and I were ready to get married, and that he would be happy to come to Baltimore. But I never saw Father Maloney after the war. Theresa wanted the priest in Saint Patrick's, the church she regularly attended, to marry us since she had known him a long time.

HOMEWARD BOUND

On June 28th, 1945 I left the mountains of Austria and started my journey back to the United States. I and the other men in the 506th and 502nd Parachute Infantry Regiments who were heading home were reassigned to Company G of the 101st Airborne's 501st PIR. The rest of the guys in the 506th, the guys with less than 85 points, were supposed to be sent to Japan, but they never were, as by mid-August the Japanese surrendered.

When we left the Austrian Alps on our trip back to the United States we were first sent back to Berchtesgaden, which was just a short distance from where we were in Austria. I figured we'd stay there for a day or two and then we'd move out to France or England and then we'd cross the Atlantic Ocean. I planned on being home in Maryland by mid-August at the latest.

Boy was I wrong! We remained in Berchtesgaden until early August—

well over a month! All we did there was stand around and wait patiently to be sent home. Our hanging around in Berchtesgaden for more than a month made no sense at all, but that's how the army is—a lot of things that soldiers are ordered to do don't make any sense.

Back home in Maryland, Theresa and my parents were just as anxious to have me back in the States as I was to get back. A lot of guys from the Baltimore area had already returned home, or were on their way. Every day the local newspapers in Baltimore would print the names of the men from the local areas who were returning. Every day throughout July and into August, Theresa and my parents would look in every local paper, hoping to see my name, but it never appeared during those months.

During the second week of August, 1945 we climbed into railroad box cars and left Germany by train once and for all. We arrived in Nancy, France three days later. The following week we were sent to the coast of France, where we joined up with the 17th Airborne Division. General Taylor had us sew the 17th Airborne Division patch onto our uniforms. Now we wore two airborne division patches: the 101st Airborne on our left shoulder sleeve and the 17th Airborne on our right.

We remained in Nancy for a couple of weeks, after which we boarded huge ships and set out to cross the Atlantic Ocean. Our destination was New York Harbor on the west side of Manhattan. About a week or so later, well into September, our ships arrived at the docks. This was the same harbor from which I had boarded the Queen Elizabeth in early October of 1942, nearly three years to the day earlier, and left the United States for Europe.

We remained in the New York–New Jersey area for a few days. During this time we were divided up and arrangements were made to send us to the military bases or forts close to our respective hometowns, where we would be discharged from the military. We said goodbye to each other as each of us was sent away. I was put into a group of other men who were from Maryland and Virginia. We were sent to Fort Meade, Maryland, the very fort that I was originally sent to on April 25th, 1941—the day that I was drafted into the army. I was officially discharged from the military at Fort Meade on September 23rd, 1945, after four years and nearly five months of service to my country.

The first thing I wanted to do after I was discharged was see Theresa.

I called to tell her that I was at Fort Meade, that I had just been discharged, and that I was about to go to her house. Theresa was all excited that I was back in Maryland. She told me that she and my mother knew that I was coming home because they had finally read it in one of the local newspapers. But they didn't know exactly when.

I told Theresa to tell my mother to spread the word that when I return to Dundalk later that day I didn't want anyone, including my father, brothers, sister, our neighbors . . . no one . . . asking me questions about what I did during the war. I also warned Theresa that my nerves were a little on edge, and that I wasn't quite the same as when we had last seen each other. In the three years that had passed I had been in three major battles. I had seen things that a person shouldn't have to see, and had to do things that a person shouldn't have to do. Combat changes a person, and I wanted Theresa to be prepared for it.

As soon as I got off the phone with Theresa I got on a bus and went over to her house. We spent the entire afternoon together, just the two of us. It was wonderful. Later that same day I got on the Dundalk trolley to go to my parents' house. By this time they and my brothers and sister knew that I was coming to Dundalk later that day.

My brother Herbert wanted to personally greet me when I stepped off of the trolley at the stop near my parents' house. He didn't know which particular trolley I had boarded, so as not to miss me Herbert waited patiently for hours at the stop for my trolley to arrive. My trolley finally arrived, and the moment I stepped off with my packed duffle bag slung over my shoulder Herbert ran up and hugged me. We shook hands and talked a bit, and then started to walk up the street towards our parents' house. Herbert stopped me, and said that since I was a hero I shouldn't have to walk to our parents' house, but should arrive in a more dignified manner. Before I could say a word back to him, Herbert lifted me over his shoulder and carried me up the street, then up our sidewalk and into my parents' house. Home at last!

47.

SETTLING BACK INTO CIVILIAN LIFE

May 7, 1945

To My Darling Theresa:

. . . I do feel awful thankful to God and you and my people for the prayers that brought me through from the beginning to the end. It's sure been a long, hard road for me. I'm just sorry that many of my buddies couldn't be here to see the final end . . .

I do feel, Theresa, that the war has had an affect on me a little. It may be hard for me to get used to living like a man should live, but I believe with lots of help from you I will make out okay."

Sgt. Jack Womer

Like a lot of World War II veterans that had just returned home, all I wanted to do was go back to work, marry my sweetheart, buy a house, have kids, and live happily ever after. I wanted to put the war behind me and get on with my life. But settling back into civilian life after having been overseas fighting a war for three years isn't as easy as one may think. Everything and everyone looked the same as when I had left, but then again nothing was quite the same. I had changed. Dundalk had changed. The world had changed.

NO QUESTIONS PLEASE

Like a lot of World War II veterans that had just returned home, I had the post-war blues. We weren't quite ready for civilian life just yet. We were out of military service, and were civilians again. But before we could get on with our lives many of us needed a little time off from everything to decompress, clear our heads and adjust back to being civilians. For about a month after I was discharged I did absolutely nothing except to visit Theresa, spend time with my parents, visit friends and relatives, and just hang around my parents' house in Dundalk, Maryland.

Theresa and I used the time to plan our wedding and our future. We were married on November 18th, 1945 in St. Patrick's Catholic Church in Baltimore. Reverend Nicholas Dohony married us. We moved into a small apartment located at 2530 Yorkway, in Dundalk, Maryland. We stayed there about three years, and then for $7,000 we bought a single family home located at 3013 Dunleer Road in Dundalk, where we lived for many years thereafter.

Like a lot of World War II veterans that had just returned home, I absolutely would not and could not talk about what I had done or experienced during the war. I would remain this way for many years. I didn't want to be reminded of the war. I wanted to forget it all. Theresa had forewarned my friends, parents, brothers and sister not to ask me questions about the war. For the most part, they didn't. Casual acquaintances and other people that I knew of in the Baltimore area would ask me questions about the war when I bumped into them while out and about. I knew they didn't realize that their questions bothered me, so I would just give them a short, vague answer and immediately changed the subject. They usually got the hint not to ask any more questions about the war.

CAN'T GET ANYTHING

While I was overseas fighting it had never dawned on me that life wasn't all that great for the folks back home in the states. For one thing, there was a shortage of everything. The demand for goods and materials to support the war effort in Europe and the Pacific theatres created shortages in the United States. When I returned to the states there was still a shortage of dishes, soap, clothes, butter, meat, furniture, gasoline, and just about everything else. Everything was in short supply and rationed. You couldn't go into a store and simply buy anything that you wanted. There were limits.

In order to obtain something you'd have to go into a store, place an order, and then wait indefinitely to receive whatever it was that you ordered. When the item you ordered finally arrived it was usually very expensive because of the shortages. A lot of items could only be obtained with ration stamps. I needed shoe stamps to buy a pair of shoes when I got out of the army. It was hard getting used to the shortages and rationing that was going on back in the states, because while I was in the army us soldiers were given anything that we needed. It would take months after I returned home before the shortages and rationing ended.

BACK TO WORK

Joe Stokes had been my superintendent at the Bethlehem Steel Mills in Dundalk, where I worked prior to the war. Joe had a reputation of being underhanded. I always felt that he didn't like me. A lot of the guys, including myself, that had worked under Joe in the steel mills and had been drafted felt that Joe played favorites with the guys.

When the draft had started in 1941, Joe had been chosen by the local draft board to rank the mill's employees for eligibility to serve in the military. In those early days of the draft, whether a mill worker would be drafted was largely in the hands of Joe. But Joe played favorites. Joe was the guy who in early 1941 had, before the war even started, recommended to my local draft board that I be drafted into military service. I guess I wasn't one of his favorites.

In late October, 1945 I returned to my old steel mill in Dundalk, to pay Joe Stokes a visit and talk to him about my plans to return to work. Bethlehem Steel was required by law to hire me back, since I had been forced to leave my job at the mill because I had been drafted into military service. Joe told me that I could not have my old job back. I asked him why. First he tried to tell me that he didn't need me, and they weren't hiring returning veterans. This was a lie because I knew of a lot of other guys that had worked at the mill and had to leave to fight the war and got their jobs back when they returned home. I mentioned some of these guys to Joe, catching him in his lie.

Joe then tried to say that he couldn't hire me back because I had been fired from the steel mill. This was another lie. I told him that was a lot of bullshit too, and that it was illegal for an employer not to hire back a former employee who was forced to leave his job because he had been drafted into military service. I knew my rights. By this point Joe had run out of excuses as to why he "couldn't" hire me back. Out of frustration, he shouted

"You're not getting your job back Womer!" I shouted back to Joe "We'll see about that!" and stormed out of his office.

I went to the main office of Bethlehem Steel Mills and spoke with a man who was Joe's boss. I told him who I was, that I had worked at the mills, but had to leave in 1941 because I was drafted into military service. I went on to say that I was a war hero and had just returned from the war, and now I wanted my job back. I told him that Joe Stokes said I could not come back to work. Joe's boss said I most certainly could return to work and that he was happy to have me back.

I returned to work a week or two later, in November, 1945, just before Theresa and I got married. When I returned, Joe Stokes was no longer working as the superintendant in my steel mill. I don't know what happened to him, but I think after my little argument with him he may have been transferred to another section of the mill or was fired.

48.

BRINGING PEACE TO THE HALE FAMILY

Corporal John Hale, or "Peepnuts," as the guys in the Filthy Thirteen used to call him, was a very good friend of mine. We were quite close. We jumped into Normandy from the same plane on D-Day. Sadly, Peepnuts was killed during the Normandy invasion. I found out about it when I met up with Joe Oleskiewicz and some of the other guys in the Filthy Thirteen about a week after D-Day. Joe told me that Peepnuts had landed in a swamp with George Radecka (Goo-Goo), and got shot in the head by a sniper. Peepnuts was shot while in the swamp, and he laid there dead, with his head down in his helmet, for two or three days before he was removed. Radecka was also killed a day or two later. The news that Radecka and Peepnuts had been killed upset me quite a bit, as I was quite fond of both of them, especially Peepnuts.

Peepnuts was the only son and the younger of the two children in his family. His life's dream was to become a medical doctor, a surgeon. At the time he entered military service he was in college, and had only one more year of pre-medicine classes to complete before he could apply for acceptance into medical school. Peepnuts was a devout Catholic, as were his parents and sister. At the time of his death he was just two months shy of his twenty-third birthday. The only personal items found on his body were two letters from home, a pen and pencil, some photographs of his parents and sister, two religious medals, and 7 dollars and 68 cents.

What I didn't know while I was in military service, was that months after the Normandy invasion my sister, Jane, took up communications with Peepnuts' sister and parents, who lived in Poulsbo, Washington, which is about twenty miles from Seattle. This communication really began in December of 1944 when Keith Carpenter, another paratrooper in my demolition platoon, wrote a letter to Mrs. Kathryn Hale, Peepnuts' mother. In his letter Keith enclosed the article on the Filthy Thirteen that appeared in the December 4th, 1944 issue of the *Stars and Stripes*. The article mentions the names of the guys in the Filthy Thirteen, their hometowns, and a brief description of what happened to them after they jumped into Normandy.

From this article Mrs. Hale obtained my parents home address, and in January 1945 she sent a very nice typewritten letter to my mother (see page 178), as well as to each of the mother's or families of the men in the Filthy Thirteen. This initial communication between Mrs. Hale and my mother soon led to a regular exchange of letters between my sister Jane and Peepnuts' older sister, who was married but was living with her parents in Poulsbo, Washington. Her husband, a U.S. Air Force pilot, was stationed overseas.

Beginning in the early part of 1945, until many years after the war had ended, Jane and Peepnuts' sister corresponded with each other on a regular basis. It was only after I returned home from the war and settled back into civilian life that I learned from Jane that she developed a friendship with Peepnuts' family.

As with many of the combat soldiers of World War II, when I came home, and for many years afterwards, I didn't want to talk about the war or the things that I had seen or done as a combat soldier. I had made it clear in letters that I wrote to my family and friends while I was still overseas that I didn't want to answer any questions about the war or discuss the war when I returned home.

But shortly after I returned home Jane started telling me all about Peepnuts' sister, mother and father. She also had pictures of Peepnuts, and his sister and his mother and father, which they had sent to Jane. I didn't want to hear about any of this, because it brought back sad memories. I wanted to forget about the war, and I particularly didn't want to be reminded of Peepnuts because he had been killed. I yelled at Jane for talking about Peepnuts and his family in front of me. I told her never to mention anything about the war to me again, and especially not to mention Peepnuts. Jane couldn't understand why, and we got into one hell of an argument over it. For months afterwards Jane and I didn't speak to one another because of our argument.

One day in the mid to late 1960s, over twenty years after the war had ended, a strange thing happened. After supper one evening I received a phone call out of the blue from Peepnuts' sister. She was now residing in, of all places, Patuxent, Maryland, which is only about 30 miles or so southwest of Dundalk. Her husband, still a military pilot, at this time was stationed at a naval base in Annapolis on the eastern shore of Maryland. When she called me she said: "Sergeant Womer, you and my brother Bob [Peepnuts] were very good friends. My mother and father are here from Poulsbo, Washington visiting my husband and me. We would like you to come to my house this Sunday for dinner, so we can meet you and you can tell us stories about Bob from when you knew him during the war."

I told her that I would go—how could I not—but I felt very uneasy about it. This whole thing seemed kind of spooky to me. Having served with Peepnuts, he and I becoming good friends, him getting killed, his sister and my sister communicating with one another all along, and then his sister moving to the east coast, close to where I live, and now her calling me out of the blue one day over twenty years after the war had ended . . . it all made me feel uneasy. But I've always believed that when strange things like this happen, there's a reason why they happen.

I spoke with my father about my uneasiness. I said "Dad, this Sunday afternoon I've got to go over and see this man and these women, who are Peepnuts' father, mother and sister, and talk about their son and brother, John, who I knew as Peepnuts and who was killed on D-Day. I don't particularly care to go, but something inside of me is telling me I need to." My father advised me not to go if I didn't want to. But I told him that I would go, and that eventually I would understand why all of this was taking place.

That Sunday Theresa and I drove over to Peepnuts' sister house in Patuxent and met her and her parents, Mr. John F. Hale and Mrs. Kathryn Hale. I could tell almost immediately that Peepnuts' father had complete control of his family. He did practically all of the speaking in his family, and when he spoke everyone in his family kept completely quiet. None of them ever once interrupted him, or in any way disagreed with anything he said. At first we talked about things in general, and then we talked about

Peepnuts. His complete name was John Robert Hale, and his sister and parents referred to him as "Bob" instead of John to avoid confusion with his father, John F. Hale.

I told them that I had first met their son in January of 1944, when I joined the Demolitions Platoon of the 101st Airborne Division's 506th Parachute Infantry Regiment. I went on to tell them everyone liked Peepnuts, and that Peepnuts and I became very good friends and spent a lot of time together. The conversation with Mr. Hale seemed to be going smoothly until we inevitably began to talk about the Normandy Invasion and how Peepnuts died.

I had just started to mention how Peepnuts got killed when his father suddenly interrupted me and began to talk. Out of respect for Mr. Hale I stopped talking and just listened. Mr. Hale went on to say that he already knew the details of how his son died. He said that he learned from Jake McNiece that Peepnuts was shot and killed after he had taken out three German machine gun nests. I was surprised to hear this, because Joe Oleskiewicz had told me Peepnuts was killed by a Kraut sniper while in a swamp.

Apparently, shortly after the war Jake McNiece went around and visited a lot of people that he knew of in different states. He wasn't married at the time, and these people would take him in and take care of him for awhile. They'd give him free room and board and he'd stay with them until he was ready to leave. On one of these trips he stayed in Poulsbo at the Hale residence. During this trip Jake told the Hales that Peepnuts was killed after he had taken out three German machine gun nests. I guess Jake told them this because the Hale's were giving him free room and board and, since Peepnuts had been killed in action, Jake wanted to make them feel proud of their only son. So he told them that Peepnuts had bravely taken out three German machine gun nests before the Germans killed him.

This of course wasn't what Joe Oleskiewicz had told me in June of 1944, while we were in Normandy after we invaded. According to what Joe told me, Peepnuts could not have destroyed any machine gun nests before he was killed. I knew immediately that Peepnuts' family had been misinformed, but out of respect for his family I didn't dare tell the family what Joe Oleskiewicz had told me about how Peepnuts had died. I thought how close I came to getting the stories crossed, and how hurtful it would have been to Peepnuts' family if I had told them what I had heard about how their son died. I just left it alone, but it was real close how they nearly found out what I had been told about the death of their son.

After Mr. Hale described how Peepnuts died, all of a sudden and out of nowhere, he became bitter and quite emotional. He went on to say that his son's death wasn't necessary at all, how the war wasn't necessary, and that America was full of shit. He condemned the American flag, and America for making Peepnuts' lose his life. His wife and daughter just sat there, obviously uncomfortable with Mr. Hale's comments, but neither dared to say a word.

Mr. Hale went on and on, until finally I couldn't take any more of it. At this point I really got on him for talking against the United States. I began yelling at him, at how wrong he was for condemning America and the American flag. I shouted to him: "America didn't start the war, the Japanese Imperial Empire and Nazi Germany started it! When they brought on the war they threatened world peace and the freedom of every American citizen. America didn't want to get involved with the war, but you know as well as I do that there was no way in hell we could have avoided taking part in it!"

Mr. Hale shouted back to me "I don't want to hear it!" I yelled back to him "I don't give a God damn what you want to hear! I'm telling you!" I was really getting on Mr. Hale because the things he said were very disrespectful to America and veterans like me, and particularly to men such as Peepnuts who gave their lives for America.

I shouted at Mr. Hale: "Your son was called upon to fight against the threat to world peace. He rose to the occasion, and gave his life fighting to keep the freedom that America provides to all Americans. Your son was just a regular guy, but he didn't die like a regular guy. He died a hero in service of his country! If it weren't for America and the American flag and all that it stands for, we'd all be goose-stepping and eating sushi right now. Yet here you are twenty years later, alive and well, and living in a peaceful world because of men such as your son, and you have the nerve to condemn America and the American flag! The American flag stands for FREE-DOM, and that's what America has given you, and that's what your son has given you, and don't you ever forget it!"

With that I got up and left the house with Theresa without saying another word. I was mad at Peepnuts' dad. Theresa was both embarrassed and mad at me for yelling at Peepnuts' dad. As we drove home that Sunday evening, Theresa yelled at me for saying what I had said. But I didn't pay much attention to her. I kept struggling to understand the reason why all this had happened. It just wasn't making any sense to me, yet I knew that there had to be a reason for it all.

The next day Peepnuts' sister called me. She said "Sergeant Womer, I've called to tell you that I'm sorry about the things that my father said yesterday, and to thank you from the bottom of my heart for taking away the dark cloud that's been over our family ever since we got the news that Bob was killed in action, more than twenty years ago. You see, my father has been carrying a lot of bitterness inside of himself all of these years, against the United States for Bob's death. My mother and I have come to terms with Bob's death, but my father hasn't.

The same things my father said to you last evening, the things that offended you, he has said to my mother and I, and others, over and over again, but no one would dare say back to him what you said, even though we know it would help him come to terms with the death of his only son. He needed to hear the things you said from someone who was close to Bob, but not part of the family . . . someone such as yourself. Until now no one has talked to my father the way you did, and I thank you for it. My mother and I feel that you have made him start to believe that his son's death was not in vain. I think you've helped my father let go of a lot of the bitterness he has felt all of these years."

I felt real good about what Peepnuts' sister said to me over the phone. When she was done speaking it finally became clear to me why all of this happened. Dear old Peepnuts had reached out to me from his grave to help his father get over his death and bring peace to the Hale family.

I said to Peepnuts' sister: "You're more than welcome. I know that Bob is in Heaven and that he watches over you, your mother and your father. I feel in my heart and soul that Bob is pleased that I've helped your father let go of the bitterness he's been burdened with all of these years. You tell your dad that when the war ended I brought home two German rifles. You also tell him if he is willing to come to my home in Dundalk, I'll give him one. He can take it and destroy it if he thinks it will make him feel even better." That's what I promised, and I meant it, but either Peepnuts' sister never told Mr. Hale of my promise, or she did and he wasn't interested in a German rifle, because he never took me up on my offer.*

---

*There are discrepancies as to exactly when, how and where John R. Hale ("Peepnuts") was killed. Aside from Jack Womer being told by Joe Oleskiewicz (who himself was later killed in Holland) that Hale was killed by a sniper in a swamp on D-Day, an article in the November 30th, 1944, London Edition of the *Stars and Stripes* stated that he died about two weeks after the invasion [i.e., about June 20th, 1944] trying to destroy an enemy machine gun nest. In the book *The Filthy Thirteen*, the story about Hale being killed after "attacking his third machine gun nest" is repeated, whereas Peepnuts' mother, Kathryn Hale reported receiving a letter dated June 17th, 1944, stating that her son had been wounded on June 9th, and then another letter dated August 1st stating that he had died on June 20th. She also received a letter from Colonel Robert Sink in early August stating that Peepnuts' "buddies" were nearby when he got killed, "but he could tell me no more." (See page 178.)

It must be remembered that in the days following the invasion on June 6, 1944, there were many hundreds of dead and missing paratroopers scattered over miles of battlefront, many of them behind German lines or on contested ground. By the time all of the dead and missing had been accounted for it was no longer possible to tell exactly when they had died or what they had been doing when they were killed. There were often discrepancies between, for example, a real time of death, the discovery of a body, and the completion of the necessary paperwork.

This author has concluded that John Hale ("Peepnuts") was killed on June 6th, 1944 (D-Day), or shortly afterward, not on June 20th. This conclusion is based on:

Jack Womer's recollection of Joe Oleskiewicz's comments to him on or about June 14th, 1944, when Jack rejoined the Filthy Thirteen;

The fact that Jack doesn't remember seeing Hale when he returned to the Filthy Thirteen or thereafter;

That according to Richard Killblane, co-author of the book *The Filthy Thirteen*, no one that he interviewed for the book said anything about Hale being with them when they advanced on Carentan on or about June 12th, and thereafter;

The official U.S. Army Journal: 506th Parachute Infantry, "Operation Neptune, S-1, S-2, S-3" reports "No Contact" (i.e., with the enemy), or any deaths of 506th soldiers in the entry for 20th, June 1944;

The details discussed in the letter (dated January 21st, 1945) that Mrs. Kathryn Hale wrote to Jack Womer's parents (page 178), and;

Finally, the natural tendency of soldiers throughout time to report that their comrades-in-arms had died heroically, rather than revealing any number of the more prosaic ways in which a soldier could die in battle.

49.

THE REMAINS OF THE DAY

I served in the military for four years, four months, twenty-seven days and six hours. Every second of this time all I could think about was getting out of the service, marrying Theresa, having a house and six children, and living happily ever after. This was my dream. It is what kept me going throughout my military service.

For the most part, my dream came true. In November of 1945, two months after I was discharged from the military, Theresa and I got married. I went back to work at the steel mill and we eventually bought a house. We didn't have six children, but we did have two: a daughter, Ellen, and a son, John. John was born about eight years after Theresa and I got married, and Ellen was born a few years after John was born.

LIFE'S UPS AND DOWNS

Theresa and I and our children shared many happy years together. We did many of the things that most families of the era did. I worked full time, while Theresa stayed at home to manage the household and care for our kids. We went on picnics, we went fishing, crabbing, had barbeques in our backyard, enjoyed the holidays together, spent a lot of time with our relatives and friends. I coached John's little league baseball teams, and taught him how shoot a rifle and hunt game. Ellen would eventually get married and have two children of her own, a son and a daughter.

But we had our share of tragedies too. My son John developed a very serious addiction to drugs, and it eventually killed him. He died tragically while a young man from a cocaine overdose, and it broke our hearts. At the time of his death he was homeless. John's drug addiction caused a lot of problems in our family, some of which still linger. Sometimes I wonder if I'm to blame for John's personal problems. Theresa was a good mother. I wasn't the father I should have been, or could have been.

THERESA DIES

For me the 1980s were filled with all sorts of life-changing events. I retired from Bethlehem Steel in 1982, at the age of 65. I had worked for Bethlehem Steel a long time. I joined the company's Sparrows Point steel mill facilities in 1936 and, except for the four-and-half years I spent in the military, worked there continuously for nearly 42 years, about 40 of which were in the number 54 slab mill. A workers union was established during my career with Bethlehem steel. But I never joined it, and I never liked being in a union shop.

Another reason why I retired is because by 1982 Bethlehem Steel was in serious financial trouble. Business had been good for Bethlehem Steel after World War II and throughout the 1950s. But during the 1960s business began to gradually spiral downward. Other less expensive materials became available that could replace the need for steel in products. In addition, more and more steel was being imported from other countries because it was cheaper, which caused less to be manufactured within the United States. By the late-1970s layoffs in the mills had become common and fewer guys were brought on to replace guys that were retiring. Bethlehem Steel was losing money. I could read the writing on the wall. It was time to retire.

I, as did lot of other World War II veterans who worked at Bethlehem Steel, retired from the company in 1982 with a comfortable pension and a good health insurance plan. But throughout the 1980s and 1990s Bethlehem Steel fell deeper into financial trouble. By 2003 the company was bankrupt, and could no longer provide their retirees and their dependants with pension, health care, and life insurance benefits.

Bethlehem Steel liquidated in May of 2003. At 86 years of age, after having worked hard for a company for over 40 years and fought in a world war for four and a half years, I found myself having no pension income and no private health insurance. The only income I was left with was that provided to me from the U.S. Social Security Administration. The only health benefits I had were those provided under the U.S. government's Medicare. A lot of World War II veterans that I had worked with were in the same boat as me. We felt cheated, and we were worried sick over it. The federal government eventually stepped-in and helped us out.

Theresa passed away unexpectedly in 1987. She died from an infection that was caused from being bitten by a blue claw crab. We caught a bunch of blue claw crabs one day and brought them home to cook. We put the live crabs in a pot on our kitchen stove, and Theresa reached over the pot to grab something. As she reached over the pot a crab reached up one of its claws and bit Theresa on her arm. At first we didn't think anything of it, because just about anyone who has ever gone crabbing for blue claw crabs has been bitten by one. It happens all the time, and it never causes a problem.

But Theresa's bite from that crab became infected. We didn't realize it but the infection spread like wild fire throughout her body, including her heart and brain. She became slightly delirious one evening shortly after being bitten, so she went to bed so she could sleep it off. I went to bed later in the evening. At about 2:30 in the morning she woke up, came over to me and kissed me on my lips, and then collapsed on the bedroom floor. She was rushed to a nearby hospital and died shortly later. The infection had severely damaged the mitral valve in her heart, and she died of heart failure. Her heart was already damaged from years of being a heavy cigarette smoker. I'm sure our son's drug addiction took its toll on Theresa's health as well.

I hardly ever cry, but when Theresa died I broke down. When it came time to plan Theresa's funeral I thought of the time when I was in Carentan, France on June 17th, 1944, when that old lady put the red rose in my top pocket and told me to send it back home to "the woman I love", meaning Theresa, which I did. I have always felt that that rose brought me luck, and ever since that old French woman placed that red rose in my pocket red roses have had special meaning to me. Not doing a very good job at holding back my tears, I told Ellen, my daughter, I wanted Theresa's casket covered with red roses, which Ellen arranged.

Theresa's obituary and funeral plans appeared in the local paper. At Theresa's wake service the very first person to arrive at the funeral home and express condolences was my old and dear friend John Polyniak. John and I had lost touch with one another for many years, even though we lived only a few miles apart. I wasn't expecting him at Theresa's wake. It was very uplifting to see him, and his being there meant a lot to me. We talked for a long time. I told him about my son's personal problems, and how he had stolen artifacts, including a beautiful Walther P38 German pistol that I had brought back from the war, and sold them to support his drug habit. What I didn't know was that John had also brought back a Walther P38 German pistol from the war. What do you think John did? He went home got his P38 pistol and gave it to me, to replace the one that my own son had stolen from me. This is the kind of man that John Polyniak was. You won't find a better man than John Polyniak.

Theresa, the love of my life, the only person that I could depend upon to help keep me from going insane throughout the war with her listening voice, her comforting letters, and her endless prayers, the one person who meant more to me than anyone else in the world, was suddenly gone from my life. When Theresa died my whole world caved in on me. It took me a long time to come to terms with her death. I do miss her so. Not too long after Theresa died I sold our house on Dunleer Road in Dundalk, and moved to a small waterfront house located at 9126 Todd Avenue in Fort Howard, Maryland, just a few miles from the house in Dundalk. I just couldn't live in the Dundalk house without Theresa. I had to get away from it. So I bought the small, waterfront house in Fort Howard, where I can go fishing and crabbing as much as I want and right from the back of my property. I've been there ever since.

BACK WITH THE GUYS

For many years I seldom ever spoke of the war. I didn't want to be reminded of it, and I put it behind me as best as I could. But there has never been a day since I left the service in September of 1945 that I haven't paused for a minute or two to think of the war and my experiences in it. The war has never left me.

It wasn't until the 1980s, over forty years after I had been drafted, that I felt comfortable about speaking openly about World War II. With the passage of time I gradually thought less of the sad times and more of the happy times of my military service. By the 1980s I found myself thinking quite a bit about the men that I served with and fought with. I wondered what had become of them, whether they were still alive and, if so, how they were doing.

I think a lot of World War II veterans began to feel the same way. During the 1980s most of the men that served in World War II were still alive and in their 60s. Our kids were grown, our home mortgages were paid-off, and many of us were now retired. We had free time on our hands. We were no longer young, but nor were we old. We were still young enough to drive long distances, board airplanes, and have fun on our own. If we were going to reconnect with our old war buddies, the 1980s was the perfect time to do so. A lot of us did.

The book *The Filthy Thirteen* discusses how the guys from the demolitions platoon of the 101st Airborne Division's 506th Parachute Infantry Regiment Headquarters Company began to contact one another and have get-togethers and reunions. It was nice to reconnect with the guys and reminisce. Many of us hadn't seen or even heard from one another in forty years. Ever since the 1980s, we've been writing or calling one another on a regular basis, attending reunions and other get-togethers.

Whenever we get together we invariably gather around a table or a sofa and spend most of our time reminiscing about the time we spent together during the war, especially the happy times. People who were born after the war love to sit near us whenever we share our memories, and we especially love it when they ask us to tell them particular war stories. No matter how many times people have heard us tell our stories they never seem to get tired of hearing them over again.

It is interesting that for many years after the war most of us would never talk about it. But from about the 1980s on we'll use any excuse to reminisce about the war. I guess with the passage of all the many years since the war we've come to terms with the things we did and saw, and the loss of our dear friends who were killed during the war.

On September 12th, 1990, over forty five years after the war ended, final closure of World War II occurred. On that day the Treaty of the Final Settlement with Respect to Germany was signed. This final settlement is a peace treaty between the World War II Allies (the United States, France, the United Kingdom, and the Soviet Union) and Germany, and brought completion to World War II. The Allied countries had occupied Germany

The five Womer brothers in a photo taken on March 31, 1971. From left to right: David, Herbert, Ben, Jack, and Douglas. After the war ended Jack returned to work for Bethlehem Steel in Sparrows Point, Maryland. *Photo: the Womer family*

Mike Marquez (left) and Jack, at one of the many reunions of the 506th Regimental Headquarters Company's Demolitions Platoon. By the time of the Battle of the Bulge Marquez had been assigned to the platoon's Filthy Thirteen section, and Jack had been promoted to buck sergeant. They remained good friends after the war until Mike passed away in October 2008. *Photo: the Womer family*

Even guys in the Filthy Thirteen like to hear war stories about the Filthy Thirteen. Jack Womer (right) is explaining to Jake McNiece how he saved all of those men from the 501st Parachute Infantry Regiment from drowning in a swamp on D-Day. Despite the fact that Jake has heard the story a million times, he's still fascinated by it. This photo was taken in June 1997 during Jack's 80th birthday celebration.
Photo: the Womer family

Jack (right) with his co-author Stephen DeVito, in Toccoa, Georgia, at a reunion of the men who served in the 101st Airborne Division during World War II, on September 25, 2003.

Jack Womer, with his daughter Ellen, while serving as the honorary Grand Marshall in the Dundalk Heritage Parade, July 4th, 2011. Jack will always be one of Dundalk's heroes, and one of the most notable people to have ever lived there. *Photo: Debbie Falbo*

Jack Womer with Ginnie Millholland Schry (left) and Harlan Smith (right), November 5th, 2011 at an event held in Cumberland, Maryland at which Jack was the guest of honor. Ginnie and Harlan are the daughters of Major Randolph Millholland, commander of the 29th Ranger Battalion. Jack thought very highly of Millholland, and when the 29th Rangers were disbanded he told the Major that he would soldier under him any day of the week. *Photo: Becky McClarran*

since the Nazis surrendered in 1945, to prevent Germany from starting another war. By signing the Treaty of the Final Settlement with Respect to Germany, the Allied countries gave up their occupation rights in Germany that had been established in August of 1945 by the Potsdam Agreement, giving Germany its full sovereignty since 1945.

The Treaty of the Final Settlement with Respect to Germany may have brought final closure to World War II as far as Germany and the Allied countries are concerned, but the war isn't over for me, or men like me. The war continues to go on in the minds and hearts of those who fought in it. We each have our own nightmares that still haunt us. I know I have mine. Despite the fact that over sixty five years have passed since the war ended, I prefer to keep to myself particular memories of combat, and things I had to do in order to stay alive.

Worse yet, a lot of combat veterans of World War II and other wars suffer from what used to be called "shell-shock" or "battle fatigue", but is now known as post-traumatic stress disorder. This is an anxiety disorder that can develop after exposure to or being involved with military combat. People with battle fatigue are often haunted by frightening thoughts and memories of their combat experiences and feel emotionally numb. They may experience sleep problems, have frequent nightmares, feel detached, or be easily excited or frightened, and become irrational and violent.

I've never suffered from battle fatigue. But the war has affected me. I don't know for sure whether anyone in the Filthy Thirteen suffered from battle fatigue, but I am damn sure that the war has affected them too. Mauh Darnell developed a serious alcohol problem. His alcoholism may very well have resulted from emotional and psychological issues that developed from having been in the prisoner-of-war camp. I know of World War II veterans that have suffered from battle fatigue. It can disrupt a person's life, make it hard for them to hold a job, or just get along with other people. I've seen it lead to alcoholism, cause marriages to break-up, and even lead to suicide. It is a terrible illness to have. People who suffer from battle fatigue should to try to avoid talking or thinking about their combat experiences, or situations or people that trigger memories of combat, and seek professional help.

What is sad is that it is only relatively recently that battle fatigue is considered to be a serious illness. Veterans from World War II, the Korean

War and even the Viet Nam War who suffered from it were largely ignored. The condition was kept quiet for a long time. Why it was kept quiet for so long, I don't know, but I suspect it was because soldiers are supposed to be strong, and having battle fatigue may be viewed by some as a weakness. Guys had to keep quiet about it. Another reason could be politics and money. Since it's an illness caused by combat, veterans are entitled to compensation from the U.S. Department of Defense. The cost of treating all of the veterans who suffered from the illness would be tremendous.

Nowadays I'm glad to see that people are more open about it, and that veterans do not need to feel ashamed about having it. In fact, the United States Department of Veterans Affairs has established the National Center for Post-Traumatic Stress Disorder, which offers help to soldiers or veterans who suffer from the disorder, as well as their families.

THE MEANING OF IT ALL

Throughout the 1990s and into the 2000s get-togethers among the Filthy Thirteen, and of the 506th Parachute Infantry Regiment have gradually become less frequent, and are attended by fewer veterans. Many of the guys I served with have died since the 1980s, and those who haven't yet passed are too old to travel. Sadly, there will come a day when all veterans of World War II will be gone, but that's how it must be.

In June of 1997 my daughter Ellen organized a surprise party at my home in Fort Howard Maryland in honor of my 80th birthday. She invited family, friends, and guys that I had served with during World War II. Herb Pierce was there, as was Jack Agnew, Jake McNiece, and a lot of other old friends. It was a very nice surprise. Jake McNiece and his wife Martha came all the way from Oklahoma. When Ellen went to pick Jake and Martha up at the airport she brought my dog tags which had my D-Day cricket attached to them. One click was to be answered by two clicks! When Jake and Martha arrived at the airport Ellen made single "clicks" on the cricket to get Jake's attention. It was a great party that lasted for several days. Most of the guys and their wives stayed in my house. Ellen filmed a lot of the party. There is nice footage of us old warriors telling our war stories and just having a lot of fun.

On November 7th, 2008, myself, Jack Agnew, Jake McNiece and Robert Cone—the surviving members of the Filthy Thirteen that jumped together on D-Day (June 6th, 1944)—were honored at an awards ceremony held at the American Veterans Conference Center in Washington, D.C. I had not seen Robert Cone since we were in that plane together on D-Day, flying over Nazi occupied France, over 64 years prior. It was wonderful to see him again. I am very grateful that I did see Cone, because he passed away less than two years later, on July 1st, 2010. Jack Agnew had passed away three months before Cone, on April 8th, 2010. At the time of this writing (March 2012), the only two surviving members of the Filthy Thirteen that jumped together on D-Day are Jake McNiece and myself.

On June 7th, 2011 my dear and long-time friend John Polyniak died. He was 92 years old. John died 67 years and a day after he and his comrades in Company C, 116th Infantry, of the 29th Division attacked Omaha Beach, Normandy, France. John, a sergeant, survived the assault on Omaha Beach, and under his leadership his group was among the first to get off of Omaha Beach and move inland. At about 9:00 am on June 17th, 1944, while I was under machine gun fire in the streets of Carentan, John was shot in his right hip by a Kraut sniper while the 29th Infantry Division was advancing into St Lo, less than 20 miles away from me. John spent every day of the rest of his life in pain and partially crippled. I went to John's wake service to pay my respects and to say goodbye to my old friend. No book will ever be written about Sergeant John Polyniak, but one should be. He was a fine man.

I'm not afraid to die. But I fear that when us World War II veterans are all gone, future generations of Americans will forget about how hard we fought and the sacrifices we made in order to stop Hitler's Third Reich and the Japanese Empire from taking over the world so as to preserve our freedom. People tend to take such accomplishments by previous generations for granted. Worse yet, many people forget about them or don't even care to take the time to learn about them.

Take for example Veterans' Day. In the United States November 11th is Veterans' Day, a national holiday in which people are allowed to be off from work to spend the day paying respect to our past and present veterans by remembering their sacrifices for our freedom. Yet instead people spend the day in shopping malls, looking for good deals and bargains from the many "Veterans' Day" sales.

I know that other combat veterans of World War II and other wars have or have had the same fear as I, that what we accomplished and sacrificed will be forgotten. This is evident in the fact that many combat veterans pen their war memories in the later years of their lives, when they finally begin to accept the fact that time is running out. It's a way for combat veterans to set the record straight and to keep it straight for future generations.

I think this is particularly true of the combat veterans of World War II. Since the 1990s a tremendous amount of books have been published that detail the training and combat missions of U.S. military units and the experiences and anecdotes of individual soldiers during World War II. Some of the books have been made into movies. In fact, plans are underway to make a feature length movie and a television miniseries of the Filthy Thirteen.

Since the 2000s, major memorials dedicated to World War II have been established in the United States by the United States Congress. The National D-Day Memorial was established in Bedford Virginia, in 2001. The National World War II Museum was established in 2003 in New Orleans. On May 29th, 2004, over sixty years after World War II ended, the United States World War II Memorial was dedicated on the National Mall in Washington DC. Each of these pay honor to the 16 million who served in the armed forces of the United States, the more than 400,000 who died, and all who supported the war effort from home.

I have had a good life. As my life comes to a close, I would like to leave this world believing that today's younger folks and future generations will take some time every now and then to visit a World War II memorial or museum or read a book written by or about World War II veterans. I ask you, the reader, not to let them forget the sacrifices that men like me made to preserve our freedom, especially men such as Lieutenant Charles Mellen, Corporal John Hale, George Radecka, Corporal Joe Oleskiewicz, and my childhood friend Harry Hendricks, who sacrificed their lives at such an early age. Remember us.